Body Massage for the Beauty Therapist

Body Massage for the Beauty Therapist

Third Edition

Audrey Githa Goldberg, MCSP, SRP
Formerly Senior Lecturer in Beauty Therapy

Lucy McDonald

BUTTERWORTH HEINEMANN

AMSTERDAM BOSTON HEIDELBERG LONDON NEW YORK OXFORD
PARIS SAN DIEGO SAN FRANCISCO SINGAPORE SYDNEY TOKYO

Butterworth-Heinemann
An imprint of Elsevier
Linacre House, Jordan Hill, Oxford OX2 8DP
200 Wheeler Road, Burlington, MA 01803

First published 1972
Reprinted 1976, 1979, 1982, 1986
Second edition 1989
Reprinted 1991, 1992, 1993, 1994, 1995
Third edition 1996
Reprinted 1997 (twice), 1998, 2000, 2001, 2002, 2003

British Library Cataloguing in Publication Data
Goldberg, Audrey Githa
  Body massage for the beauty therapist – 3rd.ed.
  1. Massage. 2. Physical therapy. 3. Massage therapy. 4. Beauty culture.
  I. Title II. McDonald, Lucy
  615.8'22'0246467

ISBN 0 7506 2453 1

For more information on all Butterworth-Heinemann publications
please visit our website at www.bh.com

Typeset by Genesis Typesetting, Rochester, Kent
Printed and bound in Great Britain by MPG Books Ltd, Bodmin, Cornwall

Contents

of the abdominal wall – Muscles of scalp and
facial expression

Foreword

I was delighted when Lucy McDonald asked me to write a foreword to this third edition of Audrey Goldberg's book.

I was trained in body massage many years ago by Audrey and the book is still widely used and recognized by beauty therapy students studying at all levels on vocational courses. Lucy has successfully updated the book to keep in line with the new schemes being offered by the colleges, BTEC, NVQ Level III, VAI and CIDESCO.

The publication combines an extensive up-to-date knowledge of body therapy treatments, comprising both manual and electrical techniques together with the ever popular and expanding alternative therapies, for example aromatherapy.

This book will be of great benefit to every student and teacher to enhance learning and teaching, keeping our high professional standards.

Sylvia Brooks
Beauty Therapy Lecturer
City College Manchester

Preface to the Third Edition

I was thrilled when I learned that there was to be a third edition of this highly recognized textbook. After the publication of the second edition, which covered most of the examination syllabuses such as CIDESCO and City and Guilds, the third edition has been updated in its body techniques over the past seven years for its use with NVQ, GNVQ, BTEC national diploma in beauty therapy, and vocational awards for international students.

Having been out of beauty therapy for many years I would like to thank a number of people without whom I could not have attempted such a challenge.

First, many thanks to Sue Diamond, Lecturer in Beauty Therapy, specializing in exercise at City College Manchester, who amended the chapter on exercise in line with current techniques.

I am most grateful to Sylvia Brooks and Adrienne Walsh from Abraham Moss Centre for giving their valuable time to advise me on the new techniques studied by today's beauty therapy students. I would also like to thank Helen Faulkner from Cheadle Beauty Salon for allowing her salon to become a photographic studio for the day and the wonderful Rebecca who posed so patiently throughout the session. I owe thanks to Malcolm Heywood, a very capable and experienced photographer who has brought the book alive and up to date.

Finally, I would like to thank all at Depilex who gave me valuable information about their range of treatments which are used in colleges and salons.

The memory of the late Audrey Githa Goldberg lives on.

Lucy McDonald

Preface to the Second Edition

Since its publication in 1972, this book has become the standard work for students of body massage in beauty therapy and has been reprinted, with revisions, on several occasions.

This new edition has been revised by my daughter, Lucy Goldberg, IEL ITec, a practising beauty therapist, and I know that it would have given Audrey the greatest pleasure to have had Lucy's co-operation on the book.

Several of the techniques have been revised and updated to cater for most examination syllabuses, especially City and Guilds and CIDESCO, and a section has been added on the important topics of aromatherapy and gyratory massage, both of which have come into prominence since the book first appeared.

Ivan J. Goldberg

Preface

Manual massage in this supersonic moon age of machinery has almost been superseded by electrical devices. But not quite. For although they can indeed produce quicker results which are far less tiring to the operator, no mechanical substitute has yet been found to replace the sensitivity of touch which exists in a pair of well-trained hands, and which is so essential to convey vital information for the correct application of massage.

It seems superfluous to say that it is a form of treatment providing physical comfort and reassurance which is as old as civilization itself. Yet in the past, massage has been badly neglected, misused, derided and degraded. The beauty therapy profession is rapidly expanding and with it the demand for massage has grown. Most people enjoy the sensuous luxury of a massage especially when well-administered and it is to the beauty therapist that they are now turning for it with confidence.

This book, covering the City and Guilds of London Institute syllabus on body massage for the beauty therapist's certificate, contains a comprehensive and useful chapter about exercises. It has been written for the student, the teacher and the beauty therapist who wish to learn, to revise or to improve their standard of massage simply and clearly without confusion. In this connection it will also be found useful by those following courses run by the National Society of Health and Beauty Therapists, the British Association of Beauty Therapy and Cosmetology Limited affiliated to CIDESCO and other examining bodies.

I am most grateful to Mr L. Sharrad, Vice Principal at the College of Fashion and Clothing Technology, London for all his help and advice. Also I would like to extend my thanks to Miss Brenda Savage, MSc, MCSP, DipTP, of the Physical Treatment Centre, Harrogate, for kindly reading the typescript and advising me on several points.

I am most indebted to Miss Hogson, Professional Consultant at the Chartered Society of Physiotherapy for her valued assistance and to Miss Willis, of City and Guilds of London Institute.

Audrey Githa Goldberg

A history of massage

The word 'massage' is thought to be derived either from the Arabic for 'press softly' or from the Greek for 'knead'. Massage is a form of treatment, coupled with exercises, which has been passed down through the centuries for thousands of years.

Records show that in ancient China over five thousand years ago there was a system of massage and exercise in use. Archaeological expeditions in Asia Minor have established that ancient Asiatic women and men used perfumed oils abundantly on their bodies and hair. It is almost certain that most races used massage and exercise in one form or another dating as far back as the prehistoric ages of man. The peoples of ancient civilizations in Persia, Japan, and Egypt practised the art of massage for cosmetic purposes, and found that they also gained therapeutic effects when they rubbed oils and perfumes into the body and skin to beautify it. Creams taken from Egyptian tombs were found to contain camel fat, almond oil, sheep fat, or castor oil mixed with various resins and tannic substances. These were for cosmetic purposes and were massaged into the skin. Anointing was the placing of a lump of fat on the head, which would gradually melt in the heat and cover the hair and body. Clothes would then cling to the body and reveal its shape. Anointing was also the expression used for rubbing oil into the body. Perfumed oils were used in three different ways by the ancient Egyptians: as offerings to their gods, as an enhancement of the body's beauty, making it smell pleasantly, and as the main ingredients for embalming the dead.

A great selection of the pots and vessels in which these oils were kept may be seen in the British Museum. They are so pretty that many designs for today's cosmetic jars are taken from them.

The Cretans in 1700 BC were great believers in personal hygiene and aesthetic beauty and they oiled their bodies when they took their daily baths. They believed that fresh air was essential for a beautiful body, and were meticulous about good ventilation producing a cooling system of breezes.

In 1000 BC Homer spoke in his Odyssey of beautiful women 'rubbing and anointing war worn heroes' to refresh and revitalize them after battle. He also described the toilet of the Greek goddess Hera in the Iliad: 'and with ambrosia first her lovely skin she purified with oil anointing'. The Greeks favoured gymnastics and believed them to be the basis of a good education. Massage, using the essences of sweet-smelling herbs and olive oil, was applied to the body. The Greek women were shy and plump but enjoyed gymnastics, and in order to acquire a graceful body they learnt dancing. Magnificent muscular physique, the Greek attribute so admired today, was due to the importance they attached so long ago to the use of exercise in building up the body.

The ancient Romans ruled by the Etruscans had quite an advanced system of massage also. Slaves always carried oils around in glass containers slung over their arms in case their masters and mistresses wanted a massage. Exercising, bathing, and sunbathing became quite organized in that order, and, as well as looking better, the Romans began to find considerable benefits both physically and mentally. The schemes of exercises which preceded the baths were carefully graded according to the age and fitness of the individual and even catered for their moods. Running, lifting dumb-bells, playing with balls and hoops were especially popular. Following all these gymnastics, sweating in the baths was recommended. The baths were taken in four stages, not unlike the varying systems followed today. First, there was a period of gradual warming-up sufficient to start sweating in mildly heated waters or steam. This led on to profuse sweating for a long period of time in a much hotter temperature. Then this was followed by the cooling-down process of a bath in tepid water. Finally, for those who were more hardy, plunging into icy cold water concluded the bathing. During all this time the slaves were expected to rub down their masters and mistresses. Together with manual massage, small brushes, not unlike curry-combs, were used. These were made of ivory or bone. Metal such as silver, copper, or iron was used if a more stimulating effect was desired, and if the skin could stand it. Sunbathing in the fresh air followed and completed the bathing routine which has changed little throughout the ages. Today certain rheumatic conditions of joints are treated with silver and gold injections and there are many people who wear copper bands in the belief that rheumatism can be prevented or relieved by doing so. Birch twigs are used by the Finns before bathing, and loofahs, scrubbing brushes, and flannels, have replaced the old idea of the curry-comb. A brisk rub-down with a rough towel after a bath or shower is only a modern idea on the old theme.

From these early beginnings of health and beauty a medical school of thought about massage arose. Around 500 BC the Greek historian Herodotus applied exercises and massage in the treatment of disease. Principles about the technique of rubbing began to be formulated. Massage was directed away from the heart, the pressure varied during the treatment, starting off by being gentle at first and then becoming deeper and quicker and petering off again slowly towards the end. Greasy mixtures were used.

In all the large cities in Greece at this time gymnastic centres were set up. Beautiful and splendid buildings were erected where students and philosophers could meet to discuss philosophy and attend lectures, while bathing and exercising at the same time. Greek games became very important and it is recorded that the body was rubbed and anointed with oil, fine sand, and powder before and after the games took place. Javelin throwing, wrestling, running, and jumping were great favourites. Many of the beautiful ruins of these gymnasia, built during the Greek civilizations, can still be seen today in Greece.

Hippocrates, the father of medicine about 380 BC, really used massage for the treatment of injuries and disease. He found that it was more beneficial if rubbing was done towards the heart, although the circulatory system was not understood then. It would seem, from his emphasis on pressure application, that Hippocrates had discovered the physiological effects of massage that are accepted today. He stated that 'hard rubbing binds; soft rubbing loosens; much rubbing causes parts to waste; moderate rubbing makes them grow.' His observations were very astute, and he advocated the use of a gentle and smooth rate and rhythm. He also advised women to sing at the tops of their voices to improve their bust line.

Galen (130–200 AD), a famous doctor during the Roman era, experimented in physiology and discovered that arteries were filled with blood, and not air as previously believed. He varied the direction of massage according to the reason for its being applied, and also greatly believed in treating injuries and diseases with it. Roman gladiators were oiled and massaged until they were glowing red and supple before commencing battle. Around this time some other terms describing massage were pommelling, squeezing, and pinching. The latter was recommended to be used all over the body to relieve neuralgia: a good counter-irritant, no doubt. Public baths modelled on the Greek style of architecture were by now more commonplace than ever before. People would gather together to exchange gossip and news. Being absolute geniuses with water their baths were quite unique. The Romans left their mark in England during the first century AD in towns where waters were considered to contain special minerals and salts of health-giving value. Harrogate, Buxton, Bath, Leamington, Droitwich, Cheltenham, Llandrindod all became spa towns famous for their springs, baths, and waters. Sulphur, magnesium, calcium, and peat of the area were utilized by the Romans in the quest for health and beauty. Many of these waters are still taken today and the towns where the ruins of the Roman baths can still be seen remain favourite and delightful attractions for tourists from all over the world.

Little seems to be recorded about massage or beauty again until the early Middle Ages, when wise women would advise on health and beauty. One Italian woman doctor about 1100 AD advised those ladies preoccupied with slimming and beauty to bathe in the sea and use deodorants which were made of herbs. Her remedy for losing weight was to be frictioned all over with cow dung mixed in medicinal herbs, and then to spend a long period of time sweating heavily in a small room, overpoweringly heated by a wood fire. Hot sand baths near the sea provided an alternative method for producing the same effect as the heated chamber. Today in Italy sand 'graves' are still to be seen near the sea in which people bury themselves up to their necks in the hot sand for the curative and slimming effect attributed to heat and sweating. Peat and mud baths are also still prescribed for rheumatism and are used as beauty treatments. Pine is the most popular essence used today in refreshing hot baths; perhaps this replaces the pungent odour of the cow dung.

During the fifteenth, sixteenth, and seventeenth centuries, Switzerland, France, Italy, Prussia, and England produced several famous physicians and surgeons who began once again to use massage in the treatment of injuries and disease. The old terminology of massage remained but new words such as pressure, kneading, and manipulations were introduced. Opinions about pressure were expressed and an Italian doctor even went so far as to state that the position of the patient should be outstretched lying down. Generally speaking, the patients were placed in most uncomfortable positions.

In the seventeenth century strange recipes for lotions and creams could be found to beautify the face and body beyond all hopes and dreams. One such lotion claimed to remove pox marks. It merely filled in the holes left by smallpox and gave an illusion of smoothness. There were quack doctors and beauty counsellors who lived by their wits, and patented medicines, potions, and creams for massage claiming fantastic results. New Bond Street opened its first beauty salon, where women would go, believing that the creams, oils, and cosmetics which the proprietress applied and sold would work miracles on their faces and bodies.

These cosmetics were outrageously expensive and the lady was eventually imprisoned for fraudulent claims. Hand creams were fashionable and ladies went to bed wearing chamois leather gloves which were saturated with cream to keep their hands soft and supple. Beauty care and cosmetics were considered to be only within the reach of high-class society, actresses, or the demimonde. Perfume was coupled with witchcraft, and laws governing the use of cosmetics were made which sentenced women to imprisonment. Massage for beauty at this time did not rate highly and most practitioners were suspect. Some of the pots which were made at this time for oils, grease, unguents, pomades, and lotions had decorative lids which are still in existence, and are eagerly hunted by 'pot-lid' collectors today.

From the end of the eighteenth century a great revival in massage really began. Many authorities wrote and expounded their theories on the subject. One extremist advocated that massage should be given with great violence, and all had different ideas about the terminology, pressure, rate, rhythm, and medium, such as oil or powder to be used, position of the patient, and the duration of treatment. Some advocated dry hands; one used a metal object covered with leather. Some suggested that four minutes' massage to any one area was sufficient; another stated that up to forty minutes could be given. Trial and error was another means of practising massage, and if it had not suited the patient one day a modification was made the next. The massage field became confused from then on with so many different opinions and descriptions. Peter Henry Ling of Sweden (1776–1839) made the most dramatic contribution to massage and exercise at this time. His influence in the early nineteenth century spread throughout all Europe and America. He was a conscientious and devoted worker, and realized that it was important to acquire a certain knowledge of anatomy and physiology before applying massage and exercises to the body. Of medicine he knew little and only treated those conditions he considered to be normal, emphasizing that all other conditions should be reviewed by the doctor. He founded the Swedish system of massage and exercise, and introduced terms such as effleurage, petrissage, vibration, and friction, as well as rolling, slapping, pinching, and several other descriptions of massage. However, despite the good work and promotion of massage by Henry Ling, it was not until the end of the nineteenth century that massage began to become favoured and accepted all over the world as an orthodox method of treatment. Perhaps this was due to the fact that training was inadequate and poor, and that those women engaged in massage were generally of ill repute and opportunists.

Doctor Mezger of Holland (1839–1901) helped to establish massage finally as a reputable means of treatment by prescribing it widely and practising it himself. Europe and America recognized and accepted its importance from then on, leaving England to be convinced. Beauty parlours in Bond Street, where facial massage became a speciality, began to flourish and their reputation grew. It was a rare sight by now to see a face unpainted or unpowdered, and oils and creams for the body and hands at the end of the nineteenth century were bought by all.

In 1894 a group of women joined together to form the Society of Trained Masseuses, in order to try to raise the standard and reputation of massage in this country. Rules and regulations for training were made. Examinations were set and the Society flourished.

In 1900 it became licensed by the Board of Trade and was called the Incorporated Society of Trained Masseuses. During the First World War its membership increased enormously. In 1920 it amalgamated with the Institute of Massage and Remedial Exercise (Manchester). A Royal Charter was then granted and it became known as the Chartered Society of Massage and Medical Gymnastics. The title was again changed in 1943 to the Chartered Society of Physiotherapy. State Registration came in 1964.

So it can be seen that massage was eventually given the stamp of respectability by the medical profession and the State in the treatment of injuries and disease, although it is little used in hospitals today. Although massage in physiotherapy had reached a high standard, it seemed as though there was an urgent need to raise the standard as practised in the beauty field.

In June 1966 City and Guilds of London Institute set up an Exploratory Committee to look into the possibility of providing further education and training for girls wishing to study beauty therapy, and of establishing a nationally recognized course. A syllabus was drawn up by a working party consisting of people from different beauty organizations, the education world, and the medical profession.

In September 1968 the first full-time courses in beauty therapy were offered in four colleges of further education by the Institute, and in May 1970 the first City and Guilds examination in this field was held.

All that remains is for beauty therapy to become a State-registered profession.

Ethics, the beauty therapist, and the salon

Qualities of the beauty therapist

The *essential* qualities of being a beauty therapist do not merely lie in the ability to give a good massage, exercises, or any other treatment. To be successful, therapists must have a strong belief that whatever they are doing is right. This involves a deep sincere liking and interest in the work they have chosen to do. It requires a high level of tolerance of human failings when dealing so intimately with people in this profession, many of whom return day after day, week after week.

Each client is an individual case for treatment and therefore should be regarded as such, and not subjected to an indifferent attitude by the therapist. Beauty therapy is a personal business and the therapist must have the ability to concentrate on the special requirements necessary for each case in hand to obtain the best possible result for the client's total benefit and well-being.

The ability to be kind, comforting and sympathetic, to be tactful and reassuring, to be cheerful and optimistic without ever promising too much should be present at all times in the therapist's disposition. These inherent qualities are an integral part of the treatment and indeed of any therapy. They are better known as the 'bedside manner'. It is often the bedside manner which effects the cure and instils confidence once again into the client. They are the trademarks of professionalism and will help to build up a good practice. Therapists must be able to relate themselves to the client sensually and mentally, without either themselves or the client becoming involved, and without the client being allowed to become dependent on them. Therefore, the duration of the course of treatment should be quite specific, serving a dual purpose; it also allows clients to feel that their goal is always in sight drawing nearer to being achieved with each successive treatment. This can always be extended and continued.

A high level of *intelligence* and *honesty* are necessary so that both the therapist and the client know and understand exactly what the massage or other treatments will accomplish. In this way therapists protect themselves from disillusion and misinterpretation. At the end of the day therapists can feel satisfied that their work has been honest, worthwhile and well done. If one form of treatment is found to be unsuitable, it is the therapist who gently guides and suggests another form rather than heavily persuading the client in order to keep a full appointment book. It is then left to the client to make the final decision either to stop, to continue, or to change the course of treatment. In this way clients will build up their trust in the therapist and will not feel cheated or let down.

Sensitivity and *respect* for the body is vital for, although it may represent a mass of fatty tissue, or a connection of bones and muscles from time to time, it does belong to somebody who has a name and a title, so that personal consideration when moving, massaging and manipulating the client should not be overlooked, especially when the client is dressing and undressing.

Rapport between the therapist and the client should be considered. If for any reason at all therapists are unable to feel in tune with the client or finds that they have insurmountable personality problems, then they should discuss the situation with their superiors or tactfully transfer treatment to another therapist whose approach to the client may be completely different, so alleviating the source of friction. If they work privately on their own and there is no other solution available, then it would be best to discontinue the treatment as soon as possible. One satisfied client's recommendation is worth more than ten dissatisfied customers. Massage is not erotic, although it produces a highly sensual feeling and if a client is suspected of requiring treatment for sexual reasons then it should be stopped immediately and further treatment discontinued. This kind of situation is very rare but requires treatment of the utmost discretion and highest integrity if it ever occurs.

Punctuality whether it is as a student in training or as a qualified practitioner is a habit which should be second nature. Keeping clients waiting and being late for appointments is sheer bad manners, being rarely justifiable. Overbooking of appointments leads to hurried and overlapping treatments, both of which are quite unnecessary. Clients usually prefer to keep the same appointment if possible each day.

Responsibility to colleagues and clients is important and being frequently absent for trivial reasons shows a complete lack of it. Dental appointments should be made out of working hours so that treatments or lectures are not interrupted, continuity is not affected, and clients feel that their beauty therapist is dependable. Personal duties however distasteful should be cheerfully and willingly accepted and carried out without question. In this way beauty therapists, or potential beauty therapists, build up their reliability and the reputation of the profession which they represent.

Physical and *mental stamina* are essential for a job which is absorbing, strenuous and exacting. As students, they will be required to work physically hard and to apply their mind intelligently to learning the theory. As qualified therapists, they should keep up-to-date with new techniques and modern treatments and should have a sound knowledge of anatomy.

Appearance should be neat and tidy. A uniform should be worn, preferably made out of a material which does not attract dirt and can be easily washed. It should give freedom of movement and not too clinical, although white always looks efficient. Buttons, hooks and eyes must be replaced immediately when lost and never substituted by safety pins. Dresses and skirts should be well above an even hemline, with nothing showing below, the sleeves should be above the elbow, again with nothing poking below them. Clean teeth, sweet breath and the regular use of a good deodorant should go without saying. Jewellery should not be worn, though this does not imply removing a wedding ring. A fine ring has always been permissible; it does not cause pressure or discomfort and cannot be felt during massage.

Shoes should be low-heeled for comfort and preferably rubber-soled for quietness and for safety (to prevent slipping on polished floors and when dealing with electricity). Beach sandals and coloured sandals look unprofessional, sloppy and undignified.

Hair, if long, should be tied well back, otherwise kept neat and tidy if short. Make-up if worn should be natural and well-applied. Nails must be short and well manicured, and if nail polish is applied a natural colour should be chosen. Naturally, together with the hands, the nails should be unquestionably scrupulously clean.

Beauty therapists should be the ambassador of their profession. Their deportment in their place of work must be calm and quiet. Their own posture should be impeccable, carrying their fresh sparkling uniform proudly. Their attitude should be one of politeness to all those around here including colleagues, super-iors, clients and those who make the tea and wash the floors. It costs nothing to open a door, or to say 'Good morning' or 'Thank you'.

Etiquette to doctors if they prescribe treatment or recommend a client to the beauty therapist is shown by carrying out their instructions implicitly. Their decision must not be discussed or queried with clients. This applies to treatment prescribed by a superior. If therapists feel that they cannot comply with the requirements or do not agree about the treatment, then they should have the courtesy to discuss the matter with the doctor and if they cannot carry out the treatment it would be prudent to give up the case. This applies in the case of those clients who knows what treatment they want. If therapists feel that it is the wrong treatment and cannot conscientiously carry it out she would do best to retract tactfully from the situation. Beauty therapists working in hospitals should always ask the person in charge of the ward if it is convenient to visit. The therapist should try to keep the beds tidy and keep out of the way of the hospital routine while giving the patient treatment.

Conversation should be limited to impersonal topics and therapists should not chatter too much to clients during the course of treatment as it can be tiring. Neither should they inflict their opinions on clients. They should be cheerful but try to dissuade clients from talking too much. However, it is often on the massage couch that clients reveal their secrets, personal problems and worries. These must be kept in strict confidence and while listening to clients they should never indulge in gossip with them, or about clients to others. They can be friendly without being familiar but it is generally a mistake to mix personal friendship with professional work. When the client asks for details about the treatment, the therapist must be prepared to explain them in simple terms without long and alarming names. Private medical information should not be disclosed without permission from the source.

Loyalty to colleagues, to superiors and to clients is essential to create an atmosphere of warmth, friendliness and trust. Criticisms of other salons and treatments by the clients is to be discouraged.

Vital requirements for massage

The first most important requirement for massage is a pair of well-schooled hands intelligently applied. They should be completely relaxed, warm and moulded to the part. Some people have a natural ability to relax them more than others but most people are capable of learning good techniques with practice.

Rate of movement should be carried out at a moderately slow speed but this depends upon the effect required.

Rhythm and flow of movement should be even, continuous and consistent. A good technique depends upon its use throughout all the massage treatments. The rhythm is produced by swaying backwards and forwards from the ankles, knees and hips.

Stance of beauty therapists while massaging is important to allow them to obtain a good rhythm and freedom of movement. A good stance also helps to avoid back strain and utilizes the body weight correctly. The positions of walk standing when working longitudinally down the length of the muscles, and stride standing when working transversely across the muscles are most frequently used. It is from these positions that the therapist is able to sway rhythmically and fluently while massaging, using the body weight effortlessly when required. Stooping not only gives a poor performance, but results in an aching back. The therapist should never lean on the client or on the couch.

Depth of pressure depends upon the area being treated and upon the sensitivity to the tissues of the therapist's hands. They should with experience be able to judge the condition of tissues, knowing when to decrease or increase the depth accordingly. The back and lower limbs require deeper pressure than that for the neck, chest and upper limbs. Most clients seem to prefer deep massage but when tissues are delicate, thin or stretched and afford little protection to the underlying bones, a light massage is advocated.

Greater depth of pressure is obtained by correct use of body weight transferred through the arms and into the hands. It is not acquired with brute force by pushing harder into the tissues or massaging quickly.

Position of clients should be such that they are well supported, accessible, warm and comfortable. Clothing should be removed completely if a general body massage is given and removed from the part locally where required. All the areas of the body which are not being treated should be kept covered with towels and blankets if necessary to ensure warmth. Pillows must support the whole of the limb and not just the area being massaged. This prevents stress and strain on joints and ligaments. For convenience and comfort clients should be either lying or prone lying unless there is some medical reason that necessitates them sitting up. Sometimes the client can be treated sitting at a small table or in a chair but this very much depends upon the area to be massaged. The ability to improvise when a couch is unavailable with the use of pillows and a table is an advantage.

Beauty therapists themselves must make the client feel at ease and welcome. Their appearance should be impressive. They should look clean and well groomed and should accompany clients to the place of treatment and show them out of the salon on completion.

Massage couch or *plinth* should be the correct working height, sturdy and with an adjustable back-rest. Therapists should not have to work on one which is either too low causing them to stoop or one which is too high so that they have to stretch, and are unable to use their body weight correctly. It should be wide enough to allow the client to turn over comfortably and yet remain near enough to the therapist without having to be moved closer. The base should be covered with a thin firm mattress and sheet.

Linen should be abundant, always freshly laundered and scrupulously clean. Clients should be covered or wrapped in a sheet and light-weight blanket. Small towels are used for covering locally exposed areas which are not being treated, for covering edges of the sheet and blankets when turned back while working on an area, and for placing under parts to afford protection from soiling the bed linen with powders and lubricants. The bed should always be kept as tidy as possible. A plentiful supply of pillows is necessary for the support and comfort of the client.

A *trolley* on quiet, well-oiled and smooth-running castors is of great value to be able to wheel equipment easily from one place to another. If there is no table by the couch then the trolley can be laid with the necessary oils, powders, tissues, tape-measure, spare towels, pillows, waste bowl and everything else that might be required during the course of treatment. It is a good place for a watch which, although necessary, should not be worn on the wrist while massaging.

Screens are vital if more than one client is being treated in the same room at once. Again these must be kept in a quiet, smoothly running condition. The curtains on them should be frequently washed as they tend to collect dust.

Electrical machines and all other equipment should be stored neatly out of the way in a corner. Suitable cupboards provided for cosmetics, powders, oils and suchlike should be kept clean and tidy. Regular stocktaking safeguards shortage of essentials.

Atmosphere and *decor* of the salon must be relaxing, friendly and welcoming. It should be tastefully furnished and decorated, making the clients feel pleased to be in such surroundings for their treatment. Carpets where possible are warm and deaden sound, but are not always practical round a working space. Here the floors should be kept clean and dry but not highly polished. Although shining floors are preferable because of their look, they can prove to be treacherously dangerous.

Warmth is an important factor and the room must be heated sufficiently for the body cools quickly when exposed. Good ventilation, however, prevents over-stiffness and airlessness.

The *reception area* requires comfortable chairs and up-to-date reading material in case the client has a short wait. Even quiet background music is conducive to a pleasant atmosphere.

Toilets should be within easy reach and as carefully and hygienically maintained as the department, with the usual washing facilities.

A *staff room* for the therapists is essential. It is in here they can relax, have a coffee, change their clothes, and check their final appearance.

Kitchen facilities that will provide the client with at least coffee or tea are always welcomed.

A *wash-basin* if possible should be near the couch so that therapists can wash their hands before and after treatment.

Business organization

A professional touch does not end with paper qualifications. If rendering a personal service to the public it should be run in a businesslike manner, whether it is a one-man band or not, and many professional people do not know how to run a business. When starting a business it is wise to seek the advice of a solicitor and an accountant on a regular basis so that it is under control at all times.

The *receptionist–telephonist* should be helpful and courteous with a ready smile to greet the client. They should have the ability to use their initiative in making appointments, taking correct messages and making decisions without interrupting the beauty therapist at work.

Accounts should be accurately maintained and recorded systematically and daily, so that a complete record of incoming and outgoing moneys can be easily checked.

The *tax inspector* will require to see books and records of wage deductions, income and all expenses.

Clients' record cards of treatment must be kept and an efficient filing system maintained. Personal details of the client, such as name, age, marital status, weight, measurements, etc. are recorded. The name and telephone number of the client's doctor is taken. Medical history should record major operations, illnesses or diseases. The date of the client's last visit to the doctor, and the reason, could be quite revealing. Any physical peculiarities must be noted such as birth-marks, scars, bruises, stretchmarks on the skin, or even varicose veins.

If therapists have any doubts about the health of the client, they should ask the client's permission to check with the doctor about the treatment proposed, which should be recorded. Any untoward effect of the treatment should be noted. The therapist must be on her guard for contra-indications of treatment which might be present or arise, and record anything extraordinary. This not only protects the client from harm but protects the reputation of the beauty therapist. Some establishments prefer their clients to sign a form accepting all responsibility of treatment. However, if no effort has been spared by the beauty therapist in setting a high standard and maintaining it, this should not be necessary.

By thorough and careful examination of the client a general picture of the client's health, fat, muscles and posture can be built up and a conclusion can be drawn as to what form the treatment should take. Even if clients only require half an hour's body massage, they should be given the kind of massage suitable for their type, arrived at by a detailed recorded analysis. Individuality of treatment can be guaranteed by the up-to-date maintenance of efficient record cards. Apart from the benefit to the client in the long run, the standards of the beauty salon will be high and as a business its reputation should grow in esteem.

Manipulations and massage technique

Massage can be defined as a scientific method of manipulating body tissues. It can be performed mechanically by the use of electrical equipment, and manually by hand. The following pages are concerned only with the classification and technique of manual massage. Students must bear in mind that there are different schools of thought on every subject. Massage is no exception but generally speaking classification of manipulations used in massage falls into four main groups. These groups in turn are further subdivided according to their functions and use upon the body tissues. Some French terminology is retained for convenience of description.

Groups of manipulations

There are four groups:

1 **Stroking**
   Effleurage
   Stroking
2 **Pressure**
   Kneading
   Picking up
   Wringing
   Rolling
   Frictions

3 **Percussion**
   Hacking
   Clapping
   Beating
   Pounding
4 **Shaking**
   Vibrations
   Shaking

Technique of manipulations

Part of good technique in massage is to ensure that the client's muscles are completely relaxed. Only if clients are relaxed will the massage by truly effective, although, of course, massage itself can be a means to an end by inducing a state of relaxation. However, the client's comfort and support with adequate pillows, blankets, the atmosphere of the salon, and the attitude of the therapist will provide the right medium to work in, and enhance good technique making sure the manipulations are effective.

Stroking manipulations

Effleurage

Effleurage is derived from the French word 'effleurer' meaning 'to skim over'. Effleurage can be deep or superficial. The technique for both is identical, except that the pressure varies.

For *deep effleurage* the pressure is finer and deeper. For *light* or *superficial* effleurage the pressure is superficial and lighter.

Technique

It is a stroking movement performed with the whole palmar surface of the hands. It follows the direction of the flow of blood back to the heart, i.e. venous return, and also along the flow of lymphatic vessels ending in a group of lymph glands. On smaller delicate areas such as the toes, fingers or face the padded palmar surface of the fingertips or thumbs may be used.

The hands may be used alternately, both together, or one may support the area while the other is used on its own. Whichever way they are used, the hands must be completely relaxed and moulded to the shape of the limb or part being treated.

The movement must be smooth and rhythmical; pressure is increased slightly at the end of the stroke, which ends whenever possible in a group of lymph glands, following the course of the veins and lymphatics from the distal end to the proximal end of the limb. The lymph glands for the arm are in the axilla (or armpit); those just above the clavicle are called the supra-clavicular glands. For the face massage, the lymph glands are at the back of the ear; for the leg, they are in the groin, or femoral triangle (see Figure 3.1). Those behind the knee are known as the popliteal lymph glands. At the end of the stroke the hands can glide back with no pressure exerted at all. This maintains continuity and rhythm of movement; contact with the client is unbroken. Some schools of thought prefer to lift the hands off the part at the end of the stroke, and move them back relaxed through

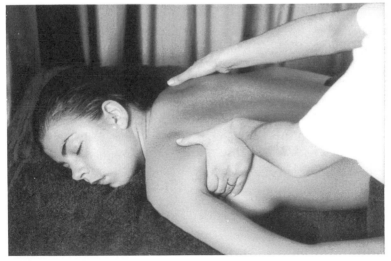

Figure 3.1 Effleurage into the axillae

the air before commencing again in effleurage. It very often depends on the client's reaction, and if the client appears to find the return gliding movement irritating then the latter technique can be employed.

The length of stroke depends upon the part being treated. Effleurage is usually performed slowly, as it is generally a manipulation aimed at the slow circulation.

Effects and uses of effleurage

1 Promotes the flow of blood in the veins, therefore helping to increase and improve the general circulation.
2 Increases the flow of lymph to the tissues and therefore waste products, amino-acids and carbon dioxide are more speedily removed into the lymphatic system where they are dealt with and absorbed.
3 Deep effleurage is thought to improve the capillary circulation in the skin, so the nutrition of the skin is aided and the process of healing is assisted, as in a spotty skin or a dry skin. The elasticity of the skin can be improved, as the sebaceous glands secrete more sebum keeping the skin soft and supple.
4 Superficial or light effleurage has a smoothing effect on the sensory nerve endings in the skin inducing relaxation in the client.
5 Effleurage helps the client to become accustomed to the therapist's touch. It gives them confidence in the hands of the beauty therapist. It is a manipulation that can provide good continuity in treatment joining up all other manipulations. All massage should begin and end with effleurage. It should be used generously and interspersed frequently throughout all forms of the massage manipulations, helping to emphasize their effects and removing any broken-down tissue products by any of these other manipulations (Figure 3.2).

Contraindications

1 Where the limb or area is grossly swollen, as there is a danger of breaking the skin with overstretching.

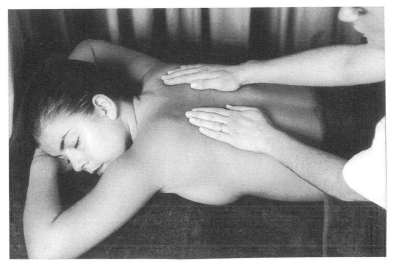

Figure 3.2 Effleurage to the back

2 Bad varicose veins where pressure may harm.
3 Hairy areas, as it is uncomfortable.
4 Any area where stretching of the skin could be harmful such as newly-healed scar tissue, or over-flabby, flaccid muscles.

Stroking

While certain points of technique of stroking are similar to effleurage, it must be entirely distinguished from it as a manipulation.

Stroking can be either:

1 Soothing.
2 Stimulating.

Technique

It is performed with a relaxed hand which may or may not be moulded to the part. It is entirely independent of the veins and lymphatics, and can be performed in any direction. However, like effleurage, it should be rhythmical. The continuity of the work and the contact should be maintained throughout. Some schools of thought consider it to be effleurage. It can be performed with the whole hand or again with the finger or thumb tips. The dorsum of the hand may be used if desired.

Soothing stroking

It is basically a gentle, slow and utterly rhythmical manipulation; the touch should be just firm enough for the client to be aware of the stroking, with the whole hand completely relaxed and moulded softly to the part. It is important for the therapist to feel as relaxed and supple as possible to enable this manipulation to be fully effective. The hand is gradually placed on and taken off the client, the return rhythm of the movement in the air being as slow, smooth and meticulous as the actual stroke, taking the same amount of time to return to the beginning.

Again, like effleurage, one hand may follow the other alternately, both hands may be used together or the stroking may be done with only one hand while the other gently supports the area. The length of the stroke varies according to the area being treated. It can be performed anywhere on the body.

Effects and uses of soothing stroking

1 It soothes the cutaneous nerves and induces relaxation.
2 It can induce sleep and help insomnia.
3 Produces a feeling of restfulness, particularly when performed on the back, from the base of the skull to the bottom of the spine, and is used to relieve tension.
4 The capillaries in the skin contract and swellings can be reduced.
5 Muscle relaxation can be promoted and tension headaches can be relieved by gentle stroking on the brow.
6 Can be used for tense, nervy clients.
7 Stroking can cool down a hot area.

Contraindications

1 When a client is irritated by stroking.
2 Marked poor circulation such as seen in chilblains and dead white fingers.

Stimulating stroking

Performed quickly and vigorously in any direction with the palmar or dorsal aspect of the hand or fingers. Pressure varies according to the treatment as does the length of the stroke.

Effects and uses of stimulating stroking

1 The cutaneous nerves are stimulated, therefore a sense of invigoration occurs. Can be used for the treatment of lethargic, obese clients where stimulation of inefficient muscles is required.
2 Involuntary muscle is also stimulated and this manipulation can be used on the abdominal organs to increase their activity if required.
3 Stimulating stroking can stimulate the central nervous system and if used firmly from the base of the head to the bottom of the spine could invigorate and tone up a tired client.
4 Stimulates the glandular activity of the hair follicles, and brisk stroking of the scalp would produce more sebum, so promoting the growth of hair.

Contraindications

1 Insomnia.
2 Tense, nervous and excitable clients.
3 Painful areas.
4 Muscle tension.
5 Poor circulation.
6 Clients who dislike stroking.

Pressure manipulations

The manipulations under this heading are sometimes referred to as petrissage. This word comes from the French 'petrir' meaning 'to knead'. Kneading incorporates varying manipulations, all of which press the tissues down on to the underlying structures.

Picking up, wringing and skin rolling incorporate the technique of lifting the tissues away from the underlying structures, namely bone. These three manipulations alone are sometimes referred to as petrissage. They are all essentially pressure manipulations and are used on individual muscles or definite muscle groups, where one end of the muscles to the other is worked upon.

Wringing and skin rolling are manipulations particularly employed for the skin and subcutaneous tissues, such as fat.

Kneading of the abdominal organs has been adapted to suit the area and the function of the organs, so the manipulations simulate the action of peristalsis.

Frictions are stationary pressure manipulations used for localized treatments or small areas where the tissues are pressed down on to the underlying structures.

Kneading

Technique

As with all massage the hands must be supple and relaxed. Kneading has many variations, according to the shape, size and bulk of the area being treated, so the kneading can be adapted accordingly. But it is all kneading. The pressure emphasis is given in the direction of the venous blood return to the heart. The tissues are pressed and relaxed against the underlying bone.

Kneading may, like other manipulations, be performed with one or both hands. It is the whole palmar surface that is used. The muscles are gently squeezed, pressed and released against the underlying structures. On relaxation of the hands they glide slowly along the muscle or muscle groups being treated. Some authorities consider the kneading as a form of petrissage.

Modifications of kneading are considered below. They consist of flat handed, squeezing, circular and finger kneading as well as ironing (double-handed kneading).

Flat handed kneading

Technique

Sometimes when working on large thin sheets of muscle, such as on the back, squeezing is impossible and the pressure decreases. This is called flat handed kneading.

Squeezing kneading

In this modification the tissues are squeezed.

Effect and use

In both squeezing kneading and flat handed kneading there is a slight increase in circulation, used for relaxation, due to its gentle rhythm and superficial effect.

No *contraindications* are necessary whenever massage is used.

Circular kneading

Technique

This manipulation is performed with one or both hands working alternately either side along the length of the limb. The muscles and soft tissues are pressed against the bone in a circular direction. The soft padded surfaces of the palms of the hands and fingers are used, great care being taken that the heel of the hand does not dig into the tissues. Rubbing the skin on bony parts must be avoided by releasing the pressure of the hands when massaging over them.

Areas around the shoulder, for example, the coracoid and acromion process of the scapula, the forearm, and the prominent shin bone in the lower leg are particular points to note with this manipulation. However, the pressure should be deep with circular kneading otherwise 'skin rubbing' results if the muscles are not massaged against the bone.

Effects and uses

1 The main effects are on the muscles. A better blood supply to the muscles is stimulated, therefore they are nourished and fed so helping to maintain elasticity and tone.
2 Improved blood supply will help to carry away fatigue products and carbon dioxide, so refreshing the muscles and helping to alleviate the feeling of stiffness after muscular exertion.
3 When performed rhythmically and slowly down the length of the limb it has a sedative effect and promotes relaxation, also easing away tension and any nervous twitching of muscles.
4 If performed down the length of the spine particularly slowly, a general feeling of restfulness can be obtained and possibly clients would become so completely relaxed that they would fall asleep.
5 If performed briskly this manipulation can stimulate the muscles and invoke a sense of alertness and well-being on perhaps a rather lethargic client.
6 Because of the pressure of the kneading against the bone, the blood supply to the periosteum is stimulated. Thus, the bone itself is fed and nourished.
7 Kneading is performed on the organs of digestion, which is aided in all its stages by abdominal massage. The end-product of a good digestive system is glowing healthy skin, always providing that the diet is well-balanced in the first place. Kneading on the abdomen can be used to help relieve constipation.

Contraindications

1 On extremely hairy surfaces.
2 On the abdomen if distended.
3 In cases where massage is completely contraindicated.
4 Where clients are excessively weak or feeble.

Finger kneading

Technique

This is a circular movement performed with the pads of the palmar surfaces of the thumb or first and second fingers localizing the massage (Figure 3.3). It can be used around the shoulder girdle, down the long back muscles, on small areas such as the face or soles of the feet or hands. It is similar to frictions but is used mainly for muscles rather than joints. Again the muscle is pressed against the bone and moved in a circular direction.

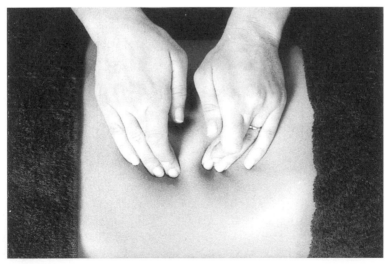

Figure 3.3 Finger kneading

Effects and uses

1 Mainly to obtain a localized hyperaemia on small muscles in hands and feet where the larger manipulation would skim over the more intrinsic muscles.
2 Used lightly for more delicate massage as on the face.
3 Used to stimulate the muscles of the arches of the foot and to improve nutrition and tone to these muscles: refreshing and stimulating to someone who has been standing all day long.

Ironing

Sometimes called reinforced kneading or double handed kneading.

Technique

The technique of ironing is to reinforce one hand on the other so obtaining greater depth, together with body weight (Figure 3.4).

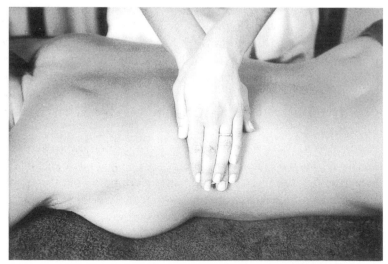

Figure 3.4 Ironing

Heavier structures can be moved against the bone, as found in the gluteal region or on the back.

Effects and uses

1 Excellent for relieving low back aches where no medical condition exists.
2 Loosens and stretches soft tissues making joints more mobile.
3 If performed slowly and rhythmically can be soothing and relaxing.

Picking up

Technique

Picking up is quite a stimulating form of petrissage. It can be performed with one or both hands, depending upon the area being treated. The movement should be like all massage, smooth and rhythmic and also continuous from one end of the attachment of the muscle to the other. The technique is to grasp the muscle with the whole hand, making sure that the thumb is completely abducted. The muscle is lifted away from the bone, squeezed and relaxed again. On relaxation of the part, the other hand, without breaking contact, grasps a fresh area and the movement is repeated in a 'plodding manner' up and down the length of the muscles, or muscle groups. Pinching between the thumb and fingers must be avoided and pressure is given in the upward direction.

If performed with one hand as on the deltoid muscle, then the muscle is grasped either side. Alternatively, one hand can overlap the other with the thumb of one hand overlapping the fingers of the other. The fingers and thumbs of each hand should be straight. This is a lovely manipulation used on the scruff of the neck, an awkward shape and area to manipulate. The muscle group or area to be massaged is treated with the whole hand lifting the tissues at a right angle and away from the underlying bone, is squeezed, and then relaxed again before moving on and a fresh grasp being made.

Effects and uses

1 Can be used in conjunction with hacking for extremely heavy or fatty areas.
2 Can be used on heavy thick tissues, such as the gluteal region or hips where there may not be much mobility of tissues.

Wringing

Technique

The technique of wringing is to lift the structures away from the bone and move them from side to side across the length of the muscle, with the fingers of one hand working with the thumb of the opposite hand (Figure 3.5). After the tissues have been grasped and stretched, the hands move alternately along the muscles from one end to the other.

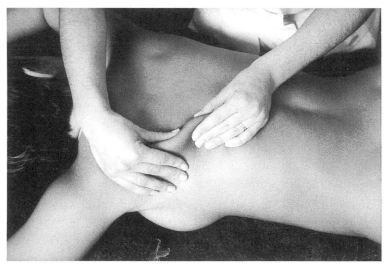

Figure 3.5 Wringing

Effects and uses

1 Like all massage it increases the circulation and thus nourishes and feeds the tissues.
2 It is chiefly used on large loose muscle groups so improving tone and elasticity, giving an overall sense of well-being.
3 It is a manipulation which produces heat quickly and absorption is assisted, so that large fatty areas are treated with this manipulation.

Skin rolling

This form of pressure massage (Figure 3.6) can only be used where there is some underlying hard bone against which the tissue can be pressed and rolled. It affects the skin and subcutaneous tissues.

Technique

The technique of skin rolling is to place the hands flat on the area. The skin and soft superficial tissues are grasped firmly between

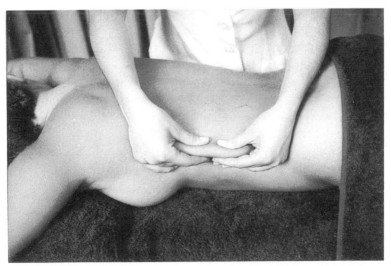

Figure 3.6 Skin rolling

fingers and thumbs and gently rolled backwards and forwards against the thumbs or fingers. It should be performed transversely across the limbs or back, and great care must be taken to ensure comfort of performance.

Effects and uses

1 Stimulation of blood and skin, increasing nutrition and functions of skin.
2 Used over fatty tissues.
3 This manipulation if performed slowly can be used to induce relaxation. If a brisk rhythm is employed, it can stimulate a client, leaving a sense of invigoration.
4 The skin can be loosened over tight areas making it soft and supple, and also relieving adhesions and releasing tensions. Elasticity of the dermis is improved and maintained.

Frictions

Technique

These are small deep movements with much pressure (Figure 3.7). Before travelling on to a new area, the pressure must be completely released. Frictions are very localized movements performed in a circular or transverse direction with the thumb or fingertips. Circular frictions gradually progress to a maximum depth into the muscle or structures being treated. Transverse frictions maintain a steady and even pressure throughout the movement across the muscle fibres. The fingers must not be hyperextended, especially when working deeply, as this strains the joints of the fingers. It is important to move the skin and superficial structures against the deeper structures with no movement taking place on the surface of the skin. Usually the part needing frictions the most is tender, such as in cases of fibrositis, so care must be taken in application of this manipulation not to cause unnecessary discomfort. Effleurage should be interspersed frequently when frictions are applied.

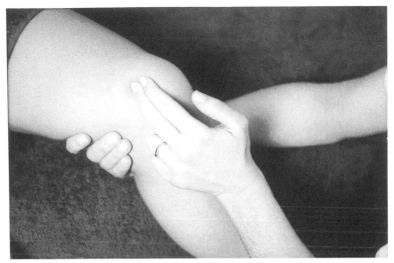

Figure 3.7 Frictions round the knee joint

Effects and uses

1 Adhesions are broken down, such as stiff joints, or in fibrositic conditions usually found in the back. Localized hyperaemia is produced and this softens the adhesions and helps to bring nourishment to the area.
2 Frictions can loosen and stretch scar tissue.
3 Spinal frictions can produce an invigorating effect through stimulating the spinal nerves leaving the client with a sensation of glowing.
4 Because of the localized hyperaemia, joint structures can be nourished, possible arthritic conditions prevented, and mobility of joints increased and maintained.

Contraindications

1 All cases of acute inflammation or severe pain.
2 Over joints which are deformed by rheumatoid arthritis.
3 Whenever massage is generally contraindicated.
4 On bony surfaces.

Percussion manipulations

These are sometimes referred to as a tapotement. They consist of a series of manipulations which strike the body. Both hands are used alternately. The wrists are kept loose and mobile so that the movements produced are light, springy and stimulating.

Hacking

Technique

This is a movement performed with the elbows bent and arms abducted (taken away from the mid-line of the body). The wrists are extended but the fingers should be fairly relaxed (Figure 3.8). The movement is of pronation and supination of the forearm allowing the ulnar side but dorsal surface of the fifth, fourth and third fingers to strike the part being treated. The sound should be like falling raindrops and the action should be as sharp and as

Figure 3.8 Hacking

rapid. If a deeper effect is required, as on the heavy gluteal structures, then the ulnar border only of the hand and fingers can be used. Care must be taken to avoid bony areas and prominences with hacking. Hacking can be performed with the tips of the fingers for more delicate areas such as the face, the movement consisting of flexion and extension of the wrists. This is sometimes known as point hacking, tapping or digital tapotement.

Effects and uses

1 If light hacking is performed across the muscle fibres, it can stimulate them to contract without nerve stimulation; therefore hacking can be used to tone up muscles.
2 Its stimulating effect leads to a sensation of invigoration and refreshment to the muscles treated.
3 The client will also experience a glowing sensation due to the increased flow of blood to the muscles, so raising the metabolism due to the increase in temperature.
4 The increased blood supply raises the temperature to the part and hacking can be used for warming up a cold area.
5 A roll of fat can be picked up and hacked with one hand.
6 Hacking tones up the muscular and circulatory systems throughout the body.
7 Hacking down either side of the spine stimulates the spinal nerves and is refreshing.
8 Hacking over the abdominal organs stimulates their actions and aids digestion.

Contraindications

1 Hacking must never be used over bony areas.
2 On areas which are tending to contract and shorten.
3 On spastic muscles.
4 In cases of excitability or nervousness.
5 In painful conditions.

Clapping

Technique

This manipulation (Figure 3.9) is used for the limbs, back and chest. Again as with all percussion, the wrists must be flexible. Clapping is a movement performed with the palmar surfaces of the hands, which are slightly cupped. The movement of flexion and extension takes place in the wrist. The fingers can either be placed on the part and the heels of the hands are lifted and dropped quickly, or the whole of the cupped hand can be lifted and dropped on to the area being treated. In both instances the hands must spring off the part lightly and quickly, creating a hollow, cupping sound.

Effects and uses

1 Increases blood flow to the skin and so improves condition of skin.
2 Increases blood flow to the lungs in the thorax, therefore there is a better interchange of gases in the lung capillaries. In turn,

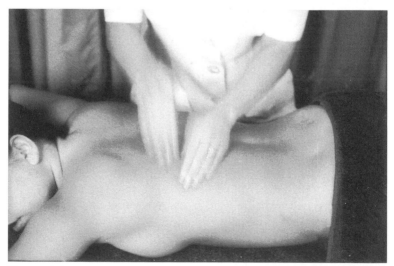

Figure 3.9 Clapping

more oxygen will be carried to the tissues of the body and the gaseous waste products exhaled.

3 Loosens mucus to hollow organs, such as the lungs.
4 Because of the increase of activity of the lung tissue their resistive powers to infection can be said to be increased.
5 Increases the circulation of the area treated and causes increased nutrition and a sensation of warmth.
6 This manipulation can be used again over fatty tissue.

Contraindications

1 The same as for hacking.
2 Where the client has had tuberculosis of the lungs, to the chest only.
3 Never applied over abnormally contracted muscles.

Beating

Technique

Beating is a heavier manipulation similar to clapping, but it is performed with a loosely clenched fist, so the dorsal part of the fingers strike the client and the heel of the hand comes into contact with the part to be treated. The hands again work alternately, but one only can be used, for example over the sacrum or liver.

Pounding

Technique

This is another form of heavy percussion. It is a movement similar to hacking, the loosely clenched fist striking the part to be treated with the ulnar border of the hand.

Effects and uses of beating and pounding

1 Used over the liver they will stimulate cell activity. More bile will be produced and therefore sluggish digestion aided. This in turn shows its improved effects in the tissues of the body.
2 Can be used to stimulate the nerves in the sacral area. This in turn helps to quicken peristalsis, improve digestion, and relieve constipation.
3 Can be used on areas where the subcutaneous fact is dense and heavy, so helping to soften the adipose tissue.
4 Imparts a healthy glow to the part being massaged and tones up the muscles.
5 With each striking movement the muscles first contract and then relax as the fingers are removed from the body. Muscle activity is increased with this manipulation.
6 All other effects as for hacking and clapping.

Contraindications

1 Where tissues are thin and delicate.
2 Over bony areas to prevent bruising.
3 In cases of general weakness and where the client is excessively thin, as these manipulations are far too heavy.
4 All other contraindications as for hacking and clapping.

Shaking manipulations

Vibrations

Technique

Vibrations are a fine trembling-like movement performed with one or both hands, using either the whole palmar surface of the fingertips. The movement consists of small quick flexions and extensions at the fingers and wrist joints. The therapist's arms and hands must be completely relaxed as it is a tiring manipulation, and will not be effective if tension in the operator's muscles is produced. The vibrations can be *static*, that is performed in one place, or they can be *running* where the hand or fingertips travel over the part while still vibrating. They can be fine, or coarse and more vigorous.

Effects and uses

1 Scar tissue can be loosened.
2 Fine vibrations have a sedative effect and can be used over nerves and nerve centres to relax a client.
3 Relieves flatulence in the abdominal organs.
4 Coarse vibrations are stimulating.
5 Vibrations performed down the spinal column with the fingertips will stimulate a lethargic client and produce a sensation of alertness and refreshment.

Contraindications

1 Coarse vibrations as for tapotement where all cases for stimulation are undesirable.
2 Fine vibrations are contraindicated where massage in all forms in contraindicated.

Shaking

Technique

Shaking is similar to vibrations, being performed with relaxed hands. It is a shaking movement of the hands moving the part up and down, or from side to side or in and out.

Effects and uses

1 The same effects as for percussion.
2 Loosens mucus in lungs.
3 Stimulates liver cells.

4 If used to shake the limbs, the bone marrow is said to be stimulated thus increasing output of red blood corpuscles and therefore enriching the blood stream.

5 Can increase the vitality and functional activity of the abdominal and thoracic organs; therefore it is of great value to the body generally.

Contraindications

As for percussion.

Summary of effects of massage

All the various manipulations of massage have to some extent the same effect. The chief effect of massage is definitely on the circulation and, in turn, by this manner can influence the various tissues and organs of the body. There is little effect on the activity of the muscles and therefore the tone, which can only be improved effectively by active exercise.

Correcting faulty eating habits by well-balanced diets is the best means for reducing fatty tissue. However, each manipulation has its own special effect on some particular tissue and students should learn which manipulation to apply for the kind of effect they are hoping to bring about.

Effleurage chiefly affects the flow of lymph, the blood back to the heart and the circulation. It is useful in cases of fatigue, aids absorption of waste and broken-down products, helps healing processes and increases the nutrition of the tissues. It is used for nourishing the skin, so improving its function.

Stroking affects mainly the nerve endings in the skin. It is useful in relaxing or stimulating a client according to whether soothing or stimulating stroking is used.

Pressure manipulations stimulate muscle or muscle groups, increasing their circulation and so improving nutrition, helping to restore tired function and improve tone, especially after exercise when stiffness can be alleviated. Used most frequently in an abdominal massage, improving the functioning of the abdominal organs.

Wringing and *skin rolling* is used especially on adipose tissue to soften and break down fatty masses. Good for loosening muscles and adherent skin, maintaining elasticity.

Picking up is often applied to muscle bellies and to a lesser degree to the tendons.

Frictions bring about a local hyperaemia and quite definitely aid absorption of inflammatory products. Mostly used around joints, so increasing mobility, also in the long muscles of the back and around all tender spots on the back, breaking down tension areas causing pain. Can be used to loosen scar tissue and stimulate the spinal nerves. Care must be taken not to cause a deadening sensation with too much pressure, unless specifically required

Percussion is used to stimulate nerves and muscles and give a feeling of increased tone. It also stimulates nerves, leaving a general exhilarating and glowing sensation. Again, too much percussion on one spot can deaden the area. It can be used to soften fatty tissue for weight reduction. Combined with picking up, hacking can help to break down subcutaneous fat. Also used in loosening mucus in the lungs, therefore promoting a better gaseous interchange and allowing more oxygen to be taken to the muscles. It also stimulates deep organs in the abdomen to better functioning.

Vibrations and *shakings* especially affect nerves and organs. According to the effect required and manipulation used, they can soothe or stimulate nerves, thus producing a relaxation of the client, or invigoration. They also loosen mucus in the lungs and stimulate the cells of the abdominal organs. Useful for constipation, sluggish liver and poor digestion.

Psychological effects of massage

Massage has been endowed with powers of magic beyond all imagination and it is as well to bear in mind its limitations. However, the psychological effects produced are unlimited and cannot be underestimated by any manner of means. The marvellous tonic effect of massage is not only confined to the healthiest and most normal person, but its value has been recognized by psychiatrists and doctors. A beauty care service organized by the Red Cross has spread up and down the country to help people in psychiatric wards and long-term patients in other hospitals throughout the country.

It is necessary for the therapist to understand that many benefits received from massage are physiologically impossible without long-term and regular treatment. This, on no account, means that its value is less. Health, both physical and mental, is the basis of beauty and in the busy average day when all systems are go, tensions mount and relaxation is impossible. These tensions of the mind and body begin to show on the face and in the body, which ages and deteriorates. Men and women alike have little time to spare for relaxation at home, and very often there is nowhere to go where their peace remains undisturbed, even if they have time.

So they visit the beauty salons to escape the hectic city life and enter the serene and pleasant atmosphere that should welcome them. Minor aches and pains caused by nervous tensions can be soothed and massaged away as the sense of relaxation seeps over the body. A glowing sensation of well-being is promoted after a well-executed massage.

Some clients who feel they are ageing fast may not look younger after treatment but feel completely rejuvenated. Some clients, young or old, need the help of massage to encourage them to stick to rigid diets, especially if they feel that the fatty tissues are being softened and broken down more quickly. Other clients merely want to avail themselves of the luxury of being pampered, soothed and being made to feel beautiful by massage; they enjoy spending time in having their bodies looked after and enhanced. Others like the pleasant sensory effect that massage can give.

Perhaps, during the course of treatment, a client needs the comfort of a sympathetic and willing ear to listen to any troubles. Clients may need reassurance about their figure, face or age and may feel that massage does much to benefit them in this way.

Many clients really feel that aches and pains are cured with massage; perhaps it is because the tensions causing the aches and pains have been reduced by a relaxing massage and very often disappear. The increased circulation does help to relieve pain also. Some clients need to feel stimulated and alert and a brisk massage will invoke a sensation of invigoration.

Feeling refreshed, invigorated, glowing and marvellous for whatever reason at the end of a treatment of massage is the keynote that it has been successful. An experienced masseuse will recognize immediately what it is that a client requires, and will endeavour to provide the conditions and massage necessary for such a treatment. Remember that beauty radiates outwards from within. Psychologically clients benefit by massage because they simply feel it is doing them good. They feel healthier and in turn look healthier.

Even if massage had no physical benefits whatsoever, the beauty salons would still be full of people requiring massage for the wonderful sensation that it produces.

General contraindications of massage

1 In recent injuries and any condition that requires medical supervision.
2 Tumours or unrecognizable lumps.
3 Over varicose veins or phlebitis or thrombosis.
4 In acute inflammatory conditions.
5 Rheumatoid arthritic joints.
6 Swollen ankles due to other causes than long periods of standing.
7 Grossly swollen limbs.
8 In pregnancy.
9 Immediately prior to and during a period, to the abdomen or sacral areas.
10 Neuritis and neuralgia.
11 Acutely painful areas.
12 When the temperature is raised.

13 Skin diseases.
14 Over especially hairy area due to discomfort.
15 Abdominal massage in cases of diarrhoea, high blood pressure and hernia.
16 In cases of lung disease.
17 Over unhealed and recently healed wounds and scars.
18 In the area of boils or carbuncles or round septic conditions.
19 Haemophilia where a client might bleed easily if accidentally bruised.
20 In older clients with a tendency to arteriosclerosis (hardening of the arteries) a vigorous massage would be contraindicated.
21 Loss of skin sensation.
22 Low blood pressure.
23 Glandular obesity.

Lubricants, oils, powder and massage creams

As far as therapists are concerned, if they are skilled enough and their technique of massage perfected to a fine art, they should not need to use any form of lubricant or powder. However, if it should be necessary from their point of view to use an aid of this kind, it should be used as sparingly as possible.

Sometimes clients request that certain oils or creams are used, according to the claims of the beauty preparations, and they will feel that their massage has added value if the benefits are massaged into the skin and body. Whatever emollient is used it should always be applied to the hands of the therapist first and not directly on to the client.

Oil

Olive oil softens and nourishes the skin and subcutaneous tissues. It will lubricate a dry skin and enable masseuses to stretch the skin without tearing or skin rubbing so that they can massage deeper into the tissues. This in turn makes the skin more supple. If deep frictions are given it is inadvisable to use oil in order to obtain maximum penetration. It is no use trying to disguise wet, sticky hands by using oil, for they will merely slide off the client, producing an irritating and unsatisfactory massage. Essential oils are becoming widely used in beauty therapy.

Powder

The finest of powders should be used and preferably one with the most innocuous smell. Fine French chalk or even a brand-named baby powder is suitable. The therapist's hands should be powdered: never under any circumstances should the therapist powder the client as though using salt and pepper on a bag of chips. The powder is of no benefit to the client, but purely to the hands of the operator, who may be a bit sticky. If the skin is dry, powder will only irritate the condition. Keep the use of powder down to a minimum. Flapping it around in the air creates a dusty atmosphere and gets in the eyes and nose of the client.

Soap, oil and hot water

These can be discreetly used in cases where the client has dirty or scaly patches of skin, until the condition is alleviated. Sometimes the soles of the feet are neglected, or on a wet rainy day the shoe dyes soak through the skin.

Cold massage cream

Cream can be used over hairy surfaces which can then be massaged satisfactorily. It can be used in the same manner and for the same reason as powder. Creams are usually more readily absorbed into the skin than oil. Again, the importance of applying it first to the hands of the masseuse cannot be stressed too strongly. Always use extra towels when applying particularly greasy lubricants. Excessive lubricants at the end of the massage can be wiped off with eau-de-cologne or surgical spirit, according to the preference of the client.

Hand exercises

Relaxation and suppleness of the hands and joints of the hands is most important. Exercises should be practised daily until all the joints are free and mobile. Both hands should be able to work equally well. They should be well-manicured, smooth and warm.

Practise the following exercises before attempting to massage.

1 Quickly make a fist clenching and stretching out the fingers.
2 Roll the thumbs round and round, first one way, then the other.
3 Roll each finger round.
4 Stretch each finger separately and then together.
5 Place index fingers and thumbs together and try to stretch them in a straight line.
6 Separate the fingers slowly and quickly.
7 Bend the fingers straight over from the metacarpo-phalangeal joint (knuckle) and back as far as they will go.
8 Flap the wrists up and down, from side to side, and in a circle until they feel completely loose, relaxed and both moving equally.
9 Bend the elbows and turn the palms first to the floor and then to the ceiling quickly in pronation and supination.
10 Shake wrists again together and then alternately.
11 Palms together, elbows out at the sides, stretch back the wrists in a prayer position.
12 Knead a soft ball.

13 Whole arm and shoulder shaking.
14 Circle wrists round and round.

Hints for practising technique

1 **Develop sensitivity** by practising feeling the shapes of different objects with the eyes closed. Anything will do at any time and any place. Then practise feeling the shape and size of the tissues to be massaged by relaxing the hands completely and drawing them gently over the areas and contours of the body.
2 **Use spirit and cologne** on moist, sticky hands. Damp hands are a disadvantage is massage but, as confidence grows, tenseness resulting in perspiring hands disappears.
3 **Practise hacking**, clapping, beating and pounding on a hard wooden surface until it can be performed with ease for ten minutes at a time painlessly.
4 **Use hand cream** to keep the hands smooth and soft.
5 **Wash hands frequently** and always before and after a massage.
6 **Soak cold hands** under a hot tap prior to massaging, although they do soon warm up and cold hands are often an advantage in massage as they rarely become sticky during treatment.
7 **Depth and strength of manipulation** is varied by the correct use of body weight. Practise the changing of the two most important positions of the feet until it becomes second nature to swivel from one into the other.
8 **Practise the smooth change** from one manipulation to another for good continuity.
9 **Use music** to practise rhythm and speed of manipulations.
10 **Try to massage a client** on a plinth or massage couch suitable to the therapist's own requirements. If the couch is too low, stand further away and bend from the hips keeping the back straight. If masseuses work with a bent back they will get backache and the treatment will be poor.

The physiological effects of massage

Effects on the muscles

When muscles work, they need a greater supply of oxygen and more waste products are produced. The waste products can accumulate when the muscles are resting and stiffness results. If muscles are massaged the blood supply is increased. This increased circulation not only feeds the muscle tissue but brings with it oxygen and absorbs the waste products. Muscles are kept in tone and functional power with massage. However it is important to realize the limitations of massage and to understand that nothing can have the same value as active exercise. An athlete will always feel refreshed after great muscular exertion when massaged, as the acceleration of the blood will help to carry away the toxic products formed in the muscles during strenuous exercise.

Due to an increased production of heat because of the improved blood supply to the muscles, the whole body will feel warmer and the temperature can be raised. So it can be seen that a vigorous massage of the muscles will produce in them a warm glow throughout the body.

Increase and improvement in tone causes an increase in elasticity and extensibility. Tense and short muscles can be relaxed and stretched with massage. This factor can be made use of when correcting postural faults. Very often with bad posture the flexor groups of muscles tend to shorten and contract, gaining tone. The extensor muscles become over-stretched and lose tone. For instance, tight pectoral muscles across the chest could be greatly massaged, bearing relaxation in mind, while the back extensor muscles are given a vigorous and stimulating treatment. This would help to stretch and relax the hollow tight chest and strengthen up the rounded back.

Again, bearing in mind that the muscular system is really dependent upon active exercise for its greatest increase in tone and size, massage can be a valuable accessory to their normal functioning. Muscles work over joints and if the mobility of the joints is impaired by any kind of adhesions, then the function of the muscles will in turn suffer, as full-range movement will be prevented. Therefore massage, such as frictions, around and into joints will help to prevent adhesions or loosen and stretch them. Mobilizing the joints in this way will indirectly help the movement of the muscles, enabling weak muscles to move more easily and increase their range. Weakened muscles, due to long periods of disuse, can be benefited by massage and more readily returned to normal, than if left unused and unaided.

The alternate pressure and relaxation on each muscle fibre causes an increased circulation to it. Blood is said to flow three times more quickly through a muscle which has been massaged. This improved blood supply increases nutrition to the muscle fibre, and in turn of the whole muscle and muscle groups.

Kneading and all other forms of pressure manipulations, including effleurage, can improve muscle tone and delay wasting away of muscles through disuse. Although beauty therapists do not practise heart massage, it should be remembered that the heart is a muscle too, and many lives have been saved by massage to this special muscle.

Effects on the bones and joints

Pressure against the periosteum stimulates the blood circulation to the bones. This feeds and nourishes the bone itself and also the joints in the neighbouring area. Indirectly, massage to the muscles of the body can affect the direction of bone growth. Bone tends to grow in the direction of the least pressure. The flexed group of muscles exert the strongest pressure and force on the bones. If the flexors are massaged to help them relax in cases of tension and the extensor group of muscles stimulated by massage then the direction of the growth of bone could be influenced in this manner by massage with regular treatment. Mild postural deformities can be helped and possibly prevented, especially in young people.

Maintaining and increasing the mobility of joints is another effect of massage when regularly applied. Certain manipulations can help to prevent adhesions and stiffness in joints improving and maintaining their full range of movement.

Effects on the circulatory and lymphatic system

Because the veins contain so many valves, regurgitation or back flow is impossible and the flow of venous blood always moves towards the heart. The smaller veins on the surface of the skin link up to the larger ones and eventually to the two large venous trunks which return the blood to the right side of the heart. This direction of flow is called 'centripetal'. The superficial veins are easily palpated and it takes only slight pressure to empty them. So it can be seen that light superficial effleurage can affect the flow of blood very easily and possibly help the work of the heart, although it is doubtful that massage can directly affect the circulation in the arteries or the heart itself. The improvement of the blood flow in the veins is made use of in massage by interspersing effleurage freely, throughout all forms of massage, in order to carry away waste products, toxins and carbon dioxide efficiently and quickly into the blood stream. In return for the quickened venous circulation, oxygen and all nutriments are brought back by way of the arteries. Gentle stroking produces a contraction of the walls of the capillaries in the skin which has a cooling effect on the body.

Effleurage and kneading also accelerates the lymphatic circulation. Kneading squeezes the lymph from the lymph spaces and the effleurage moves it on to the nearest lymph glands. Fresh lymph seeps through the walls of the capillary blood vessels to feed the tissues, absorbing products of fatigue and wear and tear of the areas. If there is a local infection then the lymph fluid will help to pass it on to the lymph glands which will become swollen and sore in an effort to fight the germs, although massage is contraindicated for local infections. When the lymphatic circulation becomes stagnant then the area becomes grossly swollen. This swelling can be considerably relieved by massage, providing there is no condition present which requires medical supervision.

Effects on the lungs

The condition of the lungs can be improved by massage. Mobilizing the joints of the thorax, strengthening and improving the tone of the respiratory muscles by massage indirectly will help with airing the lungs. Such manipulations as percussion will have a direct effect on the lung tissue. Not only will the circulation to the bronchioles be improved, thus feeding the tissues and helping to maintain elasticity, but any mucus or foreign particles, if present, can be dislodged with such manipulations. With the increased nutrition to the lung tissue, gaseous interchange is also increased, ridding the body of carbon dioxide and replenishing it with oxygen. There is a possibility that massage to large muscle groups producing an increased circulation and combustion in the tissues will increase the amount of carbon dioxide in them. This in turn could cause a need for a deeper and more thorough inspiration and expiration so effecting movement of the lungs.

Effects on the skin

Any massage manipulation affects the skin which has many functions. To a certain extent, like all other systems, these functions are made more active by massage. Circulation to the skin is improved and the secretory glands, so nourished by fresh blood, produce more sebum. This in turn makes the skin soft and supple and increases its resistance to infection. More sweat is produced by the activated sudiferous (sweat) glands which excrete urea and other waste products. By massage, the top dead layer of skin cells can be rubbed off. This enables the skin to breathe more easily, again improving the condition of the skin, and allowing tissue respiration to be assisted, imparting an overall healthy glow. If the horny layer of skin is massaged away, its functions of absorption and protection will be performed much more efficiently. In the skin too lie the peripheral nerve endings. With massage the sensory nerve endings can either be soothed, or stimulated, according to the type of massage manipulations employed and required for treatment.

Effects on adipose tissue

There is little, if any, effect that occurs when massaging the fatty tissues of the body. Fat requires a chemical reaction to take place and necessitates the presence of certain enzymes before it can be broken down or metabolized. However, the following theories have all been propounded and it is still widely believed that fat can be broken down with massage despite the scientific facts which appear to prove otherwise.

When fatty masses are treated by massage, the heat in the fatty tissue is produced more quickly by the increased circulation. This latter aids absorption of the fat and the increased metabolism of the tissues helps to burn it up. Also it is believed that the fatty globules may be released by massage and spread over a larger area for absorption into the lymphatic system.

Therefore dense areas of firm solid fat can be softened and, when massage is combined with a scheme of weight-reducing exercises plus a slimming diet, its effect will be greatly increased. If massage breaks down fatty tissue in local areas without diet and exercises it will be merely displaced and deposited elsewhere in the body. Sometimes tissue fluids are trapped around the fat globules, making fat reduction by dieting alone, a hard task. Massage with its effect of pushing the tissue fluids along and speeding up the flow of circulation can help in reducing oedema caused by fat globules retaining the fluid. Again reduction of tissue fluids makes for easier absorption of adipose tissue as it becomes more available for combustion in the body metabolism.

There are many sceptical schools of thought about the effect of breaking down fatty tissue by massage. The student and therapist should bear in mind that to be most effective the massage must be performed regularly and vigorously. For weight reduction, massage combined with diet and exercise is the ideal combination.

Effects on the nerves

The vigorous manipulations of massage, namely vibrations, frictions and percussion, generally have a stimulating and invigorating effect on the nerves of the body. Pressure on nerves sufficient to block out impulses can have a deadening effect and will temporarily relieve pain. It is a natural instinct to press a painful spot, so relieving pain. Percussion such as hacking may have a reflex effect on them, and in turn, because they are mechanically stimulated in this way, many tissues and organs in the body can be influenced to function more efficiently. For example, if the secretory nerves of the stomach are stimulated, the stomach will produce more digestive juices to aid digestion.

Another effect of massage is the soothing one which it has upon the nervous system gaining relaxation either locally or for the whole body. Slow rhythmic manipulations can produce sleep by causing the nerves to respond reflexly to this gentle stimulation. Massage of the head, neck, shoulders and back can be hypnotically relaxing. This can revive tired nerves suffering from exhaustion and revitalize them. In the same way as has already been mentioned brisk vigorous massage on the head and back will stimulate the central nervous system.

Effects on the abdominal organs

Kneading of the alimentary tract affects the involuntary muscle wall and stimulates its action, namely that of peristalsis. Peristaltic movement is increased by the pressure exerted on the stomach wall, small intestine and colon. If the manipulations are performed quickly, then stimulation of the muscular abdominal wall results. The circulation to this area is also increased.

Shaking and hacking are used over these organs to increase their vitality and function. By stimulating them with this form of percussion, more secretions are produced and digestion will be aided. Vibrations can soothe the nerves of the alimentary tract relieving flatulence and intestinal spasm (felt sometimes as 'butterflies').

Gentle stroking and kneading of the colon is said to help mechanically the flow of its contents.

Stimulating stroking over the organs of digestion has an effect reflexly on the involuntary muscle and is used when an invigorating effect is required. Massage of the liver increases and stimulates cell activity. By slow deep manipulations the liver cells produce more bile which is stored in the gall bladder until required.

Metabolism and beauty

The ability by which the body is able to convert food and other substances into suitable energy to its own use is called metabolism. It includes the taking in of food and oxygen which repairs broken-down and used tissues. The foodstuffs are worked upon by the different juices of the digestive system, broken down and then, when digested, are absorbed and rebuilt in the body's metabolic process. Chemical reactions taking place in the tissues, to produce the necessary energy for muscle actions, generation of nerve centres, and for all the other functioning of the different systems of the body, are included as part of metabolism. If food substances are not correctly metabolized then certain diseases can occur when chemical reactions are affected.

Obesity, gout and diabetes are some examples of metabolic diseases. Minor health ailments caused through incorrect metabolism for whatever reason can have a marked effect on inward and outward beauty. Take someone who is overweight but not suffering from a severe case of obesity that needs medical attention. Not only do obese people feel miserable if they look unsightly but their eating of the wrong kind of foodstuffs may well cause the digestive organs to rebel and produce indigestion. This in turn, apart from the aesthetic point of view, could register as pain on the face, possibly causing poor posture and lethargy: an ideal case for beauty treatment.

There are many people with such beauty problems, not requiring medical attention, who find their way into the beauty salons. Those who are lucky enough not to require anything more than the pure luxury that the beauty salons can give are few and far between. Spots, being overweight, greasy skins, dry skins, flatulence, poor posture and cramp are but a few of the conditions discussed with the beauty therapist. Many such problems arise from faulty metabolism for one reason or another.

One of the paths to beauty is through the stomach and the digestive system can be considered as its heart. It is from here that the metabolism of the foodstuffs begins, as has already been stated, and poor metabolism can affect the inward and outward vitality of the body health.

All the finest clothes and purest cosmetics, however skilfully applied, cannot disguise for long the malfunctioning of any of the systems of the body, particularly the digestive system.

Massage where it is not contraindicated is one of the vital tools in helping to correct the symptoms of a faulty metabolism, promoting health and beauty throughout all the systems of the body.

Order and method of work

Preparation and procedure

Salon

Before clients arrive for their massage treatment, therapists should check each client's name, record card, and time of appointment so that they can be absolutely ready on their arrival. All necessary equipment required to be used during the massage should be prepared beforehand. This includes not only the layout of the trolley with its talcum powder, oil, massage cream, tissues, and all materials which may be used during the treatment, but also spare towels, and pillows to prevent the therapist from unnecessary breaks in the massage itself because something has been forgotten. The continuity and flow of the treatment cannot be over-emphasized. If the therapist must turn to reach for something from the trolley, one hand if possible should remain in gentle contact with the client to maintain continuity.

If the masseuse is required to leave the client and break off the treatment completely then the client should be covered with a towel and a courteous apology made. Scrupulously clean linen and blankets should greet the eye of the client. No one likes to feel that they are lying between second-hand sheets or that the gowns and towels are not freshly laundered. A gown into which the client can change should be ready. If screens are necessary to ensure privacy they should be arranged in readiness around the couch. The room must be warm and an adequate supply of blankets provided, as muscles which are cold cannot be relaxed.

Lighting should be checked to see that it is not too glaring, and noise must be kept to a minimum.

Therapist

Beauty therapists must wear a clean fresh overall and check that their hair is tidy, make-up not too striking, and that their personal freshness is ensured by the liberal use of good deodorants. They should remove any rings, bracelets, or necklaces. Before the massage begins they should wash and dry their hands.

Client

Clients must be greeted warmly and directed personally to the couch or cubicle to be used. If it is their first visit to the salon a friendly chat with clients will put them at ease. During this time a record card can be filled in with all relevant information about the client, including the name, address, and telephone number of their doctor. The treatment can be discussed and the therapist can also ascertain that they have no medical conditions present which would contraindicate body massage or any other form of treatment. When clients are relaxed they can be asked to change into a gown and lie on the couch. The therapist should then examine them for scars, varicose veins, and visible contra-indications which would modify the massage. If required the client should be weighed and measured.

Position of client and beauty therapist

When settling clients comfortably, make sure that they are in such a position as to require the minimum amount of disturbance for the whole treatment. Depending upon which part of the body is to be massaged and whether the treatment is localized or generalized, so their position will vary. If only the arms are to be massaged then they could quite easily be treated comfortably sitting up. If the whole body is to be massaged it is a good idea to position them in lying either prone or supine according to requirements. Ample support from pillows is essential, however clients are placed, for their maximum support and comfort. As the body soon cools down when exposed, plenty of blankets will ensure warmth. It is important to take into consideration before asking clients to relax completely, that they are not settled too far away from the operator on the couch. This would result in ineffective massage, apart from strain on the beauty therapist's arms and back.

Incorrect positioning of the therapist or client can only result in poor technique. Therapists must place their feet in such a position as to be able to pivot freely from walk standing, which is with one foot in front of the other, into stride standing, which is with both feet a few inches apart and parallel during the massage (see Chapter 10 for positions). When working longitudinally down the length of the muscle fibres the therapist generally stands in walk standing position, but when massaging transversely across the muscle fibres swivels into stride standing. If the therapist's foot positions are incorrect, then body weight in the massage is thrown out of balance and once again, because the rhythm, depth, and smoothness are affected, technique is poor and the massage can only be bad. Apart from the client suffering and losing out, therapists will no doubt begin to develop a chronic backache as well as a diminishing clientele if, throughout a hard day's work, their positioning has been wrong.

Tension

It is because so many people are tense and unrelaxed that they have found their way onto the couch of the masseuse, for massage is a good relaxer. But total relaxation of the client does not only depend upon the benefits derived from the massage itself. To be truly effective on the muscles and tissues of the body, the mind should be completely relaxed. Therefore, from the first moment of contact with the client, the therapist must create a peaceful, calm, unhurried, and reassuring atmosphere. Even if clients are only making the appointment, their attitude and tone of voice can do much to make the client feel welcome and wanted. Most clients feel a little nervous, apprehensive and shy on their first visit to the salon. Massaging taut muscles is a difficult and tiring job, even for the most experienced masseuse. Much can be achieved to aid relaxation of clients if therapists themselves have learnt the art of relaxation.

Naturally the massage itself cannot be good if therapists' hands are stiff and unrelaxed because of their own personal irritations and tensions. Musicians, too, give a poor performance if they are unrelaxed and their fingers are wooden. There are opera singers who are so afraid of being emotionally upset before an engagement that they will not talk to anyone for forty-eight hours before a performance in case their voice is affected. One can hardly consider a massage in quite the same light but relaxation of the therapist plays a dramatic role in performance and effect. When therapists put on their overall they must leave behind their own problems. This applies when they take it off again at the end of the day. Work finished, hands washed for the last time, and overall discarded, the client's personal problems must be left behind. This is essential for the mental hygiene of beauty therapists and ultimately ensures that they start each day vitally refreshed. Chapter 11 describes some general relaxation methods which the beauty therapist can practise and teach.

The first steps towards a successful treatment will have begun when the beauty therapist appears, relaxed and unhurried, paying particular attention to the sounds around and ensuring that equipment is not clattered about. Use of the client's name and a pleasant smile ushering them gently to their cubicle will also invoke a further sense of confidence in clients, which encourages a totally relaxed state of mind and body, ready for the treatment to begin.

Order and method of general massage

Massage, like baking a cake, has certain basic ingredients and simple rules to follow. Once these are grasped, they can be adapted to suit any type of person on any part of the body, for whatever treatment is required. General massage is a complete massage of all parts of the body, except the face and head. A general massage lasts for about sixty minutes. The work throughout should be smooth and very rhythmic; the hands must follow and mould to the contours of the parts at all times. Break in continuity should be avoided, and contact maintained always. Where it is necessary to work with one hand, the other should be used to support the part of the limb worked upon and not left to dangle idly around, or used as a leaning prop on the client. When the client needs to be moved, it should be simply and quickly done without fuss or flapping of blankets, towels, or sheets.

The rate of massage depends upon the kind of treatment given. In practising technique a moderate rate should be adopted. This can be speeded up or slowed down as required, bearing in mind that a total of sixty minutes only gives a minimum amount of massage to any one area in a general body massage.

The work throughout should be deep, unless contraindicated; body weight for the back and lower limbs is essential. Walk and stride standing are the positions most frequently used by the beauty therapist.

Programme for full general body massage lasting sixty minutes

First position

The client lies supine (face upwards), pillows supporting head, back of neck, and under knees.

Order of massage

1 Right arm.
2 Left arm.

3 Neck and chest.
4 Right leg.
5 Left leg.
6 Abdomen.

Second position

The client lies prone (face downwards), pillows supporting face and neck and shoulders, under front of abdomen and hips, under front of ankles.

Order of massage

1 Back, neck, and shoulders.
2 Buttocks.

> **Note:** All areas not being massaged should be covered up, and the client should not be required to move more than is necessary.

Programme for arms (upper extremity or limb)

1 Effleurage of whole arm, covering whole arm three times.
2 Kneading upper arm three times.
3 Wringing and picking up of upper arm three times.
4 Finger kneading round elbow joint twice.
5 Kneading of forearm and hand twice.
6 Petrissage to forearm twice.
7 Finger and thumb kneading to forearm twice.
8 Finger kneading to wrist and tendons of hand joints, fingers, and palms twice.
9 Percussion to whole arm twice.
10 Effleurage three times.

Time for each arm about five minutes.

Programme for chest and neck

1 Effleurage down sides of neck and across chest to cover three times.
2 Flat handed kneading twice.
3 Finger kneading twice.
4 Light hacking twice.
5 Effleurage three times.

Time for chest about five minutes.

Programme for legs (lower extremity or limb)

1 Effleurage of whole leg covering four times.
2 Kneading to thigh four times.
3 Wringing and picking up to thigh four times.
4 Effleurage round knee twice.
5 Finger and thumb kneading round knee twice.
6 Kneading to lower leg twice.
7 Wringing and picking up to calf twice.
8 Finger kneading to anterior tibial muscles twice.
9 Finger and thumb kneading all round ankle and Achilles tendon twice.
10 Stroking round ankle and foot twice.
11 Deep kneading to foot four times.
12 Finger and thumb kneading to foot and toes twice.
13 Percussion to whole leg once.
14 Effleurage four times.

Time taken for each leg about seven minutes.

Programme for abdomen (abdominal wall)

1 Effleurage or stroking three times.
2 Kneading three times.
3 Wringing and picking up twice.
4 Hacking three times.

5 Vibrations once.
6 Stroking three times.

Time taken for abdomen about seven minutes.

Programme for back and neck

1 Effleurage covering back four times.
2 Kneading four times.
3 Ironing four times.
4 Wringing and picking up four times.
5 Finger kneading and frictions down sides of spine and round scapulae twice.
6 Skin rolling once.
7 Hacking and clapping (percussion) four times.
8 Effleurage four times.

Time taken for back and neck about ten to fifteen minutes.

Programme for buttocks

1 Effleurage to cover three times.
2 Kneading twice.
3 Reinforced kneading three times.
4 Wringing twice.
5 Percussion (beating, heavy ulnar border hacking) twice.
6 Effleurage three times.

Time taken for buttocks about seven minutes.

Note: The time taken for the above programmes of massage is only applicable as part of a general body massage. When analysed it is obvious that much more time could be spent on any one area but most general body massage treatments last for one hour. The number of times each manipulation is repeated having covered the area thoroughly once, is a helpful guide when first attempting a complete general body massage, with or without a clock. A general massage is usually started with effleurage, followed by the pressure manipulations, and completed by effleurage again.

Detailed technique for body massage

In all cases the description of the massage will relate to the client's right limbs. This will include massaging the neck and chest, the abdomen, the back, and the buttocks from the right side.

The length of time for each detailed section of massage will vary according to the requirements of the client, as will the number of times each manipulation is performed. The rate at which the massage is performed, like the depth, will again vary according to the required effect of the treatment. It is well to bear in mind that massage, if performed for too long, can become tiring and irritating to the client.

Each of the following descriptions will take into consideration that the massage can be used for independent, localized, and complete treatments, to any section or any one muscle of the body at any time, as well as being used as a method to follow for a general body massage.

Right shoulder and arm

Position of client and therapist

The client can either be settled comfortably in back lying as described in the general body massage with pillow under head and knees, or can be treated in a sitting position with back and head comfortably supported with pillows. The arm must rest well supported on a pillow and the masseuse takes left walk standing (left foot in front of the right). If clients are sitting on a chair then therapists could sit by their side, with the pillow and the client's arm resting comfortably on their knees. The arm is a difficult and awkward limb to manoeuvre, so it is of particular importance to pay attention to the most comfortable starting position for both the client and therapist. Before commencing the massage the hands should be warmed, washed, dried, and powdered if necessary.

Shoulder girdle

Effleurage is first given to the shoulder girdle. The movement begins at the back of the shoulder girdle from the cervical vertebrae across trapezius ending with firm pressure in the supraclavicular glands. The left hand performs this stroke and continues from the base of the hairline forwards again, to end firmly in the same glands increasing the pressure with each stroke. The right hand will be supporting the upper arm at the front. Effleurage is given to the front of the shoulder girdle above the pectoral muscles with the fingers and palm of the right hand to the glands, with the left hand now supporting the back of the shoulder and upper arm. This manipulation is repeated with both hands over deltoid from the top of the shoulder itself into the axillary glands, back and front of the joint.

Kneading with large circular movements is now given to the same area, with palm and fingers of hand using deep pressure over trapezius and rather lighter pressure on the anterior aspect of shoulder girdle across the pectoral muscles.

Finger kneadings and *deep frictions* follow around and deep into the shoulder joint, starting with fingers together on top of the joint and separating from each other into the axilla back and front (posteriorly and anteriorly).

Effleurage completes the massage to this area.

Upper arm

Effleurage to the whole arm from the fingertips to the axilla is the first movement. The left hand works on the back of the arm, and the right hand on the front of the limb. Care must be taken to mould the hands quite accurately to the part keeping the contact smooth and continuous. Each hand works alternately. At the end of the effleurage there should be a deliberate pause followed by gentle pressure to empty the lymph fluid into the lymph glands.

Kneading follows to deltoid, triceps, biceps; both hands press the deltoid muscle against the bone in circular kneading, starting at its origin at the apex of the shoulder and working towards its insertion. See Figure 5.1.

Alternate handed kneading can be employed to massage the anterior and posterior sections of this muscle. This alternate handed *circular kneading* glides from the deltoid muscle into the triceps at the back of the arm, and biceps on the front working again from the proximal attachment of the muscles, distally.

Double-handed kneading can be performed working down in the same manner linking up the movements with short smooth strokes. Great care is essential to massage triceps on the back of the upper arm, as massaging the subcutaneous area of the humerus is most painful, but a very common fault in this area.

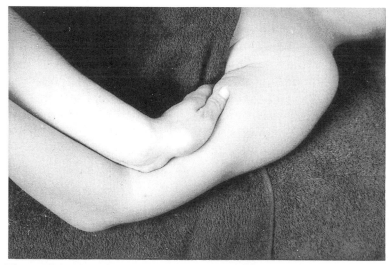

Figure 5.1 Kneading the biceps

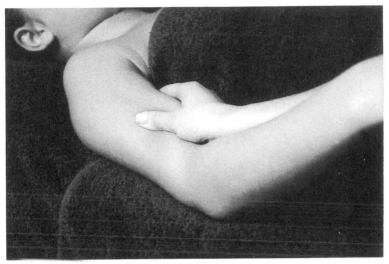

Figure 5.2 Wringing the triceps

Petrissage consisting of *picking up* and *wringing,* using one hand at a time for picking up on each of the above three muscles, is as follows (Figure 5.2). Starting again with the deltoid, the muscle is grasped firmly near its origin with the right hand. The thumb is widely abducted and the deltoid is lifted away from and squeezed against the bone in a digging-like manner. Again care with single-handed picking up must be taken so as not to pinch and press the fingers and thumb too deeply into the bone while manipulating the tissues (Figure 5.3). The right hand is used on biceps, grasping its bulk medially, beginning from its origin, and lifting the tissues away from the bone and relaxing them, while the left hand supports the back of the limb. Single-handed picking up follows on triceps with the left hand and when this manipulation is completed, it smoothly changes into *wringing* of deltoid, biceps and triceps in the same order as before starting from origin towards insertion. The beauty therapist is now working transversely across the length of the muscle fibres, and so, at the same time as changing smoothly into wringing, now swivels into stride standing. The feet should be pointing in the same direction that the hands are working. Wringing involves

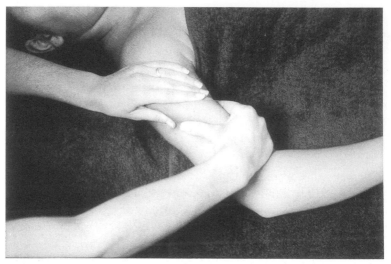

Figure 5.3 Single-handed picking up of the biceps

grasping the tissues and firmly lifting them away from the bone, gently twisting the flesh before moving onto another part in one long continuous wave-like flow.

Hacking over deltoid, biceps and triceps follows, but it often proves to be a difficult manipulation to perfect in this area without much perseverance and practice.

Divergent hacking over the deltoid starts with both hands close together at the insertion of the muscle, then fanning them out in the direction of its anterior and posterior sections, working up and down its length. The arm is then outwardly rotated, with the elbow bent and still well supported, for hacking transversely across the biceps. If the arm is then medially rotated with an extended elbow, triceps will be easily approached.

Effleurage to the whole arm as before completes the upper arm and shoulder massage. Cover this area with a towel if required.

Elbow joint

Frictions and finger kneadings are given into and around the elbow joint. To penetrate into the back of the joint the forearm should be semi-flexed and pronated. Opening up the front of the elbow joint requires that it should be supinated and extended.

The padded palmar surfaces of the fingertips of the left hand should be used on the back, and of the right hand on and around the front of the joint. Each stationary hand supports the client's wrist and hand alternately.

Forearm

Effleurage to the whole arm can be performed, if desired, after massage to the elbow joint, but, as there are no lymph glands of importance in this region, an introductory manipulation of stroking from the fingertips to the elbow joint can link up the next manipulation to the muscles of the forearm from the elbow

Alternate handed kneading of the extensor and flexor group of muscles of the forearm is next given from the elbow towards the wrist. The arm is pronated.

Single-handed picking up is given to the same two muscle groups (Figure 5.4). The left hand picks up the extensor group

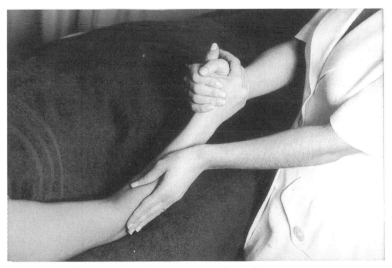

Figure 5.4 Single-handed picking up of the forearm extensor muscles

while the right hand holds the forearm in supination and slight flexion. When this movement is completed the left hand glides into supporting the client's wrist and fingers, while the right hand in a gliding stroke commences to pick up the flexor group, again from its origin to insertion.

Finger kneadings are performed on the anterior and posterior aspects of the forearm. Both hands can work together if preferred, starting with the pronated extensor group of muscles, working from the origin down towards the wrist between the radius and ulna, stimulating the circulation to the interosseus ligaments and membranes. The forearm is then supinated and the manipulation begins again just below the elbow towards the bulky flexor origin ending between the radius and ulna at the wrist on the anterior aspect of the forearm.

Hacking of both groups follows and the client's co-operation in pronating and supinating the forearm will be required to sustain continuous and effective percussion.

Wrist joint

Finger kneading and deep frictions are given to back and front of the wrist joint. When working on the posterior aspect the wrist should be flexed, but should be extended when frictioning the anterior aspect so that deep penetration into the joint occurs.

Hand and fingers

Deep palmar and dorsal kneading between the two hands is first applied from the wrist to the fingertips.

Thumb kneading with the right and left hands follows to the thenar and hypothenar eminences of the thumb and little finger (Figure 5.5). Care is taken here to massage into the crevices and spaces of the bones and into the interosseus ligaments and

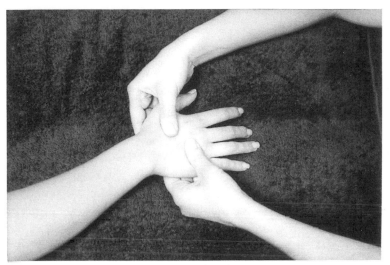

Figure 5.5 Thumb kneading to the hand

intrinsic muscles of the palm of the hand. Both its anterior and posterior aspect should be covered.

Wringing and picking up can be applied to the fleshy ball of thumb and little finger, but the technique is adapted by using the masseuse's index finger and thumb of both hands in a delicate but nonetheless deep manipulation lifting the muscles away from the bone and squeezing from side to side. See Figure 5.6.

Stroking to the fingers follows from the tips to the roots, usually pairing the ring and index finger, middle and little finger together. The thumb is treated separately, but care must be taken to cover all aspects of the phalanges.

Spiral finger kneadings are given with the fingers and thumbs of one hand, while the other supports the base of the client's palm. The movement consists of small corkscrew-like kneadings round the fingers from tip to root, maintaining firm contact, and it produces a pleasant warm sensory feeling, but special care should be taken around the joints. Stroking finishes the massage to the hand.

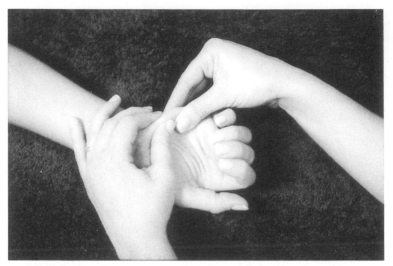

Figure 5.6 Wringing the hypothenar eminence

Hacking to the whole arm can now be applied. The therapist should stride stand at about the level of the elbow, parallel with the upper arm. With the forearm pronated working transversely from the wrist upwards, fingers striking across the forearm to the elbow. Swivelling into walk standing, the fingers turn round the elbow onto the back of the upper arm where triceps is hacked upwards towards its insertion. The operator then swivels into stride standing again, hacking across deltoid over the biceps, asking the client to supinate the slightly flexed forearm. The therapist then hacks down biceps lightly across the front of the elbow and down the medial side of the forearm to the wrist.

Effleurage to the whole limb completes the massage to the arm.

Note: Stroking is a manipulation which should be utilized as a link manipulation whenever possible to maintain continuity between all movements. It can follow the normal paths of effleurage without ending in lymph glands to act merely as a connector, or it can be used as a soothing and relaxing, or stimulating manipulation.

Right leg

Position

If the leg is to be massaged as part of a general body massage, the client would be most comfortable in back lying with an extra pillow behind the head and another pillow which will be used in varying ways to support the leg while massaging it. Alternatively the client can be comfortably settled in long sitting if the treatment is confined to limbs only. Beauty therapists must consider their stance most carefully when treating the lower limb. This applies to the back also. Body weight in both cases is essential for a thorough and effective treatment. Left walk standing is the most convenient position, swinging into stride standing when the manipulations change direction.

Full support of the heavy lower limb demands frequent changing of pillow position. The combination of the therapist's position and correct limb support requires much practice to be perfected, so that the rhythm and continuity of the massage is unaffected. It is easier to treat a leg standing, but if the plinth or couch is too low the sitting position has to be adopted to prevent strain on the therapist's back.

Once the client is comfortable, warm, and relaxed, and the therapist's hands are washed and clean, the massage begins. The leg to be treated should be resting on a pillow in relaxed outward rotation, with the hip and knee slightly flexed, and with the foot and ankle free.

The therapist stands in the left walk position at about the level of the ankle joint.

Effleurage, starting with the hands on the inner and outer sides of the foot and using body weight over the thigh, ends in the lymph glands in the groin (femoral triangle); this stroke should cover the anterior surface of the limb. The second stroke will cover the medial and lateral sides of the leg, the left hand being taken high up onto the gluteal mass laterally and returning into the groin. The third stroke must cover the posterior aspect of the limb surfacing to the front of the thigh, at the top of the leg, curving into the groin, and with slight pressure emphasis on the lymph glands at the end of the stroke.

Circular kneading, beginning with the left hand high on the gluteal mass, follows. The right hand rests on the adductor group of muscles and, when the two hands are level, alternate handed kneading continues down towards the knee. Care is taken not to massage into the femoral triangle for obvious reasons. Kneading of the anterior and posterior aspect of the thigh follows. The left hand changes onto the quadriceps muscles and the right slides to the back of the thigh onto the hamstrings (Figure 5.7). The left hand again starts the manipulation high up near to the quadriceps origin and, when level, works in conjunction with the right hand down towards the knee. The position of stride standing is adopted, and picking up is given to the adductors and quadriceps starting at the origins of the muscle groups working towards their insertions.

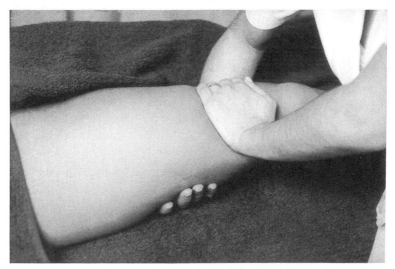

Figure 5.7 Kneading the quadriceps and the hamstrings

Double-handed picking up of rectus femoris can be applied, again from its pelvic origin down towards its insertion, and this can be followed by *wringing* to the thigh in the same way and pattern.

Hacking and clapping of these muscles is given followed by effleurage as before; the thigh is covered.

Knee joint

Position

Walk stride position is adopted and effleurage with both hands is given around the knee joint finishing in the popliteal lymph glands at the back of the knee.

Alternate handed kneading is given to the knee above and below and either side, paying particular attention to the patella (Figure 5.8).

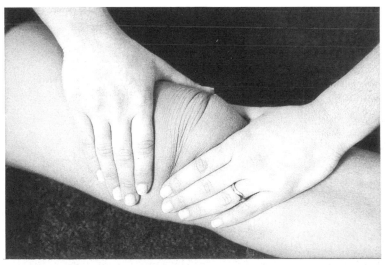

Figure 5.8 Alternate handed kneading above and below the knee joint

Finger kneading and *frictions* round the patella, into the joint round the condyles, and at the back of the joint, are followed by movements of the patella up and down and from side to side.

Note: When massaging above and below the joint with kneading change foot position to stride standing, place one hand above the patella and the other below, squeezing the tissues towards each hand in a digging-like manner. This is most effective on the deep structures of the joint.

Effleurage completes the massage.

Lower leg

Position

The beauty therapist is in walk standing position. The pillow is placed under the client's thigh, leaving the lower leg free, flexed, and relaxed.

Effleurage, in the same manner as for the thigh, ends here in the popliteal lymph glands and the back of the knee.

Kneading to the posterior calf muscles with the right hand, and the anterior tibial muscles with the left follows.

Picking up and *wringing* to the calf muscles (Figure 5.9) while smoothly changing into stride standing is next.

Single-handed picking up to the calf muscles can be given with the right hand, while the left supports the knee. Once again the operator changes into walk standing while thumb and finger kneadings are performed round the head of the fibula and anterior tibial muscles towards the ankle (Figure 5.10). Care must be taken to avoid the sharp anterior border of the tibia, or shin bone.

Light hacking with the leg rolled inwards in stride position to the same muscles is followed by hacking and clapping of the posterior tibial muscles in walk standing position, with the leg now rolled out again.

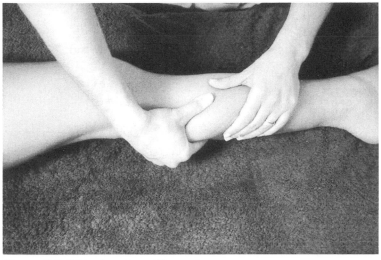

Figure 5.9 Wringing the calf muscles

Effleurage is applied to the whole limb after the pillow has once more been placed under the knee and lower leg, which should then be covered.

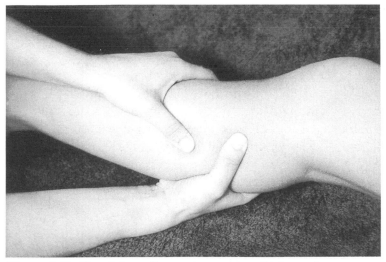

Figure 5.10 Thumb kneading to the anterior tibial muscles

Ankle joint and foot

Stroke from the toes to the back of the ankle in walk standing, the right hand on top and the left underneath the foot (Figure 5.11).

Finger knead the Achilles tendon and round the crevices of the ankle joint.

Knead the anterior and posterior aspect of the foot between the two hands, deep kneading into the sole of the foot starting from the ankle.

Thumb knead the dorm of the foot and the lateral border, starting behind the heel working towards the roots of the toes.

Stroke and *spiral finger knead* each toe from tip to root.

General hacking and *clapping* to the whole leg is followed by effleurage to the whole of the lower limb.

Back massage

For the purposes of detailed description below the back will be divided. In the programme for a general massage, it will be seen

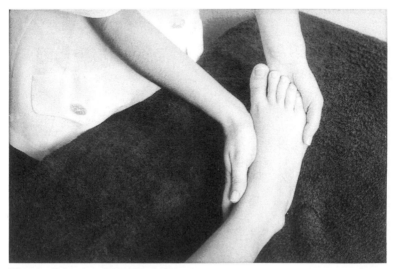

Figure 5.11 Stroking the foot

that these two areas have been combined into one whole area, that is, back, neck and shoulders.

Upper back and neck

Position

The client should be in prone lying with one pillow under the abdomen and another under the front of the ankles. The client's forehead rests on the back of their hands with elbows bent or, if they are comfortable and can turn their head sideways, with the arms slightly bent but tucked down by their sides. The beauty therapist stands in left walk. Standing on the left side of the client but should be able to massage the back from either side. Only the area to be treated should be uncovered.

Effleurage starts with both hands placed at the base of the occiput and hairline. They are drawn firmly down the neck and divide one to each side over the upper borders of trapezius to end firmly in the supra-clavicular glands. The next stroke of effleurage commences from the medial borders of the scapula and thoracic vertebrae and each hand fans out over the scapula across trapezius into the corresponding axilla.

Finger kneading either side of the cervical spine down the lateral side of the neck and across the upper border of trapezius follow. Careful attention is paid to the supra- and infra-spinatus muscles. This area is bony, and too much pressure can cause discomfort.

Double-handed picking up of the neck follows (first to seventh cervical vertebrae) from the root of the hair downwards to the upper borders of trapezius, where the hands separate picking up independently, but with the pressure working towards each other over the upper borders of trapezius as the tissues are lifted and squeezed. See Figure 5.12.

Wringing is next, from the scalp downwards, covering the whole of this area across the scapulae and neck.

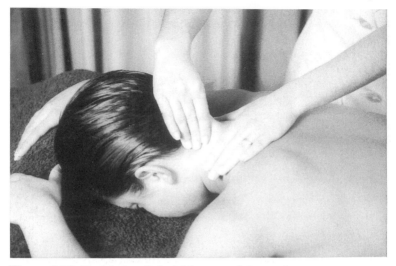

Figure 5.12 Double-handed picking up of the neck

Frictions down either side of the spine, into trapezius erector spine and around the bony edges of the scapulae, are followed by hacking.

Divergent hacking over the scapular muscles and across the upper borders of trapezius can be performed still in walk standing (Figure 5.13). Or as in wringing the therapist can swivel into stride standing and hack the whole area transversely across.

Effleurage as before completes the work in this area.

Lower back, neck and shoulder massage

Position

The client is prone lying with pillow under abdomen and ankles. The back is uncovered from the iliac crests upwards. The beauty therapist stands in the walk position using the body weight.

Effleurage with both hands from the iliac crests either side of the spine to the supra-clavicular glands is the first stroke (Figure 5.14). Each succeeding stroke begins at the iliac crest but nearer

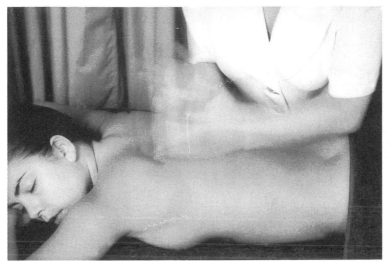

Figure 5.13 Divergent hacking over the scapular muscles

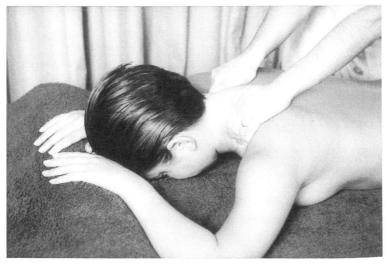

Figure 5.14 Effleurage to the supra-clavicular glands

towards the lateral side of the back, and ends in the axilla until the whole of this area is covered. This usually takes three strokes. Firm pressure is used on the upward stroke, only light contact being maintained on the return journey with the fingertips, to start to effleurage again.

Circular kneading

The hands work on either side of the spine with deep pressure, either alternately or both together. The same order as effleurage is followed to cover the back, but the manipulations all begin at the top of the back, either side of the neck working downwards to the pelvis.

Ironing is the next manipulation. Swivel into stride standing. Place the left hand reinforced with the right hand near the axilla on the right side of the trunk. Iron with slightly flexed elbows so directing deep pressure against the bone. Work downwards towards the iliac crests, then up again and across the top of the shoulders, back down, and up, until the whole area has been completely covered. It will be found that there is some difficulty in treating the side of the body nearest to the operator and so the hands can be turned either up or down to overcome this problem. Gentle rotation from the hips and ankles can help to obtain deep pressure and rhythm, emphasizing the use of body weight.

Picking up and *wringing* are excluded in a general massage of the back if it is too thin and bony as the back muscles are flat and thin. However, on most backs there is usually sufficient adipose tissue to enable these manipulations to be performed most comfortably (Figure 5.15). This stage of the general body massage is very often the most relaxing and pleasing part of the whole massage for the client. If the technique of these petrissage manipulations is well executed the client may drift into a light sleep. The same stance and order of work as for ironing is adopted for wringing and picking up, covering the whole back smoothly and methodically without any breaks between one manipulation or the other. Body weight again is used and emphasis is placed on rhythm according to the manipulation.

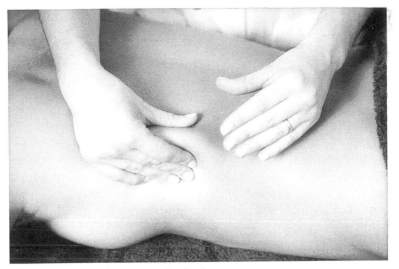

Figure 5.15 Picking up on the back

Finger kneading and *frictions* follow but the position of stride standing is once again changed to that of left walk standing. Kneading and frictions begin from the base of the skull and hairline down either side of the spine of the vertebrae. Deep pressure is essential here to be effective on the erector spinae muscles which lie mainly between the transverse processes and the spine of the vertebrae. Also the joints and ligaments of the spine will be benefited. Care is taken to avoid pressure on the bony joints but to massage deeply round them, and round the borders and spine of the scapulae. Here and across the upper borders of the trapezii trigger spots of muscle tension may be found, so care must be taken not to cause discomfort.

Skin rolling transversely across the back is performed in stride standing. Starting at the axilla, roll the tissues in over the shoulders towards the spine. Move inch by inch smoothly down the back until one side has been completely covered. The side of the back furthest away from the operator poses a little difficulty and the tissues on this side are rolled by the thumbs from the spine towards the lateral side of the back, to the mid-axillary line, but again starting across the top of the shoulder girdle.

Percussion

The client slightly flexes their neck, supporting it on the pillow or hands. *Longitudinal light hacking* down the cervical vertebrae changes into heavier hacking down the thoracic and lumbar regions with the therapist positioned in walk standing. Still in the same position divergent hacking starts with hands together in the cervical region fanning them outwards across the muscles. The hacking continues down the length of the back, bringing each stroke into the centre of the spine to diverge again. Stride walk position is adapted for transverse hacking and clapping (Figure 5.16), which starts at the right axilla, and works down and up the back, until it has all been covered on either side of the spine.

Effleurage concludes the back massage and the area is covered.

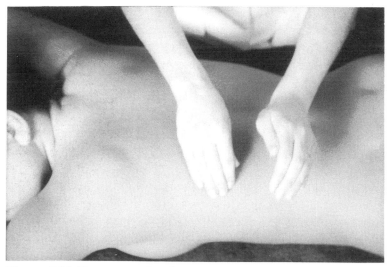

Figure 5.16 Transverse clapping

Buttocks and gluteal massage

Position of the client remains unchanged. The therapist takes walk standing position, and uncovers the area from the waist down to the top of the thigh.

Effleurage, from mid-line over the lumbar region with both hands outwards towards the groin, starts the massage. The following strokes become lower until the gluteal fold is reached.

Alternate circular kneading follows with one hand on each gluteal mass again from mid-line outwards.

Ironing each side separately can be given.

Wringing and *picking up* in this area may only be possible on the top of the hips and into the waist because of the density of these heavy tissues.

Finger kneading and *frictions* can be applied around the sacrum and deep into all the joints of this area.

Hacking, beating and *pounding* are given with the operator in stride standing and if desired over a towel to prevent any discomfort (Figure 5.17).

Effleurage completes the massage.

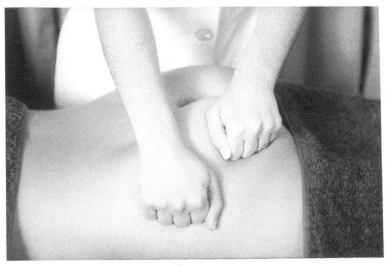

Figure 5.17 Beating the buttocks

Neck and chest

Position of the client can be in back lying or sitting up, depending on whether the massage is included as part of a general body massage, when a minimum of movement is essential. Support behind the head with pillows ensures that the neck and chest muscles are relaxed. One pillow placed under the knees takes the strain off the abdominal muscles. The therapist is in walk standing position on the right of the client. The arms should be relaxed and the area to be treated uncovered.

Effleurage down the lateral sides of the neck into the supraclavicular glands is the first stroke. The next stroke following the same path down the side of the neck with each hand fans outwards across the pectoral muscles into the axilla. An alternate method of stroking or effleurage (Figure 5.18) is to place the left hand on the lateral left side of the client's neck, drawing it smoothly downwards across the left sterno-mastoid muscle, over the sternum and right pectoral muscles, into the right axilla. The right hand then follows the same path, starting on

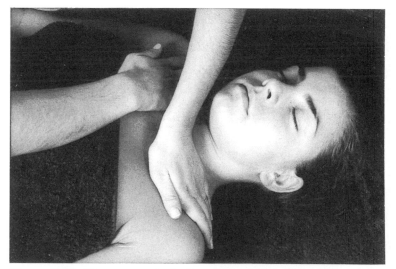

Figure 5.18 Alternate method of stroking the neck and chest

the client's right side and ending in the left axilla. Another stroke, using both hands together across the front of the chest and pectoral muscles, is to place the left hand at the fold of the left axilla and the right hand on the right fold, taking both hands across the chest and pectorals at the same time to the opposite axilla.

Finger kneading down the lateral sides of the neck and upper border of trapezius from origin to insertion follows. The sterno-mastoid muscle is finger kneaded. Care must be taken not to encroach on the front of the throat as this is most unpleasant for the client.

Light palmar kneading, if the area permits, across the pectoral muscles and chest is next, followed again by *finger kneading* round the clavicle and sternum and over platysma.

The breast tissue must not be encroached upon in this area.

Light divergent hacking and *vibrations* across the pectoral muscles, followed by *effleurage* as before, completes this massage.

Abdominal massage

An abdominal massage is often requested as a special treatment, and up to half an hour can be spent massaging the abdominal wall and the abdominal organs in order to promote digestion. However, although there are schools of thought that believe this massage serves little purpose, many people still prefer this old-fashioned method of treatment to other forms, and those who are dieting or fasting in an effort to lose weight find it invaluable and particularly useful. Therefore beauty therapists should have a good knowledge of the digestive tract and the detailed abdominal massage in case they are requested to give one. It would constitute a complete treatment in its own right and should never be hurried, nor included in a general massage of the body.

However, when an abdominal massage is included in the general programme, it is only the muscular abdominal wall which is treated; weight-conscious clients welcome this part of the massage.

Position

The client should be placed so that all strain and tension is taken off the abdominal muscles. If in back lying, the knees must be flexed and well supported. An alternative position could be to raise the back of the couch and support the client leaning backwards against pillows. The client should be well covered with only the abdomen exposed and their arms relaxed by the sides of their body. It is essential that they are as relaxed as possible, and deep breathing exercises can be practised, or shown, before the treatment commences. An abdominal massage should not be attempted until at least one hour after a meal, and the bladder should be empty otherwise it is uncomfortable.

If possible a rest of twenty minutes is advocated after the massage has been completed. Scars on the abdomen should be noted and enquired about, and gentle palpation will indicate if there is any abnormal tenderness that would contraindicate a massage in this region. Bony points in this area must be particularly noted, for excruciating pain can be caused through careless technique. The iliac crests and lower borders of the ribs are the main areas where dragging of the tissues causes discomfort. It is of the utmost importance in this area to ensure that one manipulation glides smoothly and rhythmically into the other ensuring continuity of work throughout the whole massage.

A detailed abdominal massage may build up in time from ten to forty minutes if required. The aim of an abdominal massage is to perfect digestion and absorption by promoting a better blood supply to the organs, so improving their nutrition and stimulating the cells to provide a richer flow of digestive juices. The involuntary muscle action is simulated and intestinal stasis prevented. These movements help to mix the food with the juices and push it along the different parts of the tract. When massaging the abdominal wall it is well to bear in mind its function, which is to help to empty the contents of the digestive tract, and also to support and hold in place the abdominal organs. Other effects of massage on the abdominal organs can be found in Chapter 4.

The therapist should have warm dry hands and always stand on the right side of the client, starting in the left walk position. During the abdominal massage care should be taken when working with one hand only to support the client with the other hand, and not to use it to support the therapist on the couch, or on the client.

Programme and order of work

1 Stroking of abdominal wall (muscles and fat).
2 Stomach.
3 Liver.
4 Small intestine (Figure 5.19).

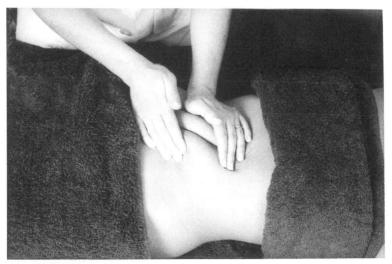

Figure 5.19 Kneading of the small intestine

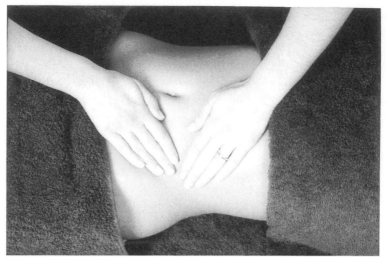

Figure 5.20 Stroking the ascending and transverse colon

5 Colon (ascending, transverse, and descending) (Figure 5.20).
6 Abdominal wall (detailed massage).

Abdominal wall

Stroking from the back of the waist forwards and obliquely downwards towards the groin introduces the abdominal massage. It can be performed either with one hand following the other covering the whole abdominal wall, or with both hands on either side working together. This accustoms the client to the therapist's touch, helping to promote complete relaxation which is so essential in this massage. See Figure 5.21.

Stomach

Stroking in stride standing is first given from the left lateral side of the stomach forwards to its exit into the duodenum at the

Figure 5.21 Kneading the abdominal wall

pyloric sphincter. Each hand works alternately giving firmer pressure with every new stroke. Care must be taken not to drag the tissues across the iliac crest and not to lean on the abdomen with the forearms at any stage in this massage. This is a common fault easily made.

Kneading using the right hand consists of a squeezing and relaxing manipulation lifting the ulnar border of the hand under the lower ribs as though trying to cup the stomach in the hand itself. This starts from the left side of the waist and works forwards to the pylorus.

Stroking as before completes the stomach massage.

Liver

The client turns a little to their left side.

Stroking begins from the back over the area of the liver and works forwards with alternate hands. The pressure should be firm and deep as the liver is protected by the ribs.

Kneading follows. Place the left hand over the back of the area of the liver and the right hand over its anterior surface, on the front of the lower ribs. The kneading should be slow and deep, each hand working alternately, cupping the lower border of the liver upwards with the ulnar side of the right hand.

Percussion, consisting of stimulating hacking, is given over the whole area of the liver.

Stroking as before completes the massage.

Small intestine

Kneading in stride standing is first given. The kneading over the small intestine is modified to the shape of the structures to be stimulated in the following way. The two hands are placed transversely across the abdomen. The tissues are moved with a gentle pushing movement from the padded heels of the hands on the right side of the navel towards the fingertips on the left side. They are then pulled back in reverse to the heels of the hands. The procedure begins again. This movement almost resembles the swell of a wave on the sea. It is thought to cause a manipulation of the intestine lying underneath between the fingers and the heels of the hands, and in this way massages it and simulates its movement.

This transverse kneading slides into a form of kneading, moving the structures round the navel, first one way, and then back the other way in a clockwise and anti-clockwise direction. The heel of the left hand works towards the fingers of the right. In this way, working round the abdomen, the whole of the intestine may be mechanically stimulated. The hands then glide obliquely across the abdomen and the tissues are squeezed and relaxed between them, the fingers and ulnar border of one hand working with the heels of the other.

Vibrations using either the right hand by itself or reinforced with the left, move transversely across the abdomen from the left side of the abdominal wall to the right, working back to the beginning and repeating the movement several times across the abdomen over the whole area of the intestine.

Colon

Stroking, again following the direction of the flow of the contents of the digestive tract, begins from the right side of the pelvis and travels up over the area of the ascending, across the transverse, and down the area of the descending colon.

Different methods of stroking are employed here and it entirely depends upon the therapist which method is adopted. One technique is to stand in stride standing and place the left hand pointing to the groin over the area of the ascending colon drawing it upwards towards, and deeply into, the right side of the waist. Now the left hand is turned and stroked across the area of the transverse colon, turning it again at the left side to stroke downwards along the path of the descending colon. The right hand firmly traces the same path the left hand has travelled, ending over the descending colon in the left pelvic area with firm pressure.

This stroking of the colon should be repeated several times with gently increasing pressure along its course.

Kneading follows. Because of the situation and shape of the structures being treated the hypothenar eminence of the right hand is used to knead the ascending colon. The therapist stands in left walk standing and starts from the right-hand side of the pelvis working up over the ascending colon into the waist. The kneading should be fairly deep. At the waist the beauty therapist swivels into stride standing and kneads across the transverse colon with the palmar surface of the hand. At the left side the therapist once again turns into left walk standing and at the same time continues to knead deeply downwards over the area of the descending colon towards the left groin, with the thenar eminence of the right hand. This enables the therapist to cup the kneading into the iliac fossa without dragging the tissues across the bony iliac crest.

Vibrations, either with the fingertips or the whole hand, follow the same course as the other manipulations over the area of the colon.

Stroking as before to the colon completes the massage of this organ.

Abdominal wall

This massage to the abdominal wall can either be done at the beginning or at the end of a detailed abdominal massage, but not in the middle of the massage of the organs.

Stroking is the first manipulation to be performed. The therapist is in the left walk position and, placing both hands on either side of the waist well to the back, draws them firmly down to the groin. The stroking can be performed with one hand at a time or both hands together covering the whole of the abdominal wall in three strokes. Transverse stroking from the left side of the waist and lower ribs towards the right side with alternate hands over the transverse muscle, and oblique stroking from one side of the abdomen and lower ribs to the opposite groin following the direction of the oblique muscles, is another method of stroking the muscular abdominal wall.

Kneading follows in walk standing with the left and right hands placed on either side of the lower ribs, briskly working towards the middle and downwards to the pubis.

Wringing and *picking up* deep into the waist over the lower ribs, and if possible over the anterior wall of the abdomen, follows. If the client is well endowed with adipose tissue, and has poor muscle tone, wringing and picking up will be most beneficial on the anterior wall of the abdomen; otherwise it is confined to the lateral sides, at the tops of the hips and waist regions, where there is more fat and protection from underlying bone.

Light hacking, changing into stride standing, across the whole of the abdominal wall starting from the left side working up and down towards the right, is the last manipulation.

Stroking as before completes the abdominal wall massage.

Modification of treatments
Special points to be considered
Obesity

In cases of obesity the work required will have to be vigorous, heavy, and deep. Skin rolling may well replace kneading, especially round the great trochanter on the thigh and around the medial condyles of the femora. Where the upper arm is obese care should be taken when employing skin rolling because it can be most uncomfortable and result in a burning sensation. Skin rolling may be performed over the lower ribs and around the waist in such cases but is completely contraindicated over the anterior wall of the abdomen under all circumstances, as there is no bone to protect the underlying organs or against which to roll the fatty tissues.

Breast massage for any condition is not performed in beauty therapy. Skin rolling may be used for obese clients over the gluteal muscles but generally speaking, even in extremely fatty clients, the tissues here are too dense to put this manipulation into practice. Wringing, picking up, hacking and clapping, beating and pounding can be applied where there is much adipose tissue. All the manipulations should be brisk and deep.

Relaxation

When a client requires a treatment purely for relaxation all stimulating manipulations should be avoided. Emphasis is placed on the back massage. The manipulations should be monotonously slow and rhythmic. Ironing and kneading prove to be the most relaxing and soothing; stroking replaces effleurage. This takes the form of long slow strokes from the occiput to the sacrum with the touch firm but light and gentle.

Stimulation

For a client who lacks energy and feels debilitated a brisk stimulating massage would incorporate light manipulations with the accent on percussion, petrissage (wringing, picking up and skin rolling), and brisk stroking. They would be carried out at a fairly quick but even rhythm. Deep vibrations and hacking performed down the vertebrae over the exit of the spinal nerves are said to stimulate the central nervous system and the effect should leave the client feeling refreshed, alive and invigorated. Local vibrations and hacking performed with the fingertips over the peripheral nerves will produce a similar effect.

General aches and pains

Providing there is no medical condition the relief of rheumaticky aches and pains, knots of tension, or accumulated fatigue products can be effected by deep massage. Frictions into thickened structures and around joints down the long back muscles can be performed. Deep petrissage and ironing of muscle groups interspersed with plenty of effleurage will prove to be most beneficial. Usually clients themselves indicate the whereabouts of their particular ache of the day and the therapist can concentrate on this area, incorporating the appropriate manipulations, with deep pressure requiring much use of body weight.

Overtoned and contracted muscles

Percussion is completely omitted.

Requires careful slow rhythmic kneading and petrissage. Stroking would replace effleurage. This can be most effective over the pectoral muscles, for example, where percussion would be contraindicated if the client were round-shouldered and the pectorals contracted and shortened. In cases of muscular cramp where the muscles go into spasm, deep slow kneading helps to relax and stretch out the spasm. A shortened tendo-achilles or tight hamstrings would benefit by the above treatment, including finger kneadings, providing it were deep and slow, discouraging further contraction. Bulky well-toned muscles would require a relaxing massage without any percussion.

Slack and flabby muscles

Untoned muscles which are slack and flabby and have lost their elasticity can be nourished and stimulated with brisk massage. Usually it is the ageing processes of the body, as well as the kind of life led, which contribute to the sagging muscles and skin. Drastic dieting and weight loss is another contributory factor. Finger kneadings, vibrations, and light hacking in the region of platysma over the neck and chest will help to provide this area with the tonic effect it may need. Brisk kneadings, clapping, and hacking are used over the other areas where the tissues have lost tone and where nourishment and stimulation are the first consideration. Later on, petrissage can be incorporated into the treatment, as the tone improves and further stimulation is required without fear of over-stretching the skin.

Oedema

Too much standing and drinking cups of tea can lead to gravitational oedema. The ankles and feet are puffy and possibly the hands may appear swollen too. Under these circumstances the client can be given a special massage to help the lymph carry away the retention of fluid. The arms would be supported with pillows above the level of the axillae and the legs would be raised above the groin. Squeezing kneading, starting from the proximal end of the limb combined with effleurage, would proceed down its length, section by section, working up over the massaged segments again each time a new area is squeezed. The hands squeeze the tissues together until the whole limb has been covered slowly and methodically, interspersing effleurage at every stage. There would be no doubt at all in the therapist's mind if a medical condition were present due to varying causes. The area would pit, leaving finger marks if medical attention was indicated. These would fill with fluid again, and the skin would be pale and cool.

Sometimes the face, legs and hands swell before menstruating and many doctors prescribe a diuretic at this time, to rid tissues of excess fluid. Water retention, overweight, and 'it's my glands' often go hand in hand with obesity, but abnormal water retention in the body could lead to the abdomen, hips and thighs being grossly distended. This is easily distinguishable from the normal fatty layers, for the skin is shiny, the navel protrudes, and there would be a rippling of the tissue fluids as the client moves, across the abdomen and thighs. Where there is any doubt ask clients to consult their doctor.

Head and scalp massage

Position

The client can either sit on a chair in a forward leaning position with the forehead and arms resting comfortably on several pillows supported on a table, or can be treated in prone lying with the forehead resting on the back of the hands in a forward position. The massage is given in walk standing with the hands on either side of the head.

Stroking starting from the brow with the fingertips to the base of the occiput is first given. The fingers are drawn slowly through the hair several times with slight pressure on the scalp.

Finger kneadings are next applied, again working from the hair-line of the brow to the base of the occiput; care must be taken to move the scalp on the skull for full effect and to deepen the pressure over any areas of tension.

Running vibrations starting from the brow and vibrating to the base of the occiput through the hair are next given, with the hands on either side of the head, as in the previous manipulations.

Stroking as before completes this massage.

Face massage

Position

The client can be in back lying with the head supported by pillows or sitting in a backward reclining position again well supported. The therapist stands or sits behind the client.

Stroking with both hands diverging from the centre of the brow to the sides of the temple in front of the ear begins this delicate but firm massage. The next strokes are given with padded surfaces of the thumbs. Starting from the bridge of the nose over the cheek bones with a lifting movement towards the ear; from the upper lip outwards towards the ear, continuing above the chin still accenting the pressure in an upwards direction over the lower cheek, again towards the ear; with the last stroke being performed by the pads of the fingers from under the chin, throat, and jaw to the ear.

Finger kneading midline to the forehead to the ears follows. This is performed with the pads of either the middle or the index fingers working on all the small muscles of the face from midline outwards and upwards, towards the ear. Special attention must be paid to finger knead into the tempero-mandibular joint in front of the ear.

Point hacking is an adaptation of hacking because of the delicacy of the facial structures. It consists of light hacking using the padded parts of the fifth, fourth, and third fingers in a tapping-like manner and is given over the brow, cheeks and chin lifting the tissues upwards.

Vibrations either with the fingertips or flat hand can be given over the same areas, and especially over the exit of the facial nerve in front of the mastoid process.

Stroking as before completes the massage.

Special points to be considered

Eyes

The eyes should be closed throughout the massage and the following massage incorporated into the general facial massage.

Stroking, starting at the outside corner of the eyes, continues lightly over the lids with the pads of the thumb or index fingers to the inner corner.

Finger kneading, superficial and delicate, follows in the same manner to the upper lids, with the tip of the index finger.

Stroking follows as before.

Stroking continues around the eyes starting this time from the inner corner below the eyes and finishing at the inner corner above in a circular direction.

Finger kneading follows in the same direction around the orbicularis occuli muscle.

Stroking in a circular direction as before completes this massage.

Mouth

Particular attention must be paid to the area around the mouth, care being taken to lift the corners of the mouth when applying all the manipulations.

Time

Time for both the head and face can last between twenty and thirty minutes each.

Modification of treatment for head and face

Special points to be considered

Relaxation

If a client has difficulty in relaxing, a head and facial massage can be most beneficial, especially as tension very often shows in the face. All percussion would be omitted; frictions and finger kneadings to the scalp would be emphasized. Double-handed picking up could be incorporated in the head massage to the 'scruff' of the neck rhythmically and slowly.

Gentle stroking from mid-jawline encroaching outwards across the shoulders can be included in the facial massage, while the finger kneadings from the jawline can continue round the back of the neck along the base of the hair-line, upper borders of trapezius, and into the sterno-mastoid muscle from origin to insertion.

Slack skin and muscles

In the area of throat, face, and neck, these require stimulating brisk manipulations lifting but not stretching the tissues further. Tapping under the chin or point hacking will have a tonic effect. Cream or oil could be used in conjunction with a facial massage.

Note: Whenever a tonic effect on muscles is required in the body, or a weight loss is desired, it would be advisable for the client to practise a scheme of active exercises and to follow a suitable diet, for the massage to be fully effective.

Modifications for stiffness in the joints

Providing that the beauty therapist knows why the joint is stiff and that no medical condition exists, the following modifications can be incorporated into a general body massage. If the cause of stiffness is in doubt the advice of a doctor should be sought before massage is given.

Shoulder joint

Massage should be vigorous to all the muscles which act on the joint. This includes the shoulder, arm, neck, chest, and back, and the whole shoulder girdle. Deep frictions and finger kneadings are applied to the joint itself followed by plenty of effleurage and hacking. Passive movements should be given followed by mobilizing exercises of the quick swinging variety.

Elbow joint

Massage to the whole arm, particularly the muscles above and below the joint. Frictions as above are applied to the joint structures followed by passive and active movements.

Wrist, hand and finger joints

Massage to the whole arm is given but with emphasis on the forearm and hand. Special consideration and care is taken around the wrist and small joints of the hand with frictions and finger kneadings. Passive movements and exercises particularly for mobility are stressed.

Back and spine joints

Massage should be deep and vigorous. Double-handed picking up to the back of the neck can be given, followed by deep finger kneadings and frictions to the joints of the spine, sterno-mastoid, and into the erector spinae muscles. In the lumbar and sacral regions ironing can replace wringing and picking up, which is found to be most comforting.

Hip joint

Massage with clients lying on their side with a pillow placed between their knees for comfort enables the therapist to massage the hip adequately. Particular attention is paid to the gluteal and thigh muscles and also those of the lumbar region. Passive movements followed by mobilizing exercises should be given.

Knee joint

Massage to the whole leg is given, particular attention being paid to quadriceps. Deep frictions around the knee joint and patella with the knee in semi-flexion should be followed again by passive movements, patella movements, and active exercises.

Ankle, foot and toe joints

Massage is given to the whole leg, including the muscles of the thigh, the anterior tibial muscles, and the muscles of the sole of the foot. Finger kneading and frictions are emphasized down the tibialis anterior muscle, round the crevices of the ankle joint, and into the deep short foot muscles. Passive movements to the ankle and toes should be followed by mobilizing and strengthening exercises. Faradic foot-baths are excellent in stimulating the muscles of the arches of the feet.

Scars

Massage to scars should consist of manipulations which try to lift the scar tissue from the underlying structures and prevent the muscles from becoming caught up in the healing process. Oil is the best medium to use when massaging scars for it allows a greater stretching of the skin.

Heat treatments

Wax, steam, or dry heat treatments, or baths, can be applied to the tissues or joints prior to massage. They can be used to soothe and ease pain, or merely to relax the client, or as a slimming aid.

Modification of massage for men

In men the skin is thicker, tougher and hairier. The subcutaneous layer contains little fat and so their tissues are firmer and more resistant. Also the muscles are toned and resilient. A toning massage is required for men in which the invigorating manipulations of wringing, picking up, alternate handed kneading, finger kneading, deep effleurage, and percussion are mainly used. These should be performed with greater depth, using all the body weight, at a more rigorous and faster rhythm than the general massage for woman.

A full massage for men is often condensed into half an hour. Here the arms, chest and light abdominal massage precedes the massage to the back of the legs and back massage, both of which are applied with the client in prone lying. Concentration of massage with wringing and finger kneading around the upper boarders of the trapezius muscle and upper back region relieves tension and tenseness, commonly found in this area. A good vegetable massage oil or an appropriate essential oil will enable the skin to be stretched without tearing, and greater pressure to be applied. Removal of excess oil with hot towels, or an astringent completes the treatment.

6
Bones

The study of bones is called osteology. Bones can be likened to the woodwork of a primitive cottage providing the body with its basic shape. This framework of bones is called the skeleton (Figure 6.1). The skeleton is divided into an axial part consisting of the bones of the head and trunk, and an appendicular part consisting of the bones of the limbs, or extremities (arms and legs).

The *structure* of bones is that of one kind of connective tissue, in which various calcium salts are laid down in the basic ground substance, so providing the body with one of its hardest and toughest structures. The articulating or joint surfaces are covered in hyaline cartilage, which helps to give ease and smoothness of movement in the joints. Elsewhere the outside covering of bone is called the periosteum. This is a tough membrane which provides a bed for the blood vessels, nerves, and lymphatics to rest in before branching out to feed, nourish, and supply the rest of the bone. If the bone was to be stripped of the periosteum, it would die.

Two kinds of bone are to be found in the body: *compact* or *hard dense* bone, and cancellous or spongy bone. The heavy compact bone can be found around the lighter cancellous bone, forming a hard outer layer. Red marrow fills in the centre, or

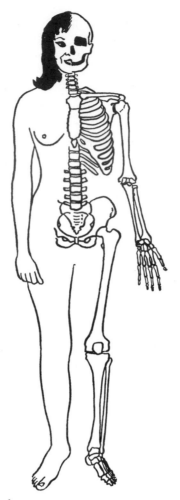

Figure 6.1 The skeleton

medulla, of the hard bones and where there is no marrow cavity as such, it is found in the space between the cancellous bone. It is mainly in the red marrow found in the cancellous bone tissue that the red blood corpuscles are found. Fat can also be found in the spongy bone tissue, and yellow marrow in the shafts of long bones. The surface of the bones sometimes is heavily ridged, roughened, or bumpy. These different features are due to the pull of the muscles which are attached to the bones.

The *function* of the bones is to give shape and support to the body. They provide rigid surfaces for the attachment of muscles, ligaments, and fascia. The bones provide the muscles with flexible levers moving at the joints which connect them up. Usually the more fixed bone is the point from which the muscle originates, and the moving bone is its insertion point. Protection is given by the skeleton to underlying organs and structures. The skull protects the brain; the vertebral column protects the spinal cord. The bony ribcage or thorax protects the heart, lungs, liver, splccn, stomach, and kidneys, while the pelvis looks after the bladder, colon, and female reproductive glands. Calcium is stored in the bones for use in the body when required.

Classification

Long bones consist of a shaft and two extremities or ends, for example the femur. The shaft is usually of compact bone, and the extremities are of cancellous bone surrounded with compact bone.

Short and *irregular bones* often consist mainly of cancellous tissue surrounded by a thin layer of compact bone and are short and irregular in shape and size, for example carpals, patella, vertebrae.

Flat bones are thin, flat, plate-like layers of compact bone sandwiched together with a filling of cancellous bone, for example scapulae, and bones of the skull and face.

There are certain features of the bones of the body which require particular mention, and for which there are special descriptive terms, devised and standardized by anatomists. Not only do these features present areas upon which the muscles are attached, or where joints articulate, but they may present bony points or places, over which massage may be contraindicated, or where the beauty therapist must take special care.

Terminology of bony features

Articular surface   Smooth area for articulation with other bones
Facet   Smooth area which may serve for articular surface
Condyle   Smooth rounded prominence
Tuberosity   Large prominence of bone rough or smooth
Tubercle   Small or large depression in a bone
Foramen   A hole or opening in a bone
Spine   Spiky bone (name given to the whole of the vertebral column)
Sulcus   Groove or a furrow
Crest   A broad ridge or a sharp ridge
Process   A localized prominence
Hamulus   A hook-like process
Cornu   A horn-like process
Epicondyle   Prominence above an articulating surface
Line   A long narrow ridge

Anatomical position

For purposes of all description the body is regarded as standing with the palms of the hand, as well as the chin and feet, facing forwards. This is called the *anatomical position.*

The *midline* of the body is taken as a line drawn down the centre of the vertebrae. It is from the anatomical position and the midline of the body that the following terminology of positions has been derived.

Terminology of positions

Anterior   In front of
Posterior   Behind
Lateral   All that is away from the midline of the body

Medial	All that is nearest to midline
Lateral	(Exterior medial) side of
Medial	(Interior medial) inside of
Superior	Above
Inferior	Below
Proximal	Near to the heart taking the heart as superior, for example upper arm is described as proximal
Distal	Furthest away from the heart, for example lower arm or forearm is described as distal
Volar	Anterior surface
Plantar	Anterior, front surface (sole of foot is the plantar surface)
Dorsal	Posterior, back surface (top of foot is the dorsum or dorsal surface)

The extremities and girdles of the body

The upper and lower extremities of the body are attached to the trunk by bones and muscles. In the upper limb the bones which serve for attachment are the scapula and clavicle, and these, together with muscles, form the shoulder girdle (Figure 6.2). In front, the shoulder girdle articulates with the sternum by means of the clavicle, but behind, it only connects to the trunk by means of muscles from the scapula. The bones which connect the lower limb to the trunk are the hip bones (os innominata). At the front these two bones fuse together at the symphesis pubis. Behind, unlike the scapula, the gap between is filled in by the base of the sacrum with which the two hip bones articulate. This girdle of bones is called the pelvic girdle (Figure 6.3) and is a much stronger and more rigid construction than the lightweight shoulder girdle.

Both the upper and lower limbs are often referred to as the arms and legs. In anatomy the arm and leg sometimes refers only to certain parts of these extremities. They are divided as follows:

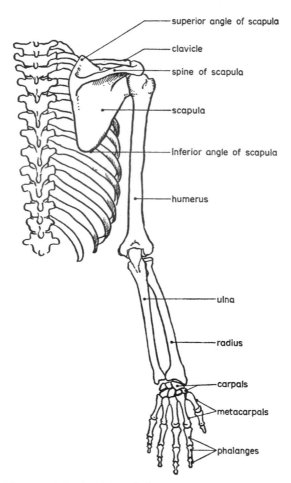

Figure 6.2 The right shoulder girdle

Bones of the upper limb (extremity)

Shoulder joint
Arm   (upper arm)
Elbow joint
Forearm   (lower arm)
Wrist
Hand   (and fingers)

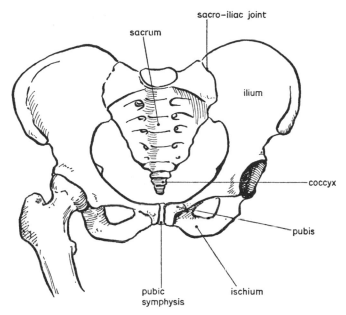

Figure 6.3 The female pelvic girdle

Bones of the lower limb (extremity)

Hip joint
Thigh   (upper leg)
Knee joint
Leg   (lower leg)
Ankle joint
Foot   (and toes)

Major features and bony prominence of the bones which are of importance to the beauty therapist will be described. Some of these features and points can be felt and identified quite clearly under the tissues, subcutaneously. While massaging the individual body types, certain massage modifications may be required over these areas.

Bones of the upper limb

Scapula (shoulder blade)

The scapula is a flat triangular-shaped bone lying on the back of the ribs occupying the space from the second to the seventh rib.

Anterior surface or *subscapular fossa* is concave and obliquely ridged.

Posterior surface or *dorsum* is convex from above downwards, divided into two fossae by the spine: the supra-spinous fossa above, infra-spinous fossa below.

The *spine* rises as a smooth triangular area from the medial border and crosses the dorsum obliquely ending in the acromion process.

Acromion process overhangs the glenoid cavity and articulates with the clavicle by a small facet on the inner border.

Three borders: superior or upper, lateral or axillary and medial or vertebral.

Three angles: superorior, inferior and external or lateral. Lateral angle forms the head and neck of the scapula.

Head is the glenoid cavity for articulation with the head of the humerus, with a supra- and infro-glenoid tubercle.

Neck is the constriction immediately below the head.

Coracoid process lies on the upper border of the scapula above the head. When the arms are by the sides the coracoid process can be felt jutting forward immediately under the outer third of the clavicle. It is very painful when pressure is applied.

Clavicle (collar bone)

The clavicle is an irregular bone situated almost horizontally at the upper and anterior part of the thorax. It has a double curve being convex forward at the inner or medial end, and concave forward at the lateral or outer end.

It is divided into two parts for purposes of description for the beauty therapist:

Outer third or flattened position.
Inner third or prismatic portion.

The *two ends* are:

Sternal end with two facets.
Acromial end with one facet.

Humerus (upper arm bone)

The humerus is a long bone with a shaft and two extremities, an upper and lower extremity.

Upper extremity

Head which is almost semispherical and directed upwards and inwards.

Anatomical neck which is a constriction in the bone immediately below the head.

Great tuberosity is large and lies uppermost and outermost.

Lesser tuberosity is small and lies on the inner side, separated from the great tuberosity by the bicipital groove, lying between the two tuberosities.

Surgical neck is the constriction of bone below the tuberosities and joins the shaft. It is the most common place for fractures of the humerus.

The shaft is cylindrical above but flattens out below, in front and behind.

Lower extremity

The lower extremity is flattened posteriorly and convex anteriorly.

Two articulating surfaces which are the capitellum and trochlea.

Three fossae which are the coronoid fossa, olectanon fossa, and radial fossa.

Two condyles:

Internal or medial condyle is the most prominent.

External or lateral condyle is fairly flat and round.

Ulna (inside forearm bone)

The ulna is a long bone lying on the inner side of the forearm. It has a shaft and two extremities.

Upper extremity

The upper extremity is formed by two curved processes which are shaped to fit and articulate with the humerus. It also articulates with the radius.

Olecranon process curves forwards from the back of the ulna and hooks into the olecranon fossa of the humerus on extension.

Coronoid process projects upwards and forwards from the front of the ulna, hooking into the coronoid fossa of the humerus on flexion.

The two processes are continuous with the shaft.

The shaft

The shaft is prismatic.

Lower extremity

This consists of the head and styloid process.

The *head* is a rounded articular eminence on the lateral side of the shaft.

The *styloid process* lies medially and projects from the head; it is at a higher level than that of the radius.

Radius

The radius (outside forearm bone) is a long bone but shorter than the ulna; it lies on the outer side of the forearm playing a small part in the elbow joint, but a large part in the wrist. The two bones are connected by an inter-osseous membrane. This membrane deserves special mention because it has a poor blood supply. Therefore the beauty therapist must take care to finger knead thoroughly between these two bones when massaging the forearm in order to promote a good blood supply.

The radius has a shaft and two extremities.

Upper extremity

The *head* is cylindrical. The *neck* is the constricted part beneath the head. *Tuberosity* (radial or bicipital) lies medially below the neck.

The shaft

The shaft is prismatic and is slightly bowed outward.

Lower extremity

The lower extremity is broad and triangular and articulates medially with the ulna.

Styloid process projects laterally and is lower than that of the ulna.

The carpus (palm bones)

The carpus consists of eight small short bones arranged in two rows. There are four in each of the proximal and distal rows. The pisiform bone is the most easily palpated bone, lying just above the hypothenar eminence of the palm; and the scaphoid can be felt above the thenar eminence on the lateral side of the palm. The other carpus can be more easily felt through the skin on the posterior surface of the hand, particularly as the carpus is convex here.

Each name describes the shape or the position of the bone. They all fit together like pieces of crazy paving.

Proximal row from lateral to medial side:

Scaphoid   Boat-shaped
Lunate   Crescent-shaped
Triquetral   Three-sided
Pisiform   Pea-shaped

Distal row lateral to medial side:

Trapezium   Four-sided, with two parallel sides (the larger bone)
Trapezoid   Four-sided, with no parallel sides (the smaller bone)
Capitate   Has a head and is the largest carpal
Hamate   Hook-like

Metacarpus (hand bones)

There are five metacarpal bones numbered from the lateral to the medial side. They are small long bones, possessing a shaft and two extremities, the head and base. The head is rounded and the base is flattened out, articulating with the carpus. The head can be felt as the knuckles on the dorsum of the hand. The first metacarpal, that of the thumb, does not lie alongside the other four. Because of its position it is able to move medially in front of the palm when it is flexed, and is a most important factor in increasing gripping power. This is called opposition.

First metacarpal is shorter and stronger than the others.
Second and *third metacarpal* are usually the longest.
Fourth metacarpal is more slender than the others.
Fifth metacarpal is the smallest.

Phalanges (finger bones or digits)

There are *fourteen* in number, two for the thumb and three for each finger. Each has a head, shaft, and base or proximal end. In each, the shaft tapers to its distal end. The distal phalanges taper to a fine, slim, non-articulating head.

Bones of the lower limb (leg)

See Figure 6.4.

Os innominatum (hip bone)

This bone consists of three united bones, which are the ilium, ischium and pubis. The junction of these bones forms the cup-like depression in the hip bone called the acetabulum, which articulates with the head of the femur and so forms the hip joint.

Ilium

The main bony point to be considered as far as the beauty therapist is concerned is the upper border of the ilium, referred to frequently as the iliac crest.

Iliac crest

The most palpable portion of the crest is situated anteriorly just below the waist and is called the anterior iliac spine. There is a superior and inferior iliac spine. This lip-like crest sweeps upwards and backwards to end in the posterior superior spine articulating with the sacrum. The crest provides an attachment place for several muscles, the bony surface being rough and stressed.

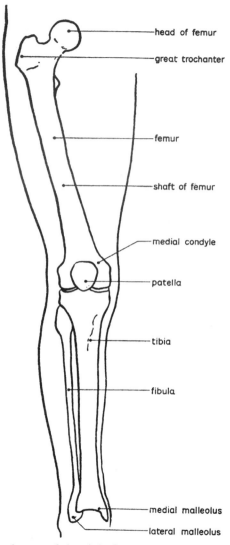

Figure 6.4 The bones of the right leg

Ischium

This projects backwards and consists of the body, ramus, and tuberosity. It is the ischial tuberosity that can be felt through thick and thin after having been seated too long on a hard seat. The beauty therapist should ensure the comfort of clients with an extra pillow if they are to be treated in a sitting position for any length of time.

Pubis

The pubis consists of a body, superior and inferior ramus, none of which can be palpated, except for the superior ramus which projects forwards to the midline of the body and articulates with the pubic bone of the opposite side.

Obturator foramen is a hole in the os innominatum between the ischium and pubis. It is oval in the male, and triangular in the female.

Femur (thigh bone)

This is the longest and largest bone in the body. It is also reputed to be the strongest. It slopes obliquely downwards and inwards, being farther apart at the hip joints and nearer together at the knee joints. Like the other long bones it has a shaft and two extremities.

Upper extremity

The upper extremity presents the head which is almost spherical, being directed upwards, inwards, and slightly forwards, and articulates with the acetabulum.

Neck connects the head to the shaft at an angle of 125°.

Great trochanter. This is a large four-sided prominence, situated at the upper and outer part of the function of the neck with the shaft. It is the area over which fatty deposits seem to be the most stubborn to reduce. It is to this great trochanter that many women can attribute their 'pear-shaped' figure, widening from the waist downwards and outwards, depending upon size and shape of this particular part of the bone.

The *lesser trochanter* lies medially at the posterior part of the neck and cannot be felt.

Tubercle lies between the great trochanter and lesser trochanter, and the gluteal ridge lies posteriorly below the great trochanter.

Shaft

This is almost cylindrical, being smooth anteriorly but strengthened behind by a prominent ridge along and into which several muscles are attached.

Lower extremity

The lower extremity consists of two condyles. Behind, between the two, lies the inter-condylar notch. In front is the patella surface. The inferior and posterior surfaces of the condyles articulate with the tibia to form the knee joint.

Internal condyle is longer than the external when the bone is vertical.

External condyle is wider than the internal condyle.

Tibia (large inside leg bone)

The tibia is situated at the front and inner side of the leg. It is the second largest bone in the body. It consists of a shaft and two extremities.

Upper extremity

The upper extremity is expanded into two condyles. The anterior sides of the condyles make a continuous surface. The posterior surface is separated by the popliteal notch, and its superior articulating surface is centred by a roughened raised area called the spine. In front of and below the tibial condyles, projecting forwards between them, lies the *tibial tubercle*. This raised 'bump' can easily be felt, especially when the knee is flexed.

Medial condyle is larger than the lateral.

Lateral condyle overhangs the shaft but presents a small surface for articulation with the fibula.

Shaft

The shaft is triangular and has three borders and three surfaces.

The *anterior border* and medial surface is subcutaneous, and is usually referred to as the 'shin'. Great care is essential when finger kneading in this area, between the tibia and fibula.

Lower extremity

The lower end of the tibia is expanded into several portions, its medial portion projecting lower than the rest of the bone, and is called the medial malleolus.

Medial malleolus is short and strong, and can be felt very easily through the skin. It is sometimes referred to as the ankle bone.

Fibula (thin outside leg bone)

This is a slender long bone, and lies on the lateral side of the leg. It has a *head*, its upper end, which can be palpated quite easily just below the lateral side of the knee and which articulates with the tibia. It has a *shaft*, and a lower end, the *lateral malleolus*, or the outside ankle bone, which projects lower than the medial malleolus of the tibia.

Patella (knee bone)

The patella is the largest sesamoid bone (or a bone that lies in a tendon). It lies in front of the knee joint in the quadriceps tendon. It is flat and triangular and can be easily palpated and passively moved. Deep finger kneadings and frictions around the patella are advocated in a detailed body massage.

Tarsus (forefoot bones)

There are seven tarsi comparable to the carpi of the hand, but much larger and stronger because of their function in the body (Figure 6.5). They are arranged in two rows:

Proximal row consists of the talus, calcaneum (heel bone) and navicular.
Distal row consists of three cuneiform bones and the cuboid.

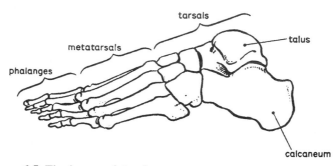

Figure 6.5 The bones of the foot

Talus lies slightly above and to the front of the calcaneum. It supports the tibia and articulates on either side with the malleoli, and in front with the scaphoid. It can be felt quite easily projecting forwards at the front of the ankle.

Calcaneum (heel bone) is the largest of the tarsal bones. It transmits the weight of the body to the ground, articulating with the talus and the cuboid bones. It can be felt as the bony heel.

Navicular bone is situated in the medial part of the tarsus and articulates with the three cuneiform bones. It can be felt through the skin below the medial malleolus.

Cuboid is the most lateral bone in the distal row of the tarsus. It lies between the calcaneum, the outer two metatarsal bones.

Cuneiform bones articulate in front with the three inner metatarsals, behind with the navicular bone, and with each other lying side by side:

Medial cuneiform is the largest.
Middle cuneiform is the smallest and wedge-shaped.
Lateral cuneiform articulates with six bones.

The metatarsus (mid-foot bones)

These bones, like the metacarpi, are mini long bones. There are
five in number and they are situated in the anterior part of the foot
in front of the tarsus. They are numbered from the medial to the
lateral side. They comprise a head (distal end), base (proximal
end), and a shaft.
The heads articulate with the proximal row of the phalanges,
and the bases articulate with the distal row of the tarsus.
First metatarsal is shortest and thickest with a strong body.
Second metatarsal is longest and has a wedge-shaped base.
Third metatarsal has a triangular-shaped base.
Fourth metatarsal is shorter than the third.
Fifth metatarsal has a tubercle which can be palpated on the
lateral side of its base.

Phalanges (toe bones)

There are fourteen in number and they correspond in general
arrangement with those of the hand. There is a proximal, middle,
and distal row. The middle row are remarkably short and small,
but broader than the proximal row. The distal phalanges are much
smaller than those in the fingers, and each has a rough tuberosity
on its plantar aspect.

The vertebral column (back bones)

There are thirty-three vertebrae in the vertebral column. The
column is made up of seven cervical, twelve thoracic, five
lumbar, five sacral, and four coccygeal vertebrae. Between each

vertebra there is a cartilaginous disc which sometimes acts as a shock absorber for harsh movements, except in the sacral and coccygeal bones which are fused together. Each group of vertebrae, while having individual characteristics, is generally constructed on the same lines, and becomes progressively stronger and heavier from the cervical region downwards.

The vertebral column is often referred to as the spine. This name is derived from the processes which are common to nearly all the bones. They can be felt quite easily down the centre of the back, and it is these particular bony prominences over which great care should be taken when massaging the back, in particular when applying frictions and finger kneadings either side of the spine, for it can be excruciatingly painful. The vertebral column or spine provides the body with its central axis round which, and from which, all movements take place. It also serves to protect the spinal cord and it supports the weight of the trunk, transmitting it through to the lower limbs.

A typical *vertebra* (Figure 6.6) is made up of a fat anterior chunk of bone called the body, behind which lies a canal which contains the spinal cord. The spinal cord is the extension of the brain and is part of the central nervous system of the body, extending from the first cervical vertebra to the first lumber vertebra where it begins to taper off down into the coccyx. It is

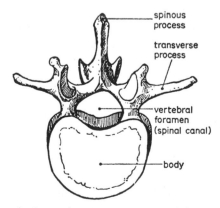

Figure 6.6 A typical vertebra

surrounded by the formation of two thin backward projecting bars of bone, extending from the body called the pedicles. The laminae extend from the pedicles and unite to form the spinous process which projects sideways. There are articulating facets on the vertebrae above and below for articulation with each other. The first and second vertebrae are called the atlas and axis. Nodding and shaking of the head is made possible by the construction of these two bones and their joints.

The thoracic vertebrae only articulate with the ribs. In the lumbar region the spines of the vertebrae are almost horizontally directed, and they are much larger than all the other vertebrae.

The *sacrum* is a triangular wedge-shaped bone. Its apex is at the inferior end of the bone, and articulates with the two hip bones, into and around which joint finger kneadings and frictions prove to be most beneficial. The *coccyx* is the rudimentary tail of humans and curves downwards and forwards from the apex of the sacrum, deep between the gluteal fold of muscle.

Curves of the vertebral column

There are four curves of the spine. Those in the thoracic and pelvic region are known as the primary curves, and are formed before birth, remaining constant after. Those of the cervical and lumbar region are only formed later after birth as the child sits and then walks. These are called the secondary curves. The cervical curve is convex forwards; the thoracic curve is concave forwards; the lumbar curve is convex forwards and the pelvic curve formed by the sacrum and coccyx, is concave forwards. Any deviation from these normal curves, generally due to poor posture, overweight, or lack of exercise, can cause deformities of the spine. Compensatory effects, causing added stress and strain throughout the body, will occur sooner or later.

The sternum (breast bone)

The sternum is a long flat bone lying in the middle and upper part of the anterior wall of the thorax. It consists of the broad *manubrium* above which articulates with the sternal end of the clavicle. It has a *body* which extends from the manubrium downwards and is fairly broad and convex in front, tapering to the *xiphoid process* below. The whole of the sternum articulates on either side with the first seven pairs of ribs. It is an extremely uncomfortable bone to have massaged and only the lightest of work is performed over and around it.

The ribs

Gray's Anatomy describes a rib as being an 'elastic arch' of bone. There are twelve ribs at each side of the vertebral column, with which they articulate. In front, the first seven pairs only are connected by cartilage to and articulate with the sternum. These are called true ribs, while the remaining five are called false ribs. The eighth, ninth, and tenth ribs are each joined, again by cartilage, to the rib above, whilst the eleventh and twelfth are free in front and known as floating ribs. Together with the thoracic vertebrae and the sternum the twelve pairs of ribs form the thorax, or rib cage.

The *thorax* is a conical-shaped cage of bone and cartilage, protecting mainly the heart and the lungs. Because of the varying shapes of the ribs, it is narrow above, flat from front to back, gradually increasing in size, from the first to the seventh rib, from side to side, decreasing and tapering from the seventh rib, to become longer behind at the twelfth rib than in front.

A typical *rib* (Figure 6.7) has a head, neck, tubercle, angle and shaft. The head and tubercle articulate with the body and the transverse process of the corresponding vertebra. The head also articulates with the vertebra above. From the angle of the rib, it is bent forward and twisted. The intercostal muscles are attached between the ribs.

On a thin person, massage over the anterior parts of the rib cage would be restricted to kneading or ironing. This applies to the back of the rib cage. Sometimes finger kneading is applied

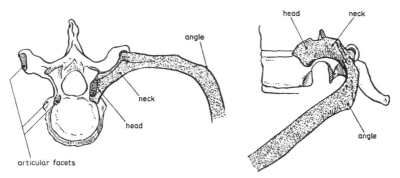

Figure 6.7 A typical rib

to the intercostal muscles in conditions such as fibrositis, but this very often proves to be a ticklish and impossible job. It is around the margins of the lower ribs (midrib) that adipose tissue seems to settle both in men and women, and it is more often than not that this spare tyre of flesh requires vigorous treatment in the form of wringing, picking up, and hacking.

The skull

The skull (Figure 6.8) consists of several flat bones which are divided into the bones of the head (cranium) and the face. With the exception of the mandible, the joints of the skull are immovable. The upper part of the cranium forms a protective box around the brain, and it is often called the vortex of the skull, the lower part being called the base.

The *forehead* is composed of the *frontal bone* which extends backwards to meet the left and right parietal bones, which form the main part of the top of the head. These two bones, sutured together, extend backwards and unite with the *occipital bone* at the base of the skull. In front of the occiput and on either side can be found the *temporal bones*, which give rise to the *mastoid process* immediately palpated behind the earlobe.

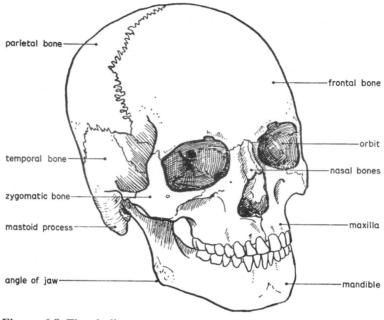

parietal bone

frontal bone

orbit

temporal bone

nasal bones

zygomatic bone

mastoid process

maxilla

angle of jaw

mandible

Figure 6.8 The skull

The *temple* is formed partly by the *temporal bones*, the other part being formed by the *sphenoid bones* sandwiched between the frontal above, and the *zygomatic bones* in front.

The *cheek* prominence is mainly formed by the zygomatic bones, which join up with the *maxillae*, forming the upper jaw and sides of the nose.

The nose mainly consists of the *nasal bones* which extend backwards into the orbits of the eyes, and these bones are called *ethmoid* and *lacrimal* bones.

The *orbits* of the eyes are two hollows formed by the shapes of the surrounding bones.

Foramen magnum is the name given to a large hole formed in the base of the skull, in the occipital bone. It is through this hole that the brain extends as the spinal cord, into the neural canal of the vertebrae.

The mandible (lower jaw bone)

The mandible is the large bone of the face. It consists of a body and a ramus which are easily identified on the living body.

The *chin* is formed by the fusion of the body of the left and right mandibles in mid-line. The triangular part of the chin is formed by the mental protuberance of either side. The lower border of the body extends backwards and forms the jaw line of the face.

The *angle* of the jaw is formed by the fusion of the body with the ramus which extends upwards into a two-pronged fork-like projection. The anterior prong of the fork is called the coronoid process. The posterior prong extends into the head of the mandible which articulates with the temporal bone, forming the temporomandibular joint. Between the prong of bone is the mandibular notch. When the mouth is opened, the mandible being depressed, the coronoid process can easily be palpated. It is round this area that special care should be taken when massaging.

Note: As the body grows older the mandible shrinks in size. This could be one reason for the tissues, skin muscle, and fat round this area becoming noticeably loose, and for the gradual disappearance of the firm contour of the jaw line.

The *hyoid bone* lies immediately underneath the interior of the temporal bones. It is the bone of the throat and is wing-shaped.

7

Joints

The study of joints is called arthrology. When two or more skeletal structures meet they form a joint or an articulation. In flat bones, such as those of the skull, it is the edges which form the joints; in irregularly shaped bones such as the tarsals it can be anywhere on their surfaces which articulate; and in long bones it is usually their extremities which form the joints, such as in the femur. Bones are united in three different ways. First, where movement is undesirable, the bones are united by fibrous tissue. Second, cartilage unites bones where a small degree of movement is necessary. Third, where a large amount of movement is called for, the bones are united by a tough membrane called the capsule; this in turn is lined by the synovial membrane.

Classification

Fibrous joints

Fibrous joints are subdivided into two types:

Sutures, such as the immovable joints found in the skull, are joints where the bones are united by strips of fibrous tissue which are continuous with the periosteum.

Syndesmosis, such as the joints between the bones in the leg and forearm, where they are united by interosseus ligaments and membranes and where movement is very limited.

Cartilaginous joints

Cartilaginous joints are subdivided into two types:

Preliminary, such as can be found in growing bones. The bones arc connected by a thin plate of cartilage which eventually becomes bone when the growth of the bone is complete. This kind of joint is only temporary and is quite fixed.

Secondary, such as the joints between the pubic bones called the symphesis pubis and between the bodies of the vertebrae. The movement is very limited in these joints and they are found in midline of the body.

Synovial joints

Synovial joints are subdivided into six types. They are freely movable joints, and nearly all the joints of the body fall into this class. Certain structural characteristics are common throughout but their classification is according to mobility.

Hinge joint, such as the elbow joint, where the movement takes place round one axis (transverse axis) which is limited to flexion and extension.

Pivot joint, such as the joint between the head of the radius and the ulna, or between the first and second cervical vertebrae (atlas and axis). Again the movement takes place round one axis (longitudinal axis) and is a rotatory movement.

Condyloid joint, such as the metacarpo-phalangeal joints of the fingers, the movements taking place round two axes, a horizontal and sagittal axis and consisting of flexion, extension, abduction, and adduction which is called circumduction.

Saddle joint, such as the carpo-metacarpo joint of the thumb, where the shape of the articulating surfaces can be likened to two inverted saddles being placed over each other at right angles. Here again the movements are bi-axial producing flexion, extension, abduction, adduction, and a combination of those four movements which is called circumduction.

Ball and socket joint, such as the hip joint where the almost spherical head of one bone fits into the cup-shaped depression of another. The extensive movements take place round an indefinite number of axes, consisting of flexion, extension, abduction, adduction, rotation, and circumduction.

Gliding joint, such as the joints between the tarsal bones in the foot and the carpal bones at the wrist. It is formed by the opposition of plane surfaces, and the gliding movement produced has no definite axis.

Structures of a typical synovial joint

Bones

Bones, which are covered on their articulating surfaces with hyaline cartilage. The elastic hyaline cartilage provides strength, allowing friction less and painless movement. It has no blood or nerve supply and obtains its nourishment from the fluid of the synovial membrane.

Joint capsule

The joint capsule is the sheath of fibrous tissue uniting the two bones creating a joint cavity. The capsule is very often reinforced by strong bands of fibrous tissue which usually blend with the periosteum.

Synovial membrane

The synovial membrane (Figure 7.1) lines the capsule and sometimes passes into the joint cavity over the hyaline cartilage.

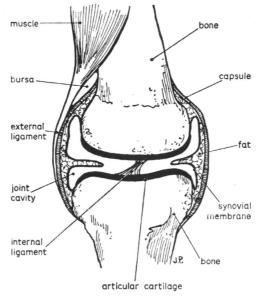

Figure 7.1 A synovial joint

It secretes a fluid which, as well as providing food for the bone ends, lubricates the hyaline cartilage assisting its smooth movement. If the synovial membrane becomes inflamed (synovitis) there is an increase of synovial fluid into and around the joint. It becomes painful and swollen.

Ligaments

Ligaments are of strong interlaced bundles of fibrous tissue. Although they are pliant they are inextensible so that they do not stretch. The direction of these fibres depends upon the stress which is put on the joint, and they are known as the accessory ligaments. Further ligaments can be found inside the capsule uniting the articular surfaces, and ligaments which deepen the articulating depression can be found in the shoulder and hip joint.

Articular discs

Articular discs may be found between the articulating surfaces.

Muscles

Muscles representing the power of the joint pass over one or two joints producing movement, often stabilizing the joint against gravity. Sometimes, between the joint capsule and the muscle, small fibrous sacs filled with synovial fluid can be found. These are called bursae and act as cushions to prevent friction.

Blood vessels

Blood vessels bring nourishment to the joint structures and so enable them to function normally.

Nerves

Nerves from the muscles which act upon the joints convey the sensory impressions to the brain from the joints, so that the brain is aware of what action the joint is taking.

Fatty pads

Fatty pads can be found inside the joint filling in the crevices.

Movements which take place in joints

The movements which take place in joints can be divided into four categories. They are gliding, angular, rotatory, and circumductory. Very often it can be found that most joints are capable of producing a variety of movements. When the articulating surfaces of the bones are reduced in size the range of movement is likely to be restricted. When they are greater in size then the range of movement will be increased, particularly on the more movable bone. The fundamental anatomical starting position, unless otherwise stated, will be used when describing the following movements:

Angular movements

Angular movement produces an increase or decrease of the angle between the two bones. It consists of two movements which take place around axes set at right angles to each other. The movements are called flexion coupled with extension, and abduction with adduction.

Flexion

Flexion is generally understood to mean the decreasing of the angle between two bones. This could be called bending. Extension is the opposite movement and could be called straightening. Bending the trunk forwards is an example of flexion in the vertebrae. Standing up straight produces extension in these joints. Flexion at the ankle joint brings the dorsum of the foot up towards the leg; this is called dorsiflexion. When the foot is stretched downwards from the ankle joint in extension it is termed plantarflexion. Flexion of the shoulder joint results in the arm being carried forwards, upwards, and medially. Flexion at the knee joint results in the leg being drawn backwards, towards, and approaching the back of the thigh.

Lateral flexion

Lateral flexion or side flexion is the term given to the movement of the vertebral column when any part of it bends sideways, either at the waist (lumbar region) or neck (cervical region) or in the more restricted middle back (thoracic region).

Eversion

Eversion is the term used when the joints of the foot turn the sole of the foot to face sideways (laterally).

Inversion

Inversion is the term used to describe the movement of the foot when the sole of the foot is turned to face inwards (medially).

Abduction

Abduction is a movement which carries the limbs away from the middle of the body, which is taken as a line drawn down the centre of the vertebrae. The fingers move away from the midline of the middle finger.

Adduction

Adduction is the movement towards midline of the body, or the fingers to the middle finger.

Elevation

Elevation is the term used to describe the movements taking place in the shoulder girdle. When the arm is abducted to shoulder level the movement which takes the arm from this point up towards the side of the head and ear is termed elevation through abduction. When the arm is flexed to shoulder level, the movement which takes the arm upwards to the side of the head and ear is termed elevation through flexion.

Depression

Depression is the term used to describe the movement of the temporo-mandibular joint when the mouth is opened.

Rotation

Rotation is a movement in which the bone moves round its long axis, as in the femur when the lower limb is turned either medially inwards or laterally outwards (medial and lateral rotation). Rotation can also take place when one bone pivots round another as in the atlanto-axial joint, which results in turning the head and chin to the left or right. Rotation of the radius round the ulna turns the palm of the hand to face backwards. This is called pronation. When the palm of the hand is turned to face forwards as in the anatomical position this is called supination. These two movements are best illustrated when the elbow is semiflexed. The palm of the hand when facing upwards is supinated and when turned downwards is pronated. Thus prone lying is lying face and anterior surface downwards. Lying supine means lying face upwards, and lying on the posterior surface of the body (on the back).

Circumduction

Circumduction presents a combination of the four angular movements. The bone describes the shape of a cone with the apex of the cone at the joint. The hip and shoulder joints are good examples for this kind of movement, in which large circles of movement can be performed.

Factors which stabilize and restrict joint movement

The stability and safety of the joints rely on several factors which limit movement. The tension of ligaments and muscles is very important in preventing excess movement in any one direction, which might strain the joint. Once a ligament has been torn or stretched it is difficult to fully repair. The stability of the joint can therefore be affected and so it is primarily the tone of the muscles which helps to prevent overstretching of the ligaments, and can restrict joint movement. It is only the perfect balance of tone between the opposing postural muscle groups that keeps the body in the erect and upright position.

No other factors play a part in stabilizing the joints in this normal position. The shape and size of the articular facets can restrict movement. On movement, contact with other bones and soft structures is another prohibiting factor, for example on flexion of the hip joint, the thigh comes into contact with the abdominal wall. The movement is therefore halted and active overstretching prevented. Tension of the capsule of the joint produces a reflex contraction in the opposing muscle group to that which is moving the joint. This in turn again prevents overstretching and tearing of the joint structures.

Poor posture and lack of tone in postural muscles can lead to stress and strain on one or more joints of the body. This can be a contributory factor in the cause of arthritic conditions, wear and tear of cartilages and discs, and many more diseases of the joints and their structures.

However, ligaments, as well as inadvertently being over-stretched, can be deliberately relaxed in order to produce a wider range of joint movement for a specific purpose, such as in sports, ballet, yoga, and even in exercising the hands and fingers to make them more supple for massage.

Joints of the upper limb

Sterno-clavicular joint

Between the sternum and the clavicle.
   Type: synovial.

Acromio-clavicular joint

Between the acromion process of the scapula and the clavicle.
   Type: synovial.

Movements

These two joints make up the joints of the shoulder girdle. The movement permitted in them is a slight gliding movement when the scapula moves.

Elevation and depression of the scapula – shrugging up and down of the shoulder girdle muscles.

Rotation forwards and retraction backwards of the scapula round the chest wall – as in punching and pushing forwards, and bracing the shoulder girdle backwards.

Rotation upwards and downwards of the scapula – as when the arm is raised above the head and brought down again. This movement involves movement in the shoulder joint.

Shoulder joint

Between the head of the humerus and the glenoid cavity of the scapula.

Type: ball and socket.

Movements

Flexion: the arm is brought upwards forwards and slightly medially across the chest.

Extension: the arm is drawn downwards and backwards behind the trunk.

Abduction: the arm is raised sideways to shoulder level away from midline of the body.

Adduction: the arm is drawn down towards midline of the body and side of the trunk.

Medial or inward rotation: the hand is turned inwards and round towards the body as far as possible so that the palms face backwards.

Outward or lateral rotation: the hand is turned outwards as far as possible so that the palm faces laterally and sideways.

Elevation is a movement of the shoulder girdle which is the movement of the arm above the head from shoulder level, either taking it up through flexion or abduction.

Circumduction is the circling round of the arm which can take place when all the above movements are combined together. The hand can describe a huge cone, the apex of the cone being at the shoulder joint.

Elbow joint

Between humerus and ulna, and the humerus and radius.
   Type: hinge joint.

Movements

Flexion: the forearm is bent up towards the upper arm.
   Extension: the forearm is stretched away from the upper arm straightening out. Because of the shape of the lower end of the humerus when the forearm is extended it does not lie in a straight line with the upper arm. It is displaced laterally away from the body at an angle to the upper arm. This angle is called the 'carrying' angle. It is said to have acquired this name because of the way in which heavy loads are carried away from the side, in order to avoid bumping the body.

Radio-ulnar joints

Superior and inferior joints between the upper and lower ends of the radius and ulna (and a connection between the two bones by an interosseus membrane).
   Type: synovial and pivot joints.

Movements

See Figure 7.2.
   Pronation is a movement of the radius which turns the palm from its anatomical position (palm when facing upwards), when the elbow is semi-flexed, downwards.
   Supination is a corkscrew-like movement which turns the palm, when the elbow is semiflexed, upwards. Pronation and supination are movements that can be confused with medial and lateral (outward) rotation of the shoulder joint if performed when the arm is by the side.

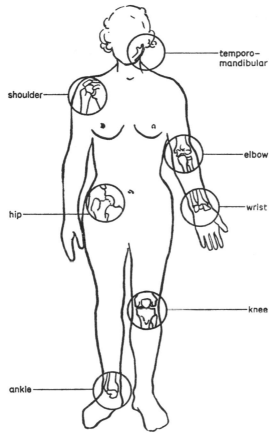

Figure 7.2 Joints

Wrist joint

The wrist joint or radio-carpal is formed between the distal end of
the radius, the scaphoid, lunate and triquetral bones.

Type: synovial joint.

Movements

Flexion: the fingers and palm of the hand are drawn forwards
towards the front of the forearm.

Extension: the dorsum of the fingers and hand drawn backwards towards the dorsal aspect of forearm.

Abduction: the hand is moved away from midline of the body.

Adduction: the hand is moved towards midline of the body.

Circumduction is a movement combining all four of the above movements to circle the wrist round.

Intercarpal and midcarpal joints

Between the proximal and distal row of carpals.

Type: plane joints.

Movements

A small degree of gliding movement is permitted in the intercarpal joints.

Flexion, extension, abduction, and *adduction* of the mid-carpal joints in conjunction with the wrist and fingers.

Carpo-metacarpal joint of the thumb

Between trapezium and first metacarpal bones.

Type: saddle joint.

Movements

Flexion of the thumb results in a sideways movement across the palm of the hand and is combined with opposition, in which the thumb can stretch over to the base of the other four fingers. There is also a slight degree of rotation.

Extension takes the thumb out sideways away from the palm.

Abduction takes the thumb forwards and at right angles to the palm of the hand.

Adduction brings the thumb back to the side of the hand.

Circumduction is a combination of all the above movements of the thumb circling it round.

Carpo-metacarpal joints of fingers

These are between the carpals and metacarpal bones of the second, third, fourth, and fifth metacarpals.

Type: plane joint.

Movements: gliding.

Intermetacarpal joints

These are between the metacarpal bones and joined together by interosseus ligaments.

Type: synovial.

Movement: gliding.

Metacarpo-phalangeal joints

These joints (knuckles) are between the metacarpal bones and the bases of the proximal phalanges.

Type: condyloid.

Movements

Flexion bends the fingers into the palm from the knuckle.

Extension straightens them back in line with the palm.

Abduction takes the index, ring, and little finger away from the midline of the middle finger.

Adduction brings them back towards the midline.

Circumduction: circular movement combining the four angular movements.

Interphalangeal joints

Between the phalanges.
   Type: hinge joints.

Movements

Flexion is a movement of bending the fingers towards the palm of the hand.

   Extension is the opposite movement of straightening and stretching the fingers backwards away from the palm of the hand.

Joints of the lower limb

Pubic-symphesis joint

Between the two pubic bones.
   Type: secondary cartilaginous.
   Movements: limited movement, except in pregnancy when relaxation of the ligaments allows greater freedom of movement.

Hip joint

Between the head of the femur and the acetabulum of the os innominata bone.
   Type: ball and socket.

Movements

Flexion draws the thigh up on to the abdominal wall.
   Extension takes the thigh from flexion downwards away from the abdominal wall and backwards towards the posterior aspect of the trunk.

Abduction carries the leg away from midline of the body sideways.

Adduction carries the leg in towards midline of the body.

Medial rotation (inward) turns the whole lower limb inwards from the hip.

Lateral rotation (outward) is the movement which turns the whole lower limb out.

Circumduction is a combination of all the above movements in circular motion.

Knee joint

Between the condyles of the femur and tibia, and an articulation between the patella and femur.

Type: hinge joint.

Movements

Flexion bends the leg backwards to the back of the thigh.

Extension draws the leg straight forwards in a line with the thigh.

Medial rotation at the knee joint occurs mainly when the knee is semiflexed and involves a small inward turning of the leg on the thigh.

Lateral rotation occurs mainly when the knee is semiflexed and turns the leg slightly outwards on the thigh.

Gliding occurs slightly with the patella and femur.

Ankle joint

Between the bones of the lower end of the tibia, fibula and talus.

Type: hinge joint.

Movements

Dorsiflexion: the foot and toes are pulled upwards towards the front surface of the leg.

Plantarflexion: the foot and toes are pointed downwards.

Gliding movements are possible.

Intertarsal joints

Formed between the bones of:

1 Calcaneum and talus.
2 Cuneiform bones and navicular.
3 Calcaneum and cuboid.
4 Cuneiform bones.
5 Cuboid and navicular.
6 Inter-cuneiform.
7 Cuneiform and cuboid.

Types:

1 Plane.
2 Ball and socket.
3 Saddle.
4 Plane.
5 Plane.
6 Plane.
7 Plane.

Movements

Gliding of the bones on each other intensifies the flexibility of the foot.

Rotation occurs on inversion and eversion.

Inversion: the sole of the foot (plantar surface) is turned to face inwards.

Eversion: the plantar surface of the foot is turned to face outwards.

Tarsal and metatarsal joint

Between the cuneiform, cuboid, and metatarsal bones.
   Type: plane.
   Movement: gliding.

Intermetatarsal joints

Between the metatarsal bones.
   Type: syndesmosis.
   Movement: slight gliding movement.

Metatarso-phalangeal joints

Between the metatarsal and proximal phalanges.
   Type: condyloid.

Movements

Flexion: toes are bent downwards and forwards.
   Extension: toes are stretched upwards and backwards.
   Abduction: the big toe, third, fourth and fifth toes move away from the second toe.
   Adduction: the big toe, third, fourth and fifth toes move toward the second toe.

Interphalangeal joints

Between the phalanges.
   Type: hinge joint.

Movements

Flexion: curling the toes over and down.
   Extension: uncurling and straightening the toes.

Joints of the vertebral column

As a whole are between the bodies and arches of the vertebrae.
   Type: cartilaginous and plane.

Movements

Flexion: forward bending of the head and trunk.
   Extension is a backward stretching and arching.
   Lateral flexion (side-flexion): sideways bending of the head
and trunk.
   Rotation is a movement which turns the trunk from side to
side.

Joints of the ribs

These are between the bones of the ribs and corresponding
vertebrae posteriorly and the ribs and sternum anteriorly.
   Type: synovial.

Movements

The movement of the ribs is brought about by the mechanism of
respiration, when the lungs take in air and expand on inspiration.
The thorax or rib cage increases all round in size, rather like
opening a Venetian blind. The sternum is pushed forwards at the
same time. On expiration the rib cage collapses, the size of the
thorax being decreased again as the air is driven out of the
lungs.

Sacro-iliac joint

Between the sacrum and ilium bone at the base of the spine.
   Type: plane joint.

Movements

Very little movement takes place in the sacro-iliac joint normally but a little interplay between the bones is permitted. The joint surfaces lock into each other on movements such as jumping and act as a shock absorber together with the cartilaginous discs between the bodies of the other vertebrae. During pregnancy and childbirth the range of movement at this joint increases to allow more room and greater mobility in the pelvis. However, as the body ages, this joint stiffens and fuses together, mobility being lost. It is a common area for chronic backache. The joint itself is one which can be strained, together with the joints in the lumbar region, especially if poor posture and the wrong standing position is adopted, for both young and old alike.

Joints of the skull

These are between the bones of the cranium and are called sutures; there is no movement between them.
   Coronal suture: between the frontal and parietal bones runs across from side to side of the skull.
   Sagittal suture: between the two parietal bones, runs from the front to the back of the skull.
   Lamboid suture: between the parietal and occipital bones, runs downwards and forwards at the back of the skull.

Temporo-mandibular joint

This joint (the jaw) is between the temporal and mandible bones.
   Type: hinge joint.

Movements

Depression: opening the mouth (mandible or jaw).
   Elevation: closing the mouth (mandible or jaw).
   Protrusion: jutting forward of the mandible.
   Retraction: pulling backward of the mandible.
   Lateral movement: sideways movement of the mandible as in chewing.

In many joints of the body, accessory (additional) movements to those described above can be found. One kind of accessory movement can be produced when an active movement is resisted, enabling another one to be produced. The movement permitted in the play between the articulating surfaces, which are themselves accessory movements during added stress and strain of a joint, is made use of in passive movements. These movements are performed on the relaxed muscles and joints by the beauty therapist. All active movements which are performed on the body are brought about by the action of specific muscles which pass over the joints.

Muscles

Myology is the name given to the study of muscles. Muscles are considered to be the meat and flesh of the body, and it is mainly the muscles of the body which are manipulated in massage. Not only is it important for the beauty therapist to know how the muscles lie in the body so that individual muscle or muscle groups can be treated and massaged correctly, but it is essential to know the name, origin, insertion, and action of the muscles if corrective and helpful schemes of exercises are to be planned, in conjunction with massage and a good diet. Every muscle in the body serves a purpose and has a function, but only the superficial individual muscles and muscle groups will be described. These can easily be identified on the living body.

Kinds of muscular tissue

There are three kinds of muscular tissue:

1 **Involuntary** which deals with actions over which we have no control and are not conscious of doing such as the alimentary tract.
2 **Cardiac**, the specialized muscle tissue of the heart.
3 **Voluntary** muscle tissue which deals with actions over which we have control and are conscious of doing. The beauty

therapist is mainly concerned with the voluntary muscles of the body.

All the individual muscles of the body are made up of muscle fibres. The muscle fibres in turn are bound together in clusters by connective tissue, and the clusters are then connected into a large group to form an individual muscle. Sometimes individual muscles are bound together by fascia to form a muscle group. Each muscle has an origin and an insertion.

Characteristics of muscle fibres

Origin

The origin of a muscle is normally its most fixed point of attachment, and is its most proximal part.

Insertion

The insertion of a muscle is normally the most movable point of attachment, and is its most distal part.

Origin and insertion reversed

Muscles act on joints and usually move the joint nearest to the insertion first, and then in continued action will move the next joint over which the muscle passes, if any. However muscles can move the joint nearest to their point of origin first and this is called origin and insertion reversed. For example, sitting up, using the abdominal muscles, is an example of origin and insertion reversed.

Attachment

The attachment of muscles can be by muscle fibres, tendons, or fibrous bands called aponeurosis, to each other, bones, skin, ligaments, fascia, or cartilage.

Shape

The shape of the muscles depends upon how they run from their origin to their insertion, and the arrangement of the muscle fibres within this direction. Sometimes the muscles run directly and straight down from one point of attachment to the other, and sometimes they run obliquely from the origin to the insertion.

Fibres of straight running muscles can be *quadrilateral, fusiform,* or *strap-like* (Figure 8.1). All these shaped muscles give great range of movement and speed.

Fibres of obliquely running muscles usually have a central tendon with short fibres going into it (Figure 8.2). They can be *uni-pennate,* with the fibres directed to one side only of the tendon, *bi-pennate* with the fibres lying on either side of the central tendon, or *multi-pennate* where there are several small

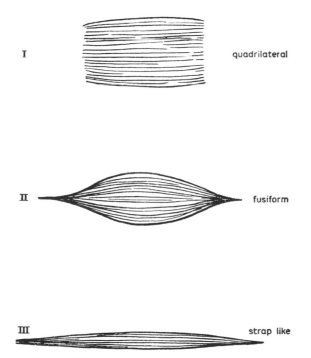

Figure 8.1 Muscle fibres

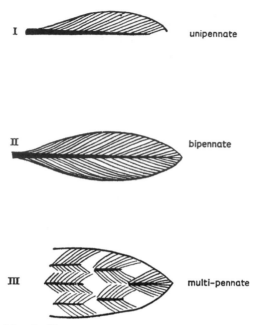

Figure 8.2 Muscle fibres

tendons into which the fibres converge. These shaped muscles are designed for power of movement.

Contraction

The contraction of muscle depends upon the shortening in length of the muscle fibres. The muscle fibres contract up to 40 per cent. However, even when a muscle appears to be tightly contracted, some of its fibres are relaxed. These remain at the ready to take over, relieving those that are working at full capacity, throughout the contraction.

Tone

The tone of muscle is that degree of slight constant contraction which remains in the muscle fibres of the most relaxed muscles.

Those muscle fibres which are not in a state of slight tension periodically take over from those that are, to avoid strain and fatigue, when the muscle appears to be at rest.

Action

The action of muscle is upon the joints, and when any particular movement takes place, several muscles or groups of muscles are brought into action to perform a specific function in a combined effort. These muscles are called protagonists, antagonists, fixators and synergists.

Protagonists are the prime movers in any muscle action, that is, the contracting muscle which produces the main action required.

Antagonists are the controlling influence upon the prime movers. They are usually the muscles which perform the opposite movement to that required and their function is to relax while the protagonists contract.

Fixators are the stabilizers of the movement. They work to fix, hold, and steady the bones either at the origin or insertion part from which the prime movers come. They cut out unnecessary movement produced elsewhere which would hinder the prime movers.

Synergists also prevent inefficiency and help the protagonists to produce the best possible movements. They fix the joints which are not required to move but over which the prime movers pass, and therefore would have to move if it were not for the synergists. By their action they place the joints not required to move in a position which ensures maximum power and efficiency for the protagnoists, e.g. making a fist requires the wrist to be extended and held in this position, the flexors of the wrist then only flex tightly the fingers and thumb.

The action of individual muscles is very difficult to define for they work together in groups and the groups come into action as a team. There may be one or more muscles involved in producing an action as a protagonist and also several muscles involved in the rest of the teamwork, as antagonists, producing, and synergistic. However, although the individual muscle can be said to have one main action, most muscles are capable of producing several other actions.

The deltoid muscle is a multi-pennate muscle, with middle, anterior, and posterior fibres. Its action as a whole produces abduction of the arm, but its anterior fibres may contract to help flex the arm and its posterior fibres can contract to extend the arm. Sometimes gravity can affect and alter the muscle groups which are brought into play during a specific movement. For example, in flexion of the trunk from the standing position, it is the flexor muscles of the trunk which start the movement. As gravity exerts its pull the back extensors take over. However, it can be seen that it is only the co-ordination of all the muscle groups together which will produce a smooth efficient performance.

Nerves

The nerves of the muscle cause the muscle to contract and convey messages to the brain which are essential for co-ordination and positioning. The brain only registers patterns of movements and not muscle contractions. It is only when the action of a muscle is known that it can be made to contract.

Blood supply

Blood supply to the muscles is rich and abundant.

Tendons and aponeurosis

Tendons and aponeurosis are the structures which connect the muscles to the bones. A tendon is a tough, fibrous, inelastic, cord-like end of a muscle sometimes called a girder or sinew. It is sometimes surrounded by a sheath which serves to prevent friction by secreting synovial fluid which in turn acts as a lubricant in the same way as for the joints. Sometimes the synovial membrane of these sheaths becomes inflamed due to strain as in 'teno-synovitis' at the wrist, when the tendons become swollen and movement is very painful. Bursae may also be present in between the tendon and bone again preventing friction. An aponeurosis is a flattened-out tendon. Both have a poor blood supply. Tendons require special attention in massage, such as finger kneadings and frictions, to stimulate the blood supply.

Fascia

Fascia of the body is a membrane of variable thickness which runs throughout the body. It is divided into two layers, a superficial and deep layer.

Superficial fascia lies directly beneath the skin over the whole body. It consists of areolar connective tissue permeated with fat. The thickness varies in different parts of the body.

Women are more evenly supplied than men and because this fatty layer is thicker in women, their contours are softer and rounder than men. It acts as a protection, and fat being a bad conductor of heat helps to prevent heat loss from the body, so that it helps to keep the body warm. It enables the skin to move easily because of its elasticity and mobility. Shielding underlying structures, it allows blood vessels and nerves to split up into it before continuing their final destination into the skin.

In the palms of the hands, feet, and in the scalp, it is tougher and more fibrous, binding down the skin to the structures beneath it. It is absent in areas such as the eyelids but abundant in the abdominal area, so this area tends to accumulate an envelope of fat. Certain muscles insert directly into the superficial fascia, for example platysma muscle.

Deep fascia lies below the superficial fascia and consists of tough inelastic fibrous membrane, binding and ensheathing muscles and muscle groups together. The muscles can contract against this strong band of tissue and sometimes originate and insert into it. In areas like the ankles and wrists the deep fascia can form thickened tunnels, separating and binding the tendons to the bone, preventing them from splaying out. In other areas it sends off fibrous partitions which dip between the muscles and separate them, blending with the periosteum. The deep fascia also surrounds the blood vessels and nerves providing them with pathways to their terminations.

Muscles of the shoulder

Table 8.1

Name	Origin	Insertion	Action
Deltoid Gives the rounded shape of the shoulder. Triangular-shaped muscle. Three sets of fibres.	Spine of scapula acromion process. Outer third clavicle.	Deltoid tuberosity on upper third of humerus.	Abduction of arm, anterior fibres flex arm, posterior extend arm.
Supra-spinatus When the muscle is sprained abduction of the arm is poor.	Supra-spinous fossa on scapula	Great tuberosity of humerus	Fixes head of humerus while deltoid works.
Infra spinatus Works with teres minor.	Infra-spinous fossa on scapula.	Great tuberosity of humerus.	Outwardly rotates the arm.
Teres major	Dorsum of lateral border of scapula.	Bicipital groove on humerus.	Inwardly rotates, adducts, and extends arm.
Teres minor	Dorsum of lateral border of scapula.	Great tuberosity of humerus.	Laterally rotates arm.
Subscapularis Works with latissimus dorsi.	Anterior aspect of scapula.	Lesser tuberosity of humerus.	Medially rotates arm.
Coraco-brachialis	Coracoid process.	Middle of medial surface of humerus.	Flexes arm, helps to adduct arm.

Muscles of the upper arm

See Figure 8.3.

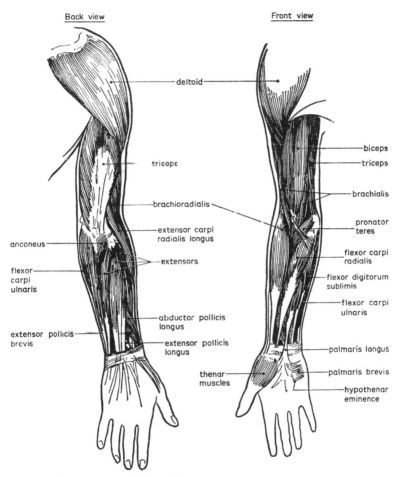

Back view

Front view

deltoid

biceps
triceps

triceps

brachialis

brachioradialis

pronator
teres

extensor carpi
radialis longus

anconeus

flexor carpi
radialis

extensors

flexor
carpi
ulnaris

flexor digitorum
sublimis

flexor carpi
ulnaris

abductor pollicis
longus

extensor pollicis
brevis

extensor pollicis
longus

palmaris longus

thenar
muscles

palmaris brevis

hypothenar
eminence

Figure 8.3 Muscles of the right arm

Table 8.2

Name	Origin	Insertion	Action
Biceps Lies on front of arm, two heads.	Supra-glenoid tuberosity on scapula. Coracoid process.	Radial tuberosity on radius.	Supinates forearm, flexes forearm, helps to fix head of humerus.
Triceps Has three heads, lies on back of arm.	Scapula and capsule of shoulder joint. Upper half humerus. Lower half humerus.	Olecranon process of ulna.	Extends the forearm.
Brachialis Lies below biceps.	Lower half humerus.	Ulna.	Flexes the forearm.

Muscles of forearm and hand

The muscles on the forearm can be divided into two groups: the anterior flexor group and the posterior extensor group of muscles. These in turn are divided into a superficial group and a deep group.

Superficial flexor group

This group consists of several muscles which originate from the medial epicondyle of the humerus and from a common flexor tendon.

Table 8.3

Name	Origin	Insertion	Action
Pronatorteres Crosses the forearm obliquely.	Common flexor tendon.	Lower shaft of radius.	Pronates forearm turning palm of hand backwards.
Palmaris longus	Common flexor tendon.	Palmar fascia.	Flexes hand.
Flexor carpi radialis	Common flexor tendon.	Second and third metacarpal bones.	Flexes and abducts hand.
Flexor carpi ulnaris	Common flexor tendon and ulnar.	Carpals and fifth metacarpal.	Flexes and adducts hand.
Flexor digitorum sublimis	Common flexor tendon, ulna and radius.	Divides into four tendons inserting into middle phalanges.	Flexes fingers and then wrist.

Deep flexor group

This group consists of muscles which lie underneath the superficial layer on the anterior surface of the forearm.

Table 8.4

Name	Origin	Insertion	Action
Pronator quadratus	Lower third of ulna.	Lower third of radius.	Pronates the forearm. Hand turns backwards
Flexor pollicis longus	Middle of radius and ulna.	Distal phalanx of thumb.	Flexes thumb.
Flexor digitorum profundus	Ulna and interosseous membrane.	Divides into four tendons inserting into distal phalanges.	Flexes fingers and wrist.

Superficial extensor group

These consist of muscles which lie on the posterior and lateral side of the forearm and arise from a common tendon originating from the lateral epicondyle of the humerus.

Table 8.5

Name	Origin	Insertion	Action
Brachioradialis Most superficial of all the muscles.	Humerus	Radius, styloid process.	Flexes elbow joint.
Extensor carpi radialis longus	Common extensor tendon and humerus.	Third metacarpal	Extends and abducts hand.
Extensor carpi radialis brevis	Common extensor tendon.	Third metacarpal.	Extends and abducts hand.
Extensor digitorum	Common extensor tendon.	Proximal phalanx of little finger.	Extends the fingers.
Extensor digiti minimi	Common extensor tendon.	Fifth metacarpal	Extends little finger.
Anconeus Assists the work of triceps, is a small triangular-shaped muscle on back of elbow joint	Lower lateral side of humerus.	Olecranon process of ulna.	Extends forearm at elbow.

Deep extensor group

These muscles all lie underneath the superficial group and cross over from the back of the forearm to the radial side.

Table 8.6

Name	Origin	Insertion	Action
Supinator	Lateral epicondyle humerus and ulna.	Surrounds upper third of radius.	Supinates forearm.
Abductor pollicis longus	Ulna and radius.	First metacarpal.	Abducts thumbs.
Extensor pollicis brevis	Radius and interroseous membrane.	Proximal phalanx of thumb.	Extends proximal phalanx of thumb.
Extensor pollicis longus	Ulna and interrosseous membrane.	Distal phalanx of thumb.	Extends distal phalanx.
Extensor indicis Lies below extensor pollicis longus	Ulna and interroseous membrane.	Second metacarpal.	Extends index finger at metacarpo-phalangeal joint and wrist.

Muscles of the hand

The muscles of the hand can be divided into three groups: the thenar eminence, which lies laterally and is the fleshy ball of the thumb; the hypothenar eminence, which is the small medial fleshy mass of the little finger; and the muscles which lie in between the metacarpal bones of the hand and palm. All these muscles are concerned with the fine movements of the fingers.

The *small muscle of the thumb* which draws the thumb across the palm is called the *opponens pollicis*. The other muscles of the thumb are *flexor pollicis brevis*, *abductor pollicis brevis*, and *adductor pollicis brevis*. They all arise from one or more of the carpal bones nearest the thumb and from the metacarpal bones. They are inserted into the phalanges or metacarpal bone of the thumb. Their actions are restricted purely to fine movements of the thumb as their name suggests, without which the hand would be almost useless. They flex, abduct and adduct the thumb.

Muscles of the *little finger* are all called digiti minimi. These muscles originate mainly from the medial carpal bones and insert into the metacarpal or proximal phalanx of the little fingers. They in turn act on the little fingers helping to flex and draw them medially so deepening the palm.

Muscles which lie between the bones are called the *lumbrical* and *interossei* muscles. They arise from the tendons of flexor digitorum profundus in the middle of the palm and insert into the extensor tendons on the phalanges. These muscles help to flex the metacarpophalangeal joint and extend the middle and distal phalanges at the same time. The interossei muscles are attached to the metacarpal bones, and fill in the spaces between these bones. They perform the action of abduction and adduction (separating and closing) of the fingers together with extending the proximal and distal interphalangeal joints.

The *index finger* and *thumb* have their own abductors and the thumb has an adductor, therefore no interossei muscles are inserted into the bones of these digits, and only one intcrossei which adducts is supplied to the little finger. The interossei which adduct are called the palmar interossei, and those which abduct are called the dorsal interossei because of their attachments.

Muscles of buttocks and thigh

In the buttock region the tissues are unusually dense and thick, because the superficial fascia in this area is exceptionally fatty, being more common in women than in men, and also because the large prominence of the buttock, which is one of the most characteristic features of the human muscular system, is composed of a coarse broad fleshy mass of muscle ensheathed in fascia called *gluteus maximus*. This muscle performs an enormous task, which is that of keeping the body upright, so that by virtue of its very function it has to be strong, tough, and unyielding. Normally, in the upright standing position, the gluteal muscles help to maintain an erect posture by working in coordination with the flexor muscles of the hip.

When the gluteal muscles work origin and insertion reversed, they can extend the trunk on the thigh, with the hamstrings. The gluteus medius and minimus are responsible for correct balance when walking. As the leg is raised on one side the muscles tilt the pelvis slightly on that side, but at the same time they pull it downwards to the supporting leg side so that the body does not topple. The deep gluteal fascia of the buttocks and thigh is called the *fascia lata*. Some of this fascia separates the muscles of the thigh into an anterior and posterior compartment. The ilio-tibial band or tract is another feature of the deep fascia in this area helping to steady the femur on the tibia. It lies on the lateral aspect of the thigh being attached above to the iliac crest and below to the lateral tibial condyle covering the tensor fascia femoris muscle completely.

Gluteal muscles

Table 8.7

Name	Origin	Insertion	Action
Gluteus maximus Most superficial and largest muscle	Iliac crest, sacral fascia.	Gluteal ridge below great trochanter, ilio-tibial tract.	Extension of thigh, lateral rotation of thigh and hip joint.
Gluteus medius Lies partly beneath gluteus maximus	Ilium (crest)	Great trochanter.	Abduction of thigh, medially rotates thigh.
Gluteus minimus Lies beneath gluteus medius and is deepest of all gluteal muscles.	Ilium (crest)	Great trochanter	Abducts thigh, medially rotates thigh.
Tensor fascia femoris Situated anteriorly and laterally on the thigh.	Ilium (anterior superior spine).	Into fascia lata below great trochanter.	Abducts thigh, inwardly rotates thigh.

Piriformis, obturator internus, and externus, gemellus superior and inferior, and quadratus femoris are all muscles deeply placed in the gluteal and hip region. Their action is to rotate the thigh outwards.

Quadriceps muscles on front of thigh

See Figure 8.4.

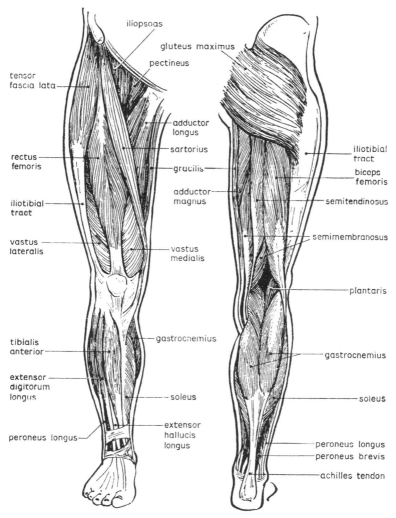

Figure 8.4 Muscles of the right leg

Table 8.8

Name	Origin	Insertion	Action
Rectus femoris Most superficial muscle.	Front of ilium, on anterior inferior spine, acetabulum.	Patella.	Extension of leg on thigh at knee joint, flexion of thigh at hip joint.
Vastus lateralis	Femur (great trochanter area).	Patella, tibial tubercle.	Extension of knee joint.
Vastus medialis	Femur (great trochanter area).	Patella, tibial tubercle.	Extension of knee joint.
Vastus intermedius Deepest of quadriceps	Upper two thirds of shaft of femur.	Patella, tibial tubercle.	Extension of knee joint.

Other muscles acting on thigh

Iliacus and psoas arise from the ilium and are inserted into the top of the femur. They are very powerful hip flexors, flexing the thigh on the pelvis.

Articularis genu lies below the quadriceps and helps to extend the knee.

Pectineus arises from the pubis and is inserted into the femur. It adducts and flexes the thigh.

Sartorius is a superficial long thin strap-like muscle extending from the anterior iliac spine crossing the front of the thigh to the medial side of the tibia. It flexes and medially rotates the leg on the thigh, and also flexes the thigh on the pelvis abducts and outwardly rotates the thigh.

Femoral triangle

The femoral triangle is an area situated on the upper and medial aspect of the thigh. When the thigh is flexed, abducted, and outwardly rotated, as in the cross-legged sitting position, it can be seen quite clearly as a triangular depression. A ligament forms its base and its boundaries are formed by the adductor longus medially, and the sartorius muscle laterally. In this area lie nerves, arteries, veins, and the important lymph glands draining the lymphatic vessels of the lower limb.

Adductor muscles on medial side of thigh

Table 8.9

Name	Origin	Insertion	Action
Adductor magnus Situated on inner side of thigh, deepest of adductor muscles, three sets of fibres.	Ischial tuberosity, ischium pubis.	Inner shaft of femur	Adducts thigh, flexes thigh. Extends thigh, outwardly rotates thigh.
Adductor longus Superficial muscle of adductor muscles on inner side of thigh	Pubis (tendonous)	Middle shaft of femur.	Adduction, outward rotation and flexion of thigh.
Adductor brevis Situated on the inner and upper part of the thigh.	Pubis (aponeurosis)	Upper shaft of femur.	Adduction, outward rotation and flexion of thigh.
Gracilis Situated near the surface on the inner side of the thigh.	Ischium pubis.	Upper part of shaft of tibia.	Inward rotation of leg and flexion. Adduction of thigh and flexion of thigh in hip joint.

Hamstring muscles on back of thigh

The hamstrings help to raise the trunk upright from the stooping position. They bend the knee.

Table 8.10

Name	Origin	Insertion	Action
Biceps femoris Two heads	Ischial tuberosity femur.	Head of fibula.	Flexes the leg at knee joint, rotates leg laterally. Extends thigh at hip joint.
Semimembranosus	Ischial tuberosity (thick tendon).	Medial condyle of tibia.	Flexes leg and medially rotates leg.
Semitendinosus	Ischial tuberosity.	Medial condyle of tibia.	Flexes legs on thigh and medially rotates it.

Muscles of the lower leg

These muscles can be divided into three groups: those on the front, those on the anterior and lateral side, and those on the medial and posterior side of the leg.

Front of leg

Table 8.11

Name	Origin	Insertion	Action
Tibialis anterior Superficial muscle on front of leg. Tendon crosses over front of ankle, lying innermost	Upper two thirds of fibula.	Medial cuneiform. First metatarsal.	Dorsiflexes foot, inverts foot.
Extensor digitorum longus Superficial muscle	Tibia, upper two thirds of fibula anteriorly, interosseous membrane.	Split tendon into middle and distal phalanges of second, third, fourth and fifth toes.	Extension of metatarsal-phalangeal joint, of four outer toes. Dorsiflexion of ankle joint.
Extensor hallucis longus Lies deep to extensor digitorum longus.	Lower two thirds of fibula.	Distal phalanx of big toe.	Extends metatarsal-phalangeal joint of big toe.
Peroneus tertius	Lower lateral third.	Fifth metatarsal.	Dorsiflexes foot, everts ankle joint.

Anterior and lateral side of leg

Table 8.12

Name	Origin	Insertion	Action
Peroneus longus Most superficial on lateral aspect of leg. Lies on outer side of leg and sole of the foot.	Upper two-thirds of fibula.	Medial cuneiform.	Plantar flexes foot, everts foot.
Peroneus brevis Lies beneath peroneus longus.	Lower two thirds of fibula.	Base of fifth metatarsal.	Plantar flexes foot, everts foot.

Calf muscles on medial and posterior side of leg
Table 8.13

Name	Origin	Insertion	Action
Superficial group			
Gastrocnemius Most superficial providing bulk of the calf.	Condyles of femur (two heads).	Calcaneum (by tendo achilles).	Plantar flexes foot, provides the push forwards in walking and running
Soleus	Fibula and tibia.	Calcaneum.	Helps gastrocnemius.
Plantaris	Lateral condyle of femur.	Calcaneum	Helps gastrocnemius.
Deep group			
Popliteus Flat triangular muscle.	Lateral condyle of femur.	Shaft of tibia.	Flexes knee joint, rotates lower leg medially.
Flexor hallucis longus	Middle of fibula.	Distal phalanx of big toe.	Flexes big toe.
Flexor digitorum longus Deep to back of leg on the inner side.	Middle of tibia.	Four tendons of distal phalanx of outer four toes.	Flexes toes, plantar flexes ankle.
Tibialis posterior Deep on posterior aspect of leg.	Fibula, tibia, interosseous membrane.	Talus, navicular three cuneiforms, second and third metatarsal.	Inverts foot, plantar flexes foot.

Muscles on sole of the foot

There are four layers of short muscles situated on the plantar aspect of the foot. They originate mainly from the tarsal bones, ligaments, and tendons of the long muscles but, as each layer deepens into the sole, their origins move forwards progressively. Their function and action is to maintain the arches of the foot which are formed by the design and shape of the bones, and to propel and push the body forwards in walking.

First layer

Abductor hallucis: abducts the big toe.
Flexor digitorum brevis: flexes the toes.
Abductor digiti minimi: abducts the little toe.

Second layer

Flexor digitorum accessorius: aids flexion of all the toes.
Lumbricals: aids extension of the toes.

Third layer

Flexor hallucis brevis: flexes the big toe.
   Adductor hallucis obliqus and transversus: adducts the big toe
and raises the metatarsal arch.
   Flexor digit minimi brevis: flexes the little toe.

Fourth layer

Interossei: extend the toes, and flex the metatarso-phalangeal
joint. There are four dorsal interossei which abduct the toes, and
three plantar which adduct the toes.

Muscle on dorsum of the foot

Extensor digitorum brevis is the only short muscle on this aspect
of the foot. It is a thin muscle and its action is to extend the outer
four toes to all the phalangeal joints but only to extend the first
phalanx of the big toe into which it is inserted. This muscle does
not exist in the corresponding hand and is essential in the foot to
give the big toe an extra push when walking.

   Popliteal fossa is the area behind the knee which contains
nerves, veins, arteries, and lymph glands. It can be seen clearly if
the knee is slightly flexed against a resistance. The floor of this
space is formed by the muscle popliteus from which the name is
derived.

   Tendo-achilles is the name given to the tendon of the gastroc-
nemius muscle which together with the soleus and plantaris is
inserted into the calcaneum. The heel of the mythical Greek hero
Achilles was his only vulnerable spot. He was shot in it by an

arrow from one of his enemies, and died. Thus the common usage of the expression 'Achilles heel' is taken to mean vulnerability, but in anatomy refers to the above-mentioned tendon.

Muscles on the back of the trunk

There are three superficial layers of back muscles (Figure 8.5). The first two superficial layers connect the upper limb and shoulder girdle to the trunk. All the muscles of the back,

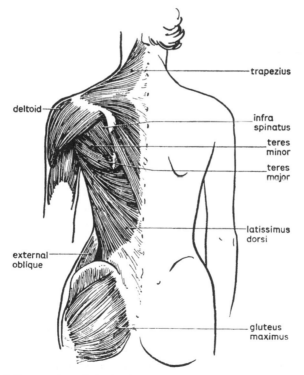

Figure 8.5 Muscles of the back

including the third and deepest layer, are concerned with extension of the spine and play an important role in keeping the body upright, raising it from the bending position.

First layer

The first layer, and most superficial, consists of the muscles trapezius and latissimus dorsi. Trapezius stretches from the base of the thorax to the occiput and out to the peak of the shoulder. One on its own is triangular in shape but both sides together are trapezoid. Latissimus dorsi is situated in the lower half of the back and spine and the upper part of the arm. It helps to form the posterior wall of the axilla.

Back muscles

Table 8.14

Name	Origin	Insertion	Action
First layer			
Trapezius	Occipit, spines of the cervical and thoracic vertebrae.	Outer third of clavicle. Acromion process, spine of scapula.	Upper fibres elevate shoulder girdle. All fibres working rotate scapula outwards to elevate arm above shoulder level. Middle fibres adduct scapula towards vertebral column. Helps extension of head origin and insertion reversed.
Latissimus dorsi Fibres are directed upwards and outwards. Its tendon twists upon itself.	Spines of lower thoracic vertebrae, lumbar fascia, spines of lumbar vertebrae, iliac crest, lower four ribs, inferior angle of scapula.	Bicipital groove on humerus.	Adducts the arm. Inward rotation of arm, and extension of arm. Raises body towards the arm when origin and insertion are reversed, as in climbing.

Second layer

Levator scapuli Situated at the back of the neck from the vertebral column to the superior angle of scapula. Fibres are directed downwards and outwards.	Upper four cervical vertebrae.	Medial border of scapula between spine and superior angle.	Rotates inferior angle of scapula inwards. Both muscles working elevates shoulder girdle. Origin and insertion reversed extends cervical spine. (Braces back shoulder girdle.)
Rhomboid minor Situated between spinal column and scapula.	Spines of seventh cervical and first thoracic vertebrae.	Medial border of scapula opposite root of spine.	Adducts scapula towards vertebral column. Inwardly rotates inferior angle of scapula. (Braces back shoulder girdle.)
Rhomboid major Situated between spinal column and scapula.	Second, third and fourth thoracic spine	Medial border of scapula below spine.	Adducts scapula towards spine bracing shoulder girdle backwards.

Third layer

This deep layer of back muscles consists of *splenius capitus* and *splenius cervicus* which lie deep in the neck of the trapezius and extend the neck when both sides work, rotating it to the same side when only one side works. Also in this layer of muscles is *serratus posterior superior* situated at the base of the neck and upper part of the thorax, and it rotates the trunk to the opposite side as well as acting on the ribs. The *serratus posterior inferior* is situated in the upper lumbar and lower thoracic region and rotates the trunk to the opposite side as well as acting on the ribs.

Deep layer of back muscles

The *erector spinae muscles* of the back lie in the deepest layer of the back muscles. The beauty therapist should note that finger frictions and kneadings are applied either side of the spine particularly for this muscle. This muscle originates from the posterior surface of the sacrum, the iliac crest, and from the spines of the lumbar vertebrae. It passes upwards attaching to the transverse processes of the vertebrae and inserts into the base of the occiput and mastoid process. As this muscle extends upwards it divides into three groups sending slips out to be attached to the ribs. It helps to extend the spine with the other deep muscles of the back, which do not unduly concern the beauty therapist.

Muscles of neck and chest

The muscles which are of important interest to the beauty therapist in this region are the sterno-mastoid, platysma, the pectoral muscles and serratus anterior (Figure 8.6).

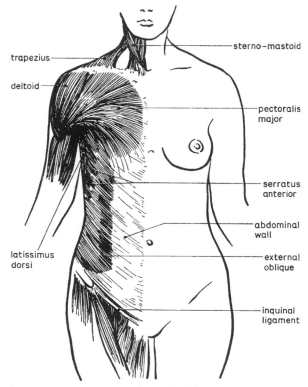

Figure 8.6 Muscles of the trunk (right side)

Diaphragm muscle is the muscle which separates the thorax from the abdomen. It is a large dome-shaped muscle originating from the sternum, the lower six ribs and the upper lumbar vertebrae. It is inserted into a strong central tendon at the peak of its dome. This muscle is the chief muscle of respiration. When it contracts on inspiration the pressures inside the thorax and abdomen are altered. On inspiration the rib cage expands and the abdominal organs descend. On expiration the diaphragm relaxes, the abdominal contents ascend and, as the rib cage collapses, air is forced out of the lungs. The diaphragm plays an important part in labour, together with the abdominal muscles, when it helps to expel the baby out of the birth canal, by pushing downwards.

Table 8.15

Name	Origin	Insertion	Action
Neck muscles			
Platysma	Fascia on front of chest.	Mandible below chin blending with fibres of muscle on opposite side.	Depresses the lower jaw.
Sterno-mastoid	By two heads from sternum and clavicle.	Occiput temporal bone.	Both together flex the head. One rotates the head to the opposite side and side flexes the head to the same side.
Chest muscles			
Pectoralis major	Clavicle, sternum, upper six ribs.	Bicipital groove of humerus.	Adducts the arm, flexes the arm with deltoid.
Pectoralis minor Lies under pectoralis major.	Third and fourth ribs.	Coracoid process of scapula.	Pulls scapula downwards and forwards.
Serratus anterior When the shoulder blade protrudes abnormally in a condition called 'winged scapula' it is because this muscle is either paralysed or very weak.	Upper eight ribs (side of chest wall.)	Vertebral (medial) border of scapula.	Pulls the scapula onto the ribs. When the arm is raised to shoulder level it helps to rotate the scapula and elevate the arm. It is the force in the punching action of the arms.

Axilla
The axilla (armpit) is the large hollow depression found underneath the top of the arm. It houses important lymph glands, arteries, veins and nerves.

Muscles of the abdominal wall

Table 8.16

Name	Origin	Insertion	Action
Rectus abdominis	Pubic crest.	Sternum and lower ribs.	Flexes spine and aids respiration. Helps in lifting legs upwards on trunk.
External oblique	Lower eight ribs	Iliac crest	When one muscle works bends trunk to opposite side, and side flexes to the same side. Flexes trunk when both work.
Internal oblique	Iliac crest, lumbar fascia.	Lower six ribs, rectus abdominis fascia.	Bends trunk to same side and side flexes trunk to same side, when one muscle works. Flexes trunk when both work together.
Transversalis	Iliac crest, lumbar fascia, lower six ribs.	Xiphoid process, fascia between umbilicus and pubis.	Aids outer abdominal muscles in all their actions and functions.
Quadratus lumborum is the muscle on the back abdomen situated in the back of the waist.	Iliac crest.	Last rib, upper four lumbar vertebrae.	Side flexes the trunk in the lumbar region, to the same side. Extends lumbar vertebrae.

Muscles of scalp and facial expression

The scalp consists of several layers. Its outermost covering of the skin is tough and thick. The next layer consists of blood vessels and nerves and the tendons of two muscles frontalis and occipitalis from the third layer running over the scalp and forehead. It is then connected to a loose layer of tissue which facilitates movement over the cranium especially when massaging. The final layer is the equivalent to the periosteum on the bones of the body, and is called the pericranium.

The facial expression muscles have very little attachment to bone and they are all inserted into the skin producing the various expressions. See Figure 8.7

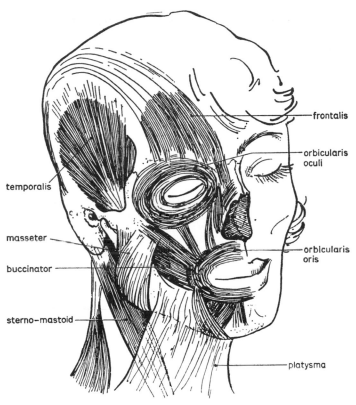

Figure 8.7 Muscles of the face

Names and actions of muscles of expression

Scalp and forehead: occipito frontalis pulls scalp backwards and produces transverse lines of forehead.

Eyelids: orbicularis oculi closes eyes gently and tightly, corrugator produces the vertical frown, *levator palpebrae superioris* raises eyelids.

Ear: auricularis twitches ear.

Nose: procerus wrinkles bridge of nose, *compressor naris* compresses the nostrils, *depressor septi* widens nostrils, *dilator naris* dilates the nostrils.

Mouth: orbicularis oris surrounds mouth, squeezes mouth tightly together, *levator labii* lifts upper lip, *levator anguli oris* lifts corner of mouth upwards, *zygomaticus* lifts mouth and cheeks upwards in laughing, *depressor labii inferioris* turns lower lip down, mentalis wrinkles chin and makes lower lip protrude, *platysma* is muscle over lower jaw and neck, *buccinator* blows out cheeks, *risorius* produces grinning

Passive movements

Passive movements are those movements given to the client which are performed by the beauty therapist alone and in which the client plays no active part. They can be divided into two groups: forced and relaxed. Forced passive movements are mainly carried out under medical supervision. It is only the relaxed passive movements which concern the beauty therapist and which will be described. They may be given as a treatment on their own, included as a part of the massage session or merely used as a method of handling the client's limbs while repositioning during the course of treatment.

Points of importance

As in massage the client must be warm and comfortable. The position of the therapist is important because therapists must be able to move the joints of the client easily and effortlessly. They should, as in massage, face the client at all times and be aware of any untoward expression that would indicate a temporary cessation or modification of treatment. The handling of the client's limbs must be firm enough to instil a feeling of complete confidence in the client, but care must be taken not to nip or squeeze too tightly with the hand grips, as this will be painful and cause tension. Once having mastered the technique of holding, grasping, and moving the joints and limbs, the same methods should be utilized and applied when merely moving a part of the body to another position. Apart from the sense of confidence and security clients feel in the therapist and treatment if their limbs are moved firmly, stress and strain on the joints, ligaments, and tendons is avoided when the limbs are adequately supported.

There is nothing more irritating and less inspiring than handling clients as though they were a wet fish, being pushed, prodded, and plonked into position. It is important to localize the movements to the joint being moved, by immobilizing the other joints above and below. Traction or a gentle pull in the long direction of the bones separating their joint surfaces is advisable to ensure a perfectly free movement. Slight over pressure at the completion of flexion, and a little extra stretching at the end of extension help to guarantee full range of movement. If the client is very tense it may take several treatments before the maximum movement possible is obtained. Forcing a movement can cause muscle spasm and tension which will restrict the movement, so defeating the object of relaxed passive movements. Sometimes it may help a client before giving the treatment if therapists demonstrate on themselves first the type of movements that are required.

Contraindications

Contraindications of passive movements would be when there are conditions present which require medical treatment. If pain is experienced on passive movements then they should be discontinued in that joint. Some chronic arthritic conditions of joints are improved by passive movements providing that the movements are only taken to the limit that the condition imposes. Where joints are hot and swollen, or the skin around them shiny, the movements are not advisable. If passive movements are properly administered there is no danger of damaging the soft structures of the joints, and therefore very few contraindications.

Effects and uses

1 Relaxation is the main effect of these kind of movements. Passive movements if performed smoothly, slowly, and rhythmically without any break in continuity have a soothing effect. A tense client can be taught to relax the whole body or any localized area.
2 Passive movements to the head can deplete the flow of blood to the head, tension in the cranial muscles is also relaxed, and tension headaches can be soothed. Strain and anxiety which soon shows on the face will be reduced.
3 Suppleness in the joints can be improved through passive movements, and this may be shown by more graceful and fluid movements in everyday functional activity.
4 Stiffness due to insufficient exercise or over-exercising may be removed by gradually increasing the range of movement, aches and pains being eased away. This in turn will give rise to a more pleasant facial expression and will relieve tension elsewhere, improving all-round general posture.
5 They may be given as a preliminary to massage to assess the type of client in order to find out whether they are tense or relaxed, and if there is any limitation of movement in the joints. The treatment can then be tailored if necessary to suit the individual requirements of the client.
6 The hand grips and support of the joints and limbs which are used in passive movements can be conveniently applied when lifting the limbs from one position to another during the course of other treatments.
7 Passive movements may encourage and prepare clients for more active exercises on their own.

8   In the joints moved, the synovial fluid is increased and therefore the joints are fed, nourished, and lubricated. Waste products are absorbed and removed, adhesions prevented, and the mobility of the joints, if not increased, is certainly maintained independently of muscular activity.

9   Muscle tone can be decreased in the muscles which pass over the joint being moved. In cases where they are shortened and tight they could be gradually eased into a state of relaxation and gently stretched. This would improve the range of movement in the joint without force although it may take several regular treatments to accomplish. The effect would be, depending upon which muscle groups are contracted, to improve the posture and carriage of the client. For instance, tight pectoral muscles can lead to round shoulders; hip flexors, or tightened hamstrings, could restrict mobility of the spine again causing a defective picture. This leads to compensatory stress and strain on other parts of the body which eventually might need medical attention.

10 Venous circulation is aided as the veins passing over the joints are squeezed and stretched by the rhythmic smooth movements. This can help warm up different areas and improve the cosmetic appearance of cold blue limbs due to sluggish circulation. The movements must be done quickly and vigorously. Circumduction of the shoulder and hip joints would be most effective in these cases. Circumduction of the hip joint will also increase the flow of blood to the abdomen, relieving abdominal stasis and aiding digestion.

11 Extensibility of the muscles passing over the joints can be increased as relaxation in them improves, although muscle tone is not effected with passive movements.

12 Sometimes passive movements are given for their stimulating effect. They could be given as a full treatment to a lethargic, tired client, or to clients who have neither time nor energy for active exercises. Although they cannot replace active exercise, they do ensure that the joints and muscles are moved through their full range. Very few people use their muscles and joints to their full limit in everyday functional activity.

With a stimulating treatment of passive movements, the joint and muscle sense is stimulated, and there is a reflex contraction in the opposing muscle group of each movement; the brain becomes aware of the movement. As the nerves, arteries, and veins pass over the joints they are alternately stretched and compressed.

Speeding up the activity of these vessels invokes a general feeling of alertness. The movements here would be done quickly and briskly, maintaining a good rhythm, but with a more staccato pattern of movement than employed when giving passive movements for their soothing effect. With the emphasis on physical stimulation by passive movements, the way could be paved for more active exercises, and the client should feel refreshed, invigorated, and raring to go.

13 Leaving the client with a sense of being thoroughly and completely treated is another effect of passive movements in beauty therapy if one or two movements are given to each joint during or after the course of a massage treatment.

Technique

Movements and grips in lying

Right arm

Shoulder joint: clients can be lying near the edge of the couch or in sitting with the therapist in stride standing beside them. The client's elbow must be slightly flexed with the hand pronated. Grasping the client's elbow firmly with the left hand, the therapist holds the client's right hand and wrist in the thumb and finger grip. This involves placing the index and middle fingers round the client's thumb and palm, with the thumb, fourth, and fifth fingers of the therapist firmly encircling the wrist to prevent movement in this joint. During all the movements of the shoulder joint the therapist's left hand pivots round the point of the elbow and the utmost care must be taken to see that full weight of the limb is borne by the therapist.

Order of movements

1 Circumduction to mobilize the joint.
2 Flexion into elevation.
3 Extension from elevation through flexion.
4 Abduction into elevation.
5 Adduction from elevation through abduction.
6 Inward rotation.
7 Outward rotation.
8 Circumduction.

Elbow joint: the beauty therapist is in walk standing with the client in the same position as for the shoulder joint. Keeping the same thumb and finger grip, the therapist's left hand slides to support the elbow from the back and just above it. The hand is supinated.

Order of movements

1 Flexion.
2 Extension.
3 Pronation to the forearm with the elbow semi-flexed.
4 Supination with the elbow semi-flexed.

Wrist joint: the position of the client and therapist remains unchanged, except that the upper arm is supported to the elbow, which is semi-flexed, with the hand in pronation. The beauty therapist firmly holds the forearm just above the wrist joint with the left hand, modifying the thumb and finger grip, by retracting the thumb and outer two fingers to below the client's wrist, leaving it completely free.

Order of movements

1 Circumduction for mobility.
2 Flexion.
3 Extension.
4 Abduction (radial deviation).

5 Adduction (ulnar deviation).
6 Circumduction.

Metacarpo-phalangeal joints: the therapist places the fingers of the left hand across the palm of the hand above the joints with the thumb across the dorsal aspect of the client's hand to isolate the movements to these joints. Each finger is moved individually at this joint.

Order of movements

1 Circumduction.
2 Flexion.
3 Extension.
4 Abduction.
5 Adduction.
6 Circumduction.

Interphalangeal joints of fingers and thumb: these are all treated individually with special emphasis being placed on traction separating the joint surfaces. Each joint is firmly held by the beauty therapist above and below its surface localizing the movement and restricting superfluous movement in the other joints.

Order of movements

1 Flexion.
2 Extension.

Saddle joint of thumb: the technique is the same as for the fingers with the palm supinated.

Order of movements

1 Circumduction.
2 Flexion.
3 Extension.
4 Abduction.

5 Adduction.
6 Opposition.
7 Circumduction.

Right leg

The position of the client remains the same as for the arm movements with the therapist in walk standing and swivelling into stride standing when required.

Hip joint: the full weight of the heavy lower limb is taken by the therapist, placing the left hand underneath the client's knee from the lateral side. The right hand is placed under the heel and sole of the client's right foot. This restricts movements in the ankle joint. The left hand of the therapist must be free to pivot around the knee as the hip is moved the knee is semi-flexed.

Order of movements

1 Circumduction for mobility with the knee in semi-flexion.
2 Flexion.
3 Extension.
4 Abduction; the therapist changes to stride standing with the client's hip and knee flexed.
5 Adduction given in the same position as for abduction.
6 Inward rotation with the leg straight is given by rolling the leg inwards on the couch.
7 Outward rotation by rolling the leg outwards.
8 Circumduction of the knee is moved into flexion and the hip joint circled round.

Knee joint: the client and therapist are in the same basic position as for the hip joint movements. The grasp is the same for movements of the knee. The hip is flexed slightly as the knee joint is moved.

Order of movements

1 Flexion.
2 Extension.

3 Medial rotation with the knee in semi-flexion.
4 Lateral rotation with the knee in semi-flexion.

Ankle joint: the grasp is modified and the therapist holds the ankle above the joint with the left hand, placing the right hand along the whole of the sole of the foot, gripping it firmly.

Order of movements

1 Circumduction.
2 Dorsiflexion.
3 Plantarflexion.
4 Inversion.
5 Eversion.
6 Circumduction.

Metatarso-phalangeal and *interphalangeal joints* of the foot are manipulated in the same way as for the hand. The left hand grasps round the ball of the big toe and the right hand across the back of the toes. Movements of the toes are more restricted than in the hand and care must be taken not to cramp the toes while performing the manipulations.

Order of movements

1 Circumduction restricted to the metacarpo-phalangeal joints.
2 Flexion.
3 Extension.
4 Abduction only to metacarpo-phalangeal joints.
5 Adduction only to metacarpo-phalangeal joints.
6 Circumduction to the metacarpo-phalangeal joints.

Movements and grips in prone lying

Before starting treatment, check the warmth and comfort of the client. Do not use pillows and blankets in this position as they restrict and hamper movements.

Hip joint

The therapist stands in stride standing at the side of the thigh on the right of the client. The therapist's right hand and forearm is placed across the sacro-iliac joint and gluteal mass. The left hand and forearm are hooked underneath the front of the right knee and thigh, supporting the weight of the knee, leg, and thigh along the upper arm and forearm. Pressure is applied with the right hand while the left hand and arm lifts the leg and thigh backwards into extension.

Lumbar spine

The left hand retains the same firm grasp of the thigh with the leg resting against the upper arm. The right hand of the therapist localizes the movements to the lumbar spine by placing it firmly with pressure over the lower thoracic vertebrae, leaving the lumbar joints free. The client's leg and hip are lifted backwards and the movement is now extended into the lumbar vertebrae.

Thoracic spine

The therapist remains in walk standing and moves to the level of the middle of the back. The therapist hooks the right hand and forearm from the back under the client's right axilla, and stretches it across the chest, with the hand holding firmly in the left axilla. Care must be taken not to place the arm across the throat. The left hand localizes each thoracic vertebra with firm pressure, starting from the first working down to the twelfth, while the head, shoulders, and back are lifted into extension by the therapist with the right arm. This procedure is then repeated on the other side with hand grips reversed.

Shoulder girdle

The beauty therapist is in walk standing at the level of the scapulae on the right of the client. Both arms, the right to the client's right and the left to the client's left, are hooked from the

back of the shoulder joint through the client's axillae, to the front
of the shoulder joint. They are then brought round gently to the
back of the client's neck. Both the client's arms are extended by
the therapist, lifting the shoulder joints backwards and pulling the
scapulae together. The pectoral muscles across the anterior aspect
of the shoulder joints and chest are gently stretched. Care must be
taken not to exert a downward thrust with the hands on the back
of the neck.

Head and neck lying

The client is in lying without any support from pillows but must
be warm and comfortable to ensure maximum relaxation. The
client's shoulders rest across the top of the couch so that the head
and neck are entirely free.

Ideally, a second therapist should hold the client's shoulders
firmly down to provide traction for the moving joints. If this is
not possible the weight of the body will provide sufficient
anchorage. The beauty therapist takes the stride standing position
at the top of the couch behind the client's head. The therapist
supports the client's head with one hand; the index finger and
thumb are widely apart and are placed round the base of the
occiput.

Care is taken to ensure that the hair is as much out of the way
as possible, otherwise the therapist's hand can glide over it, out of
the firm grip. The other hand cups the chin carefully. Traction
towards the therapist is applied firmly. In order to make the client
feel completely confident and secure the grasp must remain
consistently firm, taking the full weight of the head throughout
the whole treatment. All movements to the head and neck must be
slow, rhythmic, and very carefully and gently applied.

Order of movements

1 Circumduction.
2 Flexion.
3 Extension.

4 Right and left side flexion.
5 Rotation to the right with right hand under chin.
6 Rotation to the left with left hand under chin.
7 Circumduction.

Rest is advisable for the client after passive movements to the spine, head, and neck for at least ten minutes on completion of treatment. This will avoid a tendency to light-headedness which the client might feel. Clients should then be allowed to sit up slowly and dress themselves leisurely.

The *rate* of movements given to the spine, head, and neck should always be moderate, bordering on slow.

Repetition of each movement is unlimited but an average of four to six for each movement is usually given when passive movements are used as a complete treatment in their own right. As little as two repeats of each movement are given if they are included as part of another treatment.

Active exercises 10

Active exercises are those in which the voluntary muscles are made to contract, and clients perform the movement themselves. These movements can be performed freely by the client, or with assistance or resistance provided by gravity, by the therapist, or by equipment.

Exercises are a necessity but they need regular practice to be fully effective in maintaining and improving natural health and beauty. It is never too late to start exercising and never too early to begin. It is important for beauty therapists to have a basic knowledge about them, and to know exactly what they are trying to achieve and how to do it.

Effects and uses on the systems of the body

Muscles

When a muscle contracts it becomes thick and hard, and with repeated exercise the muscle fibres increase in size. The blood supply is increased to the working muscle, feeding and nourishing it, and leaving behind a surplus of food which is stored as muscle bulk (protoplasm). Waste products such as lactic acid are increased and these have a direct action on the walls of the blood vessels in the muscle, dilating them and producing an increased volume of blood to that area. This is called *repletion*. It is said that there is ten times as much blood in a working muscle as in a resting one. Because the working muscles are repleted, blood is taken away from other parts of the body. This is called *depletion* and this factor can be made use of to deplete the blood in the cranium by exercising the trunk and limbs, in the relief of tension headaches. Resting after a meal is to allow the blood to flow fully to the digestive organs.

Tone and strength are only built up by muscle activity, and this in turn improves the elasticity and extensibility of the muscles. It is important to bear in mind that muscles both weak and strong, if overworked, can be strained, fatigued, and weakened. Excess carbon dioxide causes the respiratory centres in the brain to be stimulated in an effort to increase the intake of oxygen. The body temperature is raised and the muscles themselves become warm as the exercises continue, remaining so for quite a while after the activity stops.

Bones

There is an increased blood supply to the bones and joints on active exercise, so that they are nourished and fed. The shape of the bones can be influenced by the pull of muscles so that general exercises ensure proper development. Many daily activities are assymetrical or restricting, and appropriate exercising counter-balances the postural deformities which can occur as a result of limited movement. While muscles are being worked the mobility of the joints is maintained and increased.

Circulation

The venous and lymphatic circulation is improved. As these vessels run over the joints there is a pumping action on them, causing them to be alternately stretched and shortened. This pushes the blood along towards the heart, regurgitation or back flow being prevented by the presence of valves in the veins. The muscles themselves on contraction are squeezed against the veins pressing out the blood and on relaxation allow them to refill. This also aids the venous return to the heart. Sometimes veins are attached to fascia which can compress them. By muscle contraction the fascia is tightened and pressure is relieved, allowing a better blood flow through the part of the vein. The arterial circulation is affected and the flow of blood to different parts of the body is greatly influenced by the active muscles. Blood pressure in the heart is raised and a greater volume of blood is pumped through it, causing it to beat at a faster and stronger rate.

Respiration

The rate and depth of respiration is increased due to the creation of an oxygen need. In this way, the excess carbon dioxide is expelled. Deeper inspiration and expiration increases the mobility of the thorax, strengthening and developing the muscles of respiration at the same time. While the increased circulation promotes the gaseous interchange, the lungs are used and aired to full capacity. Nourishment is brought to the lung tissue by the increased circulation, so increasing their resistance to infection and disease.

Digestion, excretion and secretion

Peristalsis is stimulated due to the action of the abdominal muscles against the involuntary muscle tissue of the digestive tract, and also because of the pressure exerted on the viscera during various movements. This in turn helps the passage of the contents along the alimentary tract while the improved tone of the abdominal muscles improves their excretory action. Improved circulation to the abdominal organs promotes secretion of the gastric juices and this again in turn aids digestion and absorption so that all the tissues of the body benefit. More waste products due to increased metabolism are excreted, via the kidneys. As the result of exercise there is an increased production of sweat which helps to rid the body of impurities and excess fluid, cooling the body down as it evaporates on the surface of the skin. The sebaceous glands are stimulated and more sebum being secreted lubricates the skin, providing the body surface with protection from its slight antiseptic properties.

Nerves

Co-ordination, concentration, and co-operation are developed during active exercises. This requires the complicated use of the brain and nervous system, which in order to function efficiently and accurately needs the nourishment that the increased flow of blood brings Active exercises can be used in such a way to diminish nerve impulses, decreasing all sensations and activities of the body and allowing them to be recharged with energy through rest.

Effects and uses on health and beauty

A marvellous sense of well-being and invigoration comes with exercising and keeping physically fit. Vitality improves, and the woman who seeks a new beauty image will only achieve her objective if she feels one hundred per cent fit. Regular practice of simple movements can help the determined person to overcome many trivial complaints such as tiredness, tension, stiffness, and even boredom by recharging the systems of the body. Body metabolism is raised by regular exercise and, combined with an appropriate diet, weight can be lost or gained according to the requirements of the client. Exercises can help to keep and improve the lines and contours of the body by fining, trimming, and firming flabby areas, or increasing bulk, filling out the shape where necessary.

As the body grows older, muscles tend to contract and shorten. Exercises keep the muscles stretched, supple, and strong. Although the clock cannot be turned back, some of the looks, a lot of the energy, desires, and drives of youth can be regained, keeping the body young and maintaining its activity. Normal functioning of the body is maintained and improved with exercises. In this category comes running for a bus easily, walking upstairs without puffing and blowing, bending and stretching without a backache, full mobility of joints especially for the housewife at spring cleaning time, and ending a busy day for young and old without a screaming headache.

As well as toning up the muscles of the body, exercises can help to decrease tension and promote deeper sleep through the art of relaxation, and even help to cure the insomniac. If clients can relax their body, they will be able to relax their mind, and this relaxation of mental tension can take years off the face and of the body, obviating the need to disguise lines and wrinkles under layers of cosmetics. By exercising the body regularly the heart muscle is kept functionally fit, and also ready to cope with any sudden muscular effort, or emergency. It is important to prevent the heart from becoming weak and sluggish; like a faithful dog it needs exercising regularly every day to cope efficiently in a time of stress. If clients are in poor muscular tone then in those muscles exercised, they may experience up to several days afterwards, a certain amount of muscle ache, tenderness and stiffness. This wears off gradually and decreases as the muscles are strengthened, toned, and used through their full range of movement, with carefully planned exercises. After half an hour of either localized or general exercises the client should feel glowing, radiant, pleasantly tired, but refreshed with eyes shining and bright.

A steam bath or sauna followed by a massage and rest completes, together with the exercises, one of the most revitalizing overall beauty treatments available. Popular with both men and women, young and old alike, regardless of shape or size, these basic ingredients for health and beauty have remained virtually the same for centuries.

Contraindications

1 When medically ill-advised.
2 High blood pressure or any acute heart condition.
3 Arterio-sclerosis (hardening of the arteries); usually the client is elderly and should be aware of the condition.
4 High temperatures.
5 Extreme cases of debility, general tiredness, and weakness.
6 Any advanced disease in the body.
7 Recent injuries.
8 Acute inflammatory conditions of joints, such as rheumatoid arthritis where the joints, particularly the smaller ones, would be hot, swollen, and very painful to move.
9 Fevers.
10 Health reasons, unless medically recommended.

Some mechanics of body movement

Levers

In the body the bones are used as levers to lift the limbs or different parts quickly, easily, and in a well balanced manner. The joints act as the fulcrum, the point about which the lever moves, and the power or force required to lift the weight of the limbs is provided by the muscles. Depending upon what action or movement is required, the balance, power, and speed can be altered by the position of the levers in relation to the fulcrum and the power. There are three classes of levers:

Class of levers

The classes of levers are illustrated in Figure 10.1 as follows:

1 The fulcrum or joint lies somewhere between the weight to be moved and the power. For example, in plantar flexion of the foot, the fulcrum is the ankle joint; the weight is the foot and

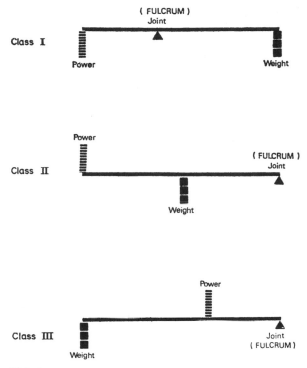

Figure 10.1 Levers

the power is the insertion of tendo-achilles. The longer the distance from the fulcrum to the power, the easier the movement. The movement is more difficult when the distance from the weight to the fulcrum is increased.

2 The weight lies between the power and the fulcrum. For example, in standing on tiptoes, the fulcrum is the metatarso-phalangeal joints, the power from the calf muscles inserted into the calcaneum, and the weight is that of the body which falls on to the tarsals. Little effort is required in these movements.

3 The power lies between the fulcrum and the weight. For example, in knee extension, the fulcrum is the knee joint, the power is the insertion of the quadriceps muscles into the tibial tubercle lifting the weight of the leg and foot. Much effort is

required in these movements. Almost every movement in the body falls into this class.

The distance from the fulcrum to the point where the power is applied is called the weight lever, and by lengthening the weight lever in free movements the movement can be made more difficult; also by increasing the resistance with added weight and placing them further away from the moving joint.

Axes and planes of movements

Movements of the body take place round an imaginary line called the axis. The axis is in the joint. Some joints are capable of producing several movements round different axes. These movements take place on an imaginary flat surface called a plane There are three axes and three planes of movement.

Axes

1 **Frontal** or transverse axis is round a line from side to side of the body which lies parallel with the forehead or the coronary suture in the skull.
2 **Saggital** axis is a line from front to back of the body parallel with the saggital suture in the skull.
3 **Vertical** or longitudinal axis is a line drawn through the body from the head to the feet.

Planes

1 **Frontal** plane is a flat surface parallel with the face and coronary suture.
2 **Saggital** plane is a surface parallel with the saggital suture.
3 **Horizontal** plane is one which is parallel to the dorsum of the foot and the ground.

Examples

1 Trunk side flexion (bending the body sideways from the waist) takes place round the saggital axis on a frontal plane.

2 Trunk rotation (twisting the body round from the waist) takes place round a vertical axis on a horizontal plane.
3 Trunk flexion (bending the body forwards from the waist) takes place round the frontal axis on a saggital plane.

Gravity

The force of gravity is the force or pull which the earth exerts on objects towards its own centre. The force acts at right angles to the earth's surface, so that if an object is dropped from a height it will fall perpendicularly downwards.

Centre of gravity of the body

The point on which the pull of gravity is the strongest in the human body is its centre of gravity. If the human body could be held straight like a plank of wood, it would be the point at which the plank balances over a pivot. In the body this point normally falls in front of the second or third sacral vertebra, but depends upon the shape, size, and weight of the individual. Each part of the body has its own centre of gravity.

Line of gravity

The direction in which gravity pulls the body is called the line of gravity. This imaginary line, either side of which the weight must be equal, normally falls from the centre of the vortex of the skull to a point midway between the feet.

From the anatomical position, this line falls from the skull in front of the ears, through the cervical and thoracic vertebrae, through the bodies of the lumbar vertebrae, hip joint, just behind the knee joint, and just in front of the ankle joint, to the point between the feet. Any movement from the normal postural attitude alters its position.

By altering the centre and line of gravity of the body exercises can be made more difficult or easier. Balance, co-ordination, and posture are also affected.

Range of movement

Movements are produced by the contraction of muscles. The extent of the movement produced is called the range or path of movement of the muscles. There are four ranges of movement:

1 **Full range** is from the most stretched point of a muscle to its most contracted point.
2 **Inner range** is from its midpoint of contraction to its most contracted point.
3 **Outer range** is from the most stretched point to the midpoint of contraction.
4 **Middle range** is from the almost fully stretched point to the almost fully contracted point.

Uses of the ranges

General strengthening exercises are given through full range. Toning, shortening, and strengthening exercises are given in inner range.

For lengthening and maintaining strength, outer range exercises are used.

Everyday functional movements are usually performed in middle range and there is a danger of stiffness in the joints and muscles if their full range of movement is not maintained properly.

Muscle work

Muscles work in three different ways when they contract. They normally work against the resistance of an outside force such as gravity. Weights and apparatus can be used if available.

1 **Concentric** muscle work is that in which the muscle becomes shorter and thicker; the origin and insertion move nearer together. Concentric muscle work produces heat in the muscles and body. It is the hardest, though most common, form of all resisted exercises. It can be used in all ranges of movement.

2 **Eccentric** muscle work is that in which the muscle lengthens and hardens, the origin and insertion being drawn further away from each other, paying out against a resistance (gravity). Eccentric muscle work is considered to be easier than concentric muscle work. It produces less heat in the body but more work, which has the tendency to make clients hold their breath and feel tired. It can be used in all ranges.

3 **Static** muscle work is that in which the muscle contracts and becomes hard and thick, with neither lengthening nor shortening and no movement. Little heat or muscle work is produced by static muscle contractions. They are given to hold positions, particularly in the correction of poor posture, where with repeated holdings of the corrected position, the postural sense is educated in the client, forming new improved automatic habits. Static contractions for a short period of time are the easiest form of muscle work; over a long period of time they produce fatigue. They are used as a starter to strengthen very weak muscles.

Components of fitness

There are five health-related components of fitness:

1 **Cardiorespiratory endurance** (stamina). This is the capacity of the heart, blood vessels and lungs to function efficiently during vigorous sustained activity, for example jogging and cycling.

2 **Muscular strength.** This is the ability of a muscle or muscle group to contract against a given resistance (weight of limb or external resistance) to bring about movement in one maximal effort.

3 **Local muscular endurance.** This is the ability of a muscle or muscle group to contract effectively and continuously over a given period of time.

4 **Flexibility.** This is the mobility or range of motion at a joint or series of joints.

5 **Percentage of body fat.** This is the percentage of fat to lean tissue in a given body.

Principles of training

When devising an exercise scheme for a client it is imperative that the principles of training are applied.

1 **Overload.** This means that for the exercise programme to be effective it must place stress on the client to a greater degree than normally experienced.
2 **Adaptation.** As a result of overload the body's physiology will adapt to cope with the increased demand.
3 **Progression.** In order to progress and not create a plateau effect further overload must be applied after adaptation.
4 **Specificity.** For training to be effective it must be designed to 'stress' the specific demand, for example if increased flexibility of the hamstrings is required then stretching exercises must be undertaken.
5 **Reversibility.** This is the adaptation principle reversed. If clients stop training their fitness level will reverse. If the level of fitness has been acquired through years of training the reversal will be slower than fitness acquired over weeks.
6 **Measurement.** There are two reasons for measurement:
   (a) To provide motivation for the client.
   (b) To evaluate the effectiveness of the training/exercise schedule prescribed.

There are other factors but these are the main principles which the therapist is concerned with.

Some important points for exercise schemes

1 The age, condition, occupation and sex of the client are the first considerations.
2 If the scheme of exercises is a general one then exercises for all parts of the body should be included.

3 Exercises which use the same muscles or muscle groups should not be given consecutively. In this way overwork of any one muscle is avoided.

4 It is important to vary the exercises in each treatment to avoid boredom. Interest must be stimulated and maintained. Music can be a helpful means to help rhythm and grace of movement. A modulated voice, with the exercise command well executed, can be most elective. Balance and co-ordination exercises always add interest and liven up the treatment.

5 Special exercises for specific problems should be emphasized if included in a general scheme of exercises.

6 A goal should be aimed for, if possible, to encourage the client to persevere and practise home exercises. These should be taught and repeated at the end of the session. The client must know exactly what exercises to do and how to do them. They should consist of natural functional movements.

7 Depending upon the kind of problem requiring attention, the choice of time should be considered. For example, relaxation exercises could be given late in the day if they are to help insomnia. Active exercises would never be given after a meal.

8 Exercises for health reasons are only given when medical permission is granted.

9 The first sessions should be short and sweet. As the muscles strengthen, the sessions can last longer by including more exercises, and repeating each exercise more often. An accurate chart must be kept, noting all details of the exercises.

10 Mobility exercises are a vital starter for all schemes; these help to warm up the muscles and loosen the joints. Muscles and joints which are cold and stiff can be torn and easily strained if they are not warmed up first. Five to ten minutes would be devoted to warming up.

11 Breathing and postural correction should begin and end all schemes of exercises. They can and should be interspersed freely throughout the whole session. The breathing exercises

will give the client a chance to rest and recoup a little energy. Sometimes the exercises can be combined with breathing instruction.

12 All muscle groups to be exercised must be statically stretched for between 8–30 seconds.

13 At the end of the session clients should feel pleasantly tired but not exhausted, and facilities should be available for them to be able to relax lying down for at least fifteen minutes if required. Clients should be suitably dressed in unrestricting clothes; the room should be airy, warm and bright.

Safety factors while exercising

The client

1 It is important that the client is dressed appropriately for exercise, that is a track suit or leotard. The clothes must be non-restrictive.

2 If the client is to undertake some form of aerobic exercise it is imperative that proper aerobic shoes with suitable support and cushioning are worn.

3 Advise the client to tie long hair back.

4 Always re-check for contraindications.

5 Do not allow the client to exercise after a heavy meal. Generally two hours later is sufficient digestion time.

6 Advise the client not to exercise with a full bladder.

7 Do not allow the client to exercise while taking pain-killing drugs or having recently consumed alcohol.

The environment

1 Ensure there is enough room for the client to move freely – at least two square metres of space.

2 The room must be warm and well-ventilated. Ensure windows open and close easily.

3 The lighting must be adequate to enable the client to clearly see the demonstration.

4 The floor should preferably be a wooden sprung floor to absorb impact and reduce the likelihood of stress impact injuries.
5 Mats must be provided for floor exercises.

Assessment/screening of the client prior to exercise involvement

The primary concern of the therapist is to ensure the safety of the client. The purpose of screening is to assess the fitness and medical history of the client and therefore prescribe the correct level and type of exercise.

A general questionnaire could be used but ideally a full fitness assessment should be carried out.

First, the general information about the client should be recorded.

The medical background should cover any recent operation, recent illness, medication, etc.

The frame size of the client can be calculated by taking three measurements as follows.

Measuring body fat by skin calipers

The apparatus

Use a calibrated caliper. See Figure 10.2.

Figure 10.2 A skin caliper

Instructions to the client

The client should stand in a natural, relaxed position with arms held freely, palms facing inwards.

Instructions for the therapist

1 Ask clients if they are right- or left-handed.
2 Use that side of the client to take four measurements.
3 The skinfold is picked up between the thumb and index finger with one hand. The other hand places the caliper about 1 cm from the finger holding the skinfold. The caliper should be held in place for three seconds and a reading taken. See Figure 10.3(a)–(c).

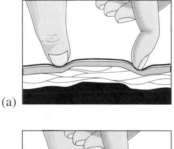
(a)

(b)

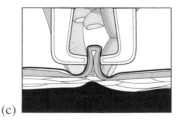
(c)

Figure 10.3 Measuring body fat

Figure 10.4 Measuring triceps

4 Measure the triceps, midway between the shoulder and elbow joints (Figure 10.4).
5 Measure the biceps, midway between the shoulder and elbow joints (Figure 10.5).
6 Measure the subscapular. Pinch the skin just below the inferior angle of the scapular (Figure 10.6).
7 Measure the supra-iliac. This is the most difficult measurement to take accurately. Look for the position of the anterior superior-iliac spine and follow the angle of the crest of the ilium. The skin above this should be pinched (Figure 10.7).
8 Add up the four readings in millimetres. The percentage body fat can be read from the Table 10.1.

Figure 10.5 Measuring biceps

9 Make sure the side that has been measured is written in the fitness assessment card.
10 The percentage of lean tissue can be worked out by taking the percentage reading away from 100 per cent.

Posture

A good professional model glides along gracefully and erect. Every movement, having been carefully considered, is elegantly made. It is all a question of correct posture remembered and practised until it becomes second nature. A client does not have

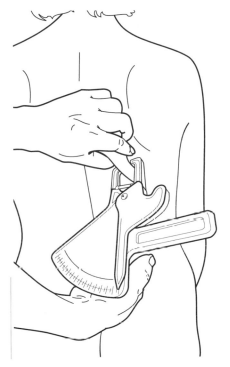

Figure 10.6 Measuring scapula

to be a model to walk tall. Even the plainest clients can look most becoming if their posture is impeccable. Some people seem to be born with a natural swing of the hips, straight shoulders, and head held high without giving it a second thought. For the client whose stance leaves much to be desired, a careful examination of the spine is essential. This will reveal exactly what kind of postural correction is indicated during the course of exercises. Perhaps only slight correction is required, or maybe a more rigorous and specific scheme of exercises will have to be devised.

Good posture relies upon the interplay and co-ordination of the flexor and extensor groups of muscles in the body. If one group of muscles becomes weak or too strong, then the whole postural

Figure 10.7 Measuring supra-iliac

balance is thrown out of line. Bad posture can lead to many side effects, including postural defects of the spine, which, apart from destroying good looks, bring their own set of problems to the body. A full length mirror is extremely useful in teaching the client postural correction. Clients can see themselves corrected, feel the correction, remember the correction, and recheck the new position again in the mirror.

Inspection of the spine from the back

Make sure that the client is suitably dressed so that the whole spine is visible. Bra and pants would be adequate. The light must

Table 10.1

Women		Men	
Total mm	*Percentage body fat*	*Total mm*	*Percentage body fat*
8	13	15	5
12	14	20	9
14	15	25	11
18	16	30	13
20	17	35	15
24	18	40	17
26	19	45	18
30	20	50	20
32	21	55	21
34	22	60	22
38	23	65	23
40	24	70	24
42	25	75	25
44	26	80	26
48	27	90	27
50	28	100	28
52	29	110	29
56	30	120	30
58	31	130	31
62	32	140	32
64	33	150	33
68	34	160	34
70	35	175	35
76	37	190	36
80	38	205	37
82	39	220	38
86	40	235	39
88	41	255	40
90	42	275	41
		295	42

Table 10.2 Body fatness rating scale up to 25 years

Rating	*Men*	*Women*
Obese	>20%	>29%
Fat	18–19%	24–28%
Average	14–17%	20–23%
Lean	11–13%	16–19%
Very lean	<10%	<15%

be good and the room warm. The beauty therapist stands behind the client to check the general posture. The client is in standing.

1 The general outline and stance of the client are first noted.
2 The ears should be level and the neck straight.
3 The shoulders should be level.
4 The medial borders of the scapulae should be at an even distance from the spine. The inferior angles of the scapulae should be level and lying flat against the back of the chest wall.
5 The angle at the waist should be evenly curved and not more apparent on one side than the other with neither hip higher than the other.
6 The ribs will be evenly spaced and not closer together on one side nor farther apart on the other.
7 The soft structures on either side should not show any signs of shortening nor abnormal signs of lengthening on the opposite side.
8 The spines themselves should be down the centre of the back, and if a finger is gently rubbed down the spines of the vertebrae they will redden, and the curve of the spine will be seen clearly.
9 The gluteal folds should be even and at the same height.
10 The arms will hang evenly near to the sides of the body.
11 Knock knees, bandy legs, or flat feet are noted.

Inspection from the front

1 Head should be high and held back, with chin tucked in and neck straight.
2 Shoulder and ear levels should be even.
3 Shoulders should be slightly back with chest and thorax out and broad.
4 Arms and hands relaxed down by the sides of the thigh, not too far forwards.
5 Even waist-line with iliac crests level.
6 Abdominal muscles slightly retracted.
7 Legs and knees straight, feet facing forwards or slightly apart with heels together.

If all these points are correct, the posture of the client should be excellent. However, what is a good posture for one person can be bad posture for another.

Active correction of posture by the therapist

1 See that the client's head is up with chin in.
2 Shoulders back, but down and relaxed.
3 Chest out.
4 Arms should lie in centre of thighs by the sides.
5 Abdominal muscles pulled in.
6 Seat muscles tight and tucked in.
7 Knees straight but not tightly braced back.
8 Inner and outer sides of feet gripping floor with arches of foot raised.

Active static muscle contractions to maintain correct posture

Static holding of a good postural position is important to learn if correction is necessary and if it requires only a simple reminder to put right. Sometimes clients can easily correct a bad posture themselves and the following static corrections would be given in the corrected standing position. The therapist would tell the client how to do the following statically.

1 Brace arm and leg muscles, hold, relax.
2 Brace neck and back of shoulder muscles, hold, relax.
3 Brace back muscles, hold, relax.
4 Brace back muscles and abdominal muscles, hold, relax.
5 Brace all muscles, hold, relax.

Specific postural conditions

Any postural condition, other than that which can be corrected actively by simple postural exercises, really needs specialized attention outside the sphere of the beauty therapist. However, in the course of treatment, there will be clients who require a course of exercises and yet have specific spinal defects. It is in these cases that the beauty therapist's guidance will be of great assistance. Therefore, it is essential for beauty therapists to familiarize themselves with conditions that may possibly confront them. They must be able to recognize them while examining the spine so that only corrective exercises are given in the course of treatment, and not exercises inadvertently prescribed which would be contraindicated for the condition.

If it is merely a matter of habitual bad posture, then corrective exercises will eventually give the client the right idea of the correct posture. It is as well to bear in mind that no two individuals are alike, and that each body type has its own characteristic postural make-up.

Pelvic tilt

The pelvic tilt is the angle which is made between a horizontal line and a line drawn from the top of the symphesis pubis to the sacral promontory. This angle varies, being greater in the female than in the male. The amount of movement possible in the pelvic angle depends upon the pelvic ligaments and joints. During pregnancy the ligaments are relaxed and movements in all these joints is increased so the pelvic tilt will alter, often increasing considerably. If the pelvis tilts forwards too much, the lumbar vertebrae can become hyperextended; if it tilts backwards too far, the curve in the lumbar vertebrae can flatten.

Lordosis

In this condition the client will appear to have a hollow back at the lumbar region. There is an exaggerated curve forwards in the lumbar region. Here the pelvic tilt is greatly increased forwards. The abdominal muscles and hamstrings are stretched and lengthened, with the lumbar muscles shortened and gluteal muscles weakened. The aim would be to give corrective exercises which would shorten and strengthen the abdominal and hamstring muscles, also to strengthen the gluteal muscles mobilizing the lumbar spine at the same time.

Kyphosis

In this condition, the normal backward curve of the spine in the thoracic region is exaggerated. Generally speaking, the client will have a poking chin and rounded shoulders as well. It is very often attributed to habitual bad posture but there are many other causes. The pectoral muscles are tight and shortened with the upper back muscles weak and over-stretched. The aim is to mobilize and loosen the tightened structures and strengthen those which are stretched, and to correct the posture.

Kypho-lordosis

This is a combination of the two latter conditions; one rarely goes without the other.

When exercises for the back are given, the lumbar spine should be corrected first so that the lordosis is not increased. When abdominal exercises are given, the thoracic region and shoulders should be straight and back so that the kyphosis is not encouraged.

Flat back

This condition is rarely seen but here the pelvis is tilted backwards, the lumbar spines are flat, and the hamstrings are shortened. The client may appear to be very erect and square-shouldered because the natural curves of the spine are almost ironed out. The aim would be to mobilize the spine and stretch the shortened muscles. Exercises for mobility would include humping and hollowing as explained for the pelvic tilt, all trunk movements including rotations, forward bendings, and side flexions done in sitting. These exercises would strengthen the spine at the same time.

Scoliosis

By scoliosis a lateral curving and rotating of the spine is meant. Unlike the exaggerated normal curves which exist in lordosis and kyphosis the curves of scoliosis are quite abnormal. A postural scoliosis where the structures of the spine have not yet altered can be corrected, but maintenance of the correct posture takes much time and practice to accomplish for long periods. If the postural scoliosis is not treated, it will eventually become permanent and changes in the muscles, ligaments, bones, and joints will inevitably take place. A postural curve consists of a single curve of the spine in one direction only in any one of the three mobile regions of the spine. That is in the cervical or thoracic or lumbar regions. Sometimes the whole spine is involved in a long 'C' curve. When the 'C' curve becomes permanent very often other compensatory curves appear in the rest of the spine in different directions, so that an 'S' curve may appear or even three and sometimes four curves can be seen in the spine. The latter are rare and are very often caused as a result of some other existing deformity. Postural curves, as the name implies, are very often the result of repeated bad postural habits.

The aim in *treating a postural scoliosis* would be to correct the general posture. The muscles maintaining the correct posture are the muscles of the head and neck, the extensors of the back, the abdominal muscles, extensors of hip and knee, and small muscles of the feet. Static contractions would be given to these muscles in lying, sitting, and standing, and the client would be encouraged to maintain a good posture while performing added arm, head and trunk exercises. More difficult exercises involving balance and co-ordination would finally be taught. It is the holding of a good posture during the exercise which is of value and not the exercise itself.

Winged scapula

This is a condition in which the vertebral border and inferior angle of the scapula protrudes backwards away from the ribs when the arm is lifted forwards to shoulder level. The client will be unable to punch the arm forward or perform forward pushing movements or lift the arm above shoulder level. It is often due to a weakness of the serratus anterior.

Weak abdominal muscles and visceroptosis

Visceroptosis is a condition in which the abdominal and pelvic organs are very often displaced downwards. It is commonly caused through over-stretched and weakened abdominal muscles. The abdominal muscles act in several ways. They flex the spine bending the trunk forwards, or draw the pelvis and legs upwards if the thorax is fixed. Together with the back muscles, the muscles of the one side flex the spine and trunk to the same side, and the obliquus muscles rotate the spine and trunk round. They also assist respiration in forced expiration and the support of the abdominal contents depends greatly on their muscle tone, together with the internal muscles of the pelvic floor. These pelvic floor muscles help with excretion, and support the contents of the pelvis and abdomen from below the pelvis like a sling preventing them from dropping out.

Very often certain body types are prone to weakness of these muscles although child-bearing, abdominal operations, poor posture, obesity, nervousness, or lack of sufficient exercise are among some of the contributory causes for weakened abdominal muscles. It is the strengthening of these abdominal muscles which is the prime concern of the beauty therapist, but it is wise to find out the cause for their weakness before commencing treatment. Visceroptosis can be a condition affecting any age and can vary in degree. Obviously not all those whose abdominal muscles are weak suffer from visceroptosis but eventually some degree or other of it may occur as a result of poor muscular tone in this area. Prevention is better than cure, and strong abdominal muscles help to avoid complications that may or may not arise.

Signs and symptoms

Clients who have weakened abdominal muscles may appear to have a prominent and bulging abdomen. They may tell the beauty therapist that they have dragging sensations, constipation, or attacks of intense pain. Very often they are nervous and highly excitable. If therapists suspect any medical condition exists whatsoever or encounters untoward signs and symptoms, they should first check with the doctor before attempting any corrective treatment. However, if clients have a severe condition of visceroptosis, it is doubtful that they would have found their way to the beauty therapist in the first place. What the beauty therapist is basically treating is the weakened abdominal muscles.

Flexibility

It is possible to measure the flexibility of the lower back and hamstrings.

Apparatus

Sit and reach box.

Instructions to the client

Clients should sit with their legs outstretched and feet flat against the box. The client should reach forward and push the slider along the box. The reading is taken.

Clients have three attempts and the best result from three is taken.

Table 10.3 Flexibility rating table

Rating	Men/boys	Women/girls
Excellent	32+	34+
Good	24–31	26–33
Average	17–23	17–25
Poor	9–16	9–16
Very poor	8 and below	8 and below

Measuring blood pressure

Why it is important to measure a client's blood pressure

High blood pressure (or hypertension) predisposes people to heart attack, strokes and kidney failure. People with this condition usually have no symptoms and may be quite unaware that anything is wrong.

The diagnosis is made by finding persistently high blood pressure on several occasions. It will be aggravataed by activities causing stress on the heart, for cxample sudden bouts of exercise, sauna and steam baths.

Blood pressure measurements are recorded as two numbers, for example 120/80. The first number is called the *systolic pressure* and represents the peak of pressure in the artery which is produced when the heart beats (that is, systole). The second number is the lowest pressure in the artery which occurs between heart beats and is called the *distolic pressure*. The units of blood pressure are millimetres of mercury (mm Hg) as the height of a mercury column is usually used to measure pressure in the arm cuff. The client should rest in a comfortable position.

Guidelines

Systolic blood pressure should be no more than 100 plus a person's age, for example for someone aged 40 not more than 140 at rest.

Blood pressure is measured by either using a battery operated blood pressure machine or a rubber cuff and stethoscope.

Resting heart rate

This is found by counting the number of heart beats per minute. The pulse can be found in the carotid artery on the left side of the neck or in the radial artery in the left wrist. Two fingers, not the thumb, should be placed gently on the chosen artery.

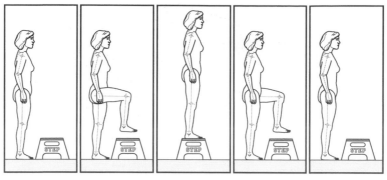

Figure 10.8 Step-by-step guide

Stamina test

This is an easy test to perform and is widely used (Figure 10.8). It works on the assumption that maximum heart rate is 195 beats per minute for young adults. It measures VO_2 maximum.

Apparatus required

1 A step-up box, 40 cm high for men and 33 cm high for women (Figure 10.9(a))
2 Metronome (Figure 10.9(b)).
3 Stop watch (Figure 10.9(c)).

Precautions

The following precautions should be taken before undertaking this test:

1 There should be a time lapse of 1–2 hours after a meal, before this test is taken.
2 If the test is taken in the morning, some carbohydrates should have been eaten for breakfast.
3 The client should not have a cold or temperature.
4 This test is strenuous and should be the first fitness test carried out. Performing other tests before the step test will adversely affect the result.

Figure 10.9 (a)

Figure 10.9 (b)

Figure 10.9 (c)

Instructions for the therapist

1 The client should sit and rest 10 minutes before taking the test and make sure the pulse can be found easily.
2 The metronome should be set for 30 beats per minute.
3 The stop watch should be set.
4 Start the test and time the client for 6 minutes.
5 Take the client's pulse for a full minute immediately after the exercise has finished. This pulse will give the recovery heart rate.

Instructions to the client

1 The client should stand facing the box.
2 One foot should be placed on the box.
3 The client should step up and place the other foot beside the first one, straightening the back and legs so that an upright position is achieved.
4 The client should immediately step down.
5 The step up rate is 30 per minute. The metronome will help clients keep in time.
6 The therapist should take the client's pulse for a full minute immediately after the exercise has finished.

Lung function test

Apparatus

Peak flow meter.

Instructions to the client

The lungs should be completely filled with air and, with a single exhalation, the client should breath out as hard as possible into the peak flow meter. Three attempts should be made and the best result recorded.

The results should be compared with those given in Figure 10.10.

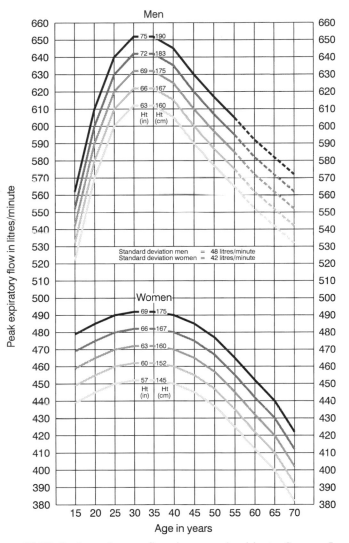

Figure 10.10 Peak expiratory flow in normal subjects. Source: Ian Gregg, A. J. Nunn, *British Medical Journal*, 1973, 3.282

Strength test

Quadriceps

Instructions for the client

Sit the client against a wall with knees at 90° and hold for as long as possible (Figure 10.11).

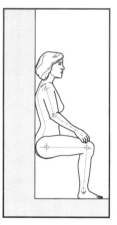

Figure 10.11 Correct position

Table 10.4 Quadriceps strength rating table

Excellent	90 seconds
Good	60 seconds
Fair	30 seconds
Poor	less than 30 seconds

Rectus abdominus

Instructions for the client

The client should lie with hands supporting the head, and elbows supporting the back. The position should be maintained at an angle of 45° for as long as possible (Figure 10.12).

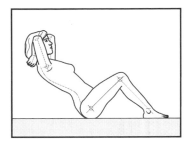

Figure 10.12 Correct position

Table 10.5 Rectus abdominus strength rating table

Excellent	25 seconds
Good	15 seconds
Fair	5 seconds
Poor	less than 5 seconds

Endurance test

Bent knee sit ups

Clients should be in the crook lying position, with their lower back pressed firmly into the floor, with their hands supporting their head and elbows supporting the back. They should then curl up to bring their shoulders and upper back off the floor, exhaling with the exertion. This exercise should be carried out for 30 seconds.

Table 10.6 Bent knee sit ups rating table

Rating	Men	Women
Very good	30	15
Good	20	10
Average	10	7
Poor	5	5

Table 10.7 Press ups rating table

Rating	Men	Women
Very good	30	15
Good	20	10
Average	10	7
Poor	5	5

Press ups

The client should lie with a straight back and the abdomen held firm and as many complete press ups as possible should be performed in 30 seconds.

Order of a general scheme of exercises

A basic general scheme of exercises should include all the principal muscle groups of the body. Not more than twelve to sixteen movements are advised. If the scheme is designed for a strenuous keep fit class, then the mobility exercises alone at the beginning of the session could last for up to twenty minutes. The following skeleton table for a simple scheme of exercises will be found a useful guide to follow, bearing in mind the above points.

Skeleton table of exercises

1 Postural correction exercise.
2 Mobility exercise for the neck.
3 Mobility exercise for the shoulder.
4 Mobility exercise for the lower back.
5 Mobility exercise for the hips.
6 Mobility exercise for the knees.
7 Mobility exercise for the ankles.

8 Static stretching for all muscle groups to be exercised.
9 Aerobic exercise, if included in the programme.
10 Muscular strength and endurance exercises for particular areas.
    (a) Rectus abdominus – abdomen.
    (b) Erector spinai – lower back.
    (c) Tricep – posterior aspect of upper arm.
    (d) Quadriceps – anterior thigh.
    (e) Hamstrings – posterior thigh.
    (f) Abductors – lateral thigh.
    (g) Adductors – thigh.
    (h) Obliques – waist.
  It is important to exercise antagonistic muscle groups to prevent an inbalance of strength and tone.
11 Static stretches for muscle exercises.
12 Deep breathing and relaxation exercises.

Health test record

A record should be completed for each client. An example of a typical form is shown in Figure 10.13.

Starting positions

It is important to consider in what position the exercises are going to be performed. In massage the aim is to make the client as comfortable as possible before commencing treatment. With exercises the aim is to ensure that the best possible effect is produced from the exercise, according to the requirements and capabilities of the client, bearing in mind that the details of correct posture are of vital importance throughout.

    There are five fundamental positions used in remedial exercises, the principles of which can be used for cosmetic exercises. They are lying, sitting, standing, kneeling, hanging. From these positions, other positions are modified, and these are

Health Test Record

NAME ———————— Date ————
Address ————————————————
Sex ——— Age ——— Occupation ————
Height ——— Weight ————
Frame size ————————

MEDICAL BACKGROUND

BODY COMPOSITION
Proportion fat to lean tissue:

Biceps ————	mm
Triceps ————	mm
Subscapular ————	mm
Suprailiac ————	mm
Total: ————	mm

Percentage of body fat: ———— %
Percentage of lean tissue: ———— %

POSTURE Spine ————
Pelvic tilt ————
Head ————
Shoulders ————
Legs ————
Feet ————

FLEXIBILITY TEST
Lower back and hamstrings ———— cm

BLOOD PRESSURE
———— systolic
———— diastolic

RESTING HEART RATE ———— bpm

CARDIO-VASCULAR TEST – STAMINA
6-minute astrand test ————
————
————
Recovery heart rate ———— bpm

LUNG FUNCTION TEST
Peak flow rate ———— litres/minutes

STRENGTH TEST
Wall sit ———— number of seconds
Abdominal hold ———— number of seconds

ENDURANCE TEST
Bent knee sit ups 30 seconds ———— number of times
Press ups 30 seconds ———— number of times

Figure 10.13 Health test record

known as the derived positions. The starting positions should be carefully considered when treating clients, and checked and corrected throughout the whole treatment. If this is not done, then the posture of the client may remain poor, and while the movements are being performed, muscles other than those used in holding the starting positions will be brought into play, defeating the aim.

Lying position

A wide flat surface should be used. Clients lie on their back with the arms resting by their sides. The legs should be relaxed, falling into slight outward rotation with the feet in relaxed plantar flexion. The head will be back with chin tucked in, chest slightly out, and shoulders gently back.

Sitting position

A stool or chair of suitable height is used. The thighs are supported from the ischial tuberosities to the back of the knees. The legs must be at a right angle to the thighs with the feet flat and slightly apart pointing forwards. The trunk is held upright, head up, chin in, shoulders back but relaxed, arms held at the sides with wrist and fingers gently extended.

Standing position

The client stands with heels together and toes very slightly apart. Head, shoulders, and arms are held as in the sitting position. The abdominal muscles are pulled in, the seat muscles tightened, and the knees straight.

Kneeling position

Kneeling on the floor, with the knees placed slightly apart, the feet are plantar flexed and the toes bent under. The thighs and trunk should be directly over the knees; the rest of the position the same as for standing.

Hanging position

Taken on wall bars, or a horizontal bar, the client's feet must be just on the floor. The hands are pronated, gripping the bar, and the arms at least shoulder-width apart with the body hanging in a straight line. The feet should be in plantar flexion.

Muscle work, effects and uses of the fundamental positions

Lying

Lying is the easiest starting position. The base is large and no muscle work is necessary to maintain the position. It can, however, restrict breathing slightly, and would be contraindicated for clients who need to see the movements of the limbs while performing them. It is a good position in which to teach relaxation, to exercise weak muscles, and to exercise after massage when this position is already used. When age and ability are a consideration, this position is also used. Lying is not a good position for anyone with a lordosis (hollow back).

Sitting

Sitting fixes the legs, hips, and pelvis, localizing movements to the upper part of the body making it easier for them to move. It is a safe steady position because the centre of gravity is low and the base is firm and large. It is a convenient starting position because it can be readily adapted to suit any requirements in a limited space. Clients who are unable to balance very well, perhaps elderly clients, can be given a variety of exercises to all parts of the body, head, and limbs which can progress into standing. Some clients unable to stand for long periods will find this an excellent position to work in, and will be encouraged to practise exercises at home if this position is adopted. Resistances can be added to movements in this position.

Muscles involved in maintaining this position are the flexors and extensors of the neck, the long back muscles, the adductors of the scapulae, the abdominal muscles and hip flexors, the extensors of the hips and knees, and the plantar flexors of the feet.

Standing

Standing is the hardest of all the fundamental positions to maintain. It is a good position in which to start with warming-up exercises as there is no restriction of movement, all joints and muscles being free. The client will be alerted and awakened in this position. Concentration and co-ordination is necessary to maintain the position because the centre of gravity is high and the base is small. The majority of clients, except the elderly, should be able to cope with any exercise given in the fundamental standing position.

Muscles involved are the same as for the sitting position in the head and trunk, the hip and knee extensors more so, the adductors of the legs and the muscles in the soles of the feet (the interossei and lumbricals), and an interplay between the plantar and dorsi flexors. The muscle work in standing relies upon the balance of the bones on each other, and upon the postural balance between the muscles on the front and back of the body.

Kneeling

Kneeling is a steadier position than standing but not a particularly comfortable one because of the pressure on the knees. It is not suitable for clients who have a lordosis, but good trunk movements and free head and arm movements can be used in this position. Although the base is large and the centre of gravity low, this position is not often used.

Muscle work involved is the same as for standing, except that the hip extensors must work more strongly to counterbalance the tendency to fall forwards. The intrinsic muscles of the feet do not work and the knee flexors work harder to maintain the balance.

Hanging

Hanging is a position used for particularly strong clients and where strengthening exercises are required to be given to the limbs and trunk. The spine and ligaments are stretched and, where postural problems need attention, hanging is an excellent starting position to stretch out mild deformities. It is particularly useful for young clients who should be able to perform strong work, and also where postural conditions are not combined with respiratory complications. The normally healthy client would feel quite invigorated after exercises given in hanging.

Muscles required to work maintaining the hanging position are the flexors of the fingers, the wrist flexors and extensors, the flexors of the elbow, the adductors of the shoulder and scapulae (latissimus dorsi, pectoralis major, rhomboids, and the middle fibres of trapezius).

Note: This position is contraindicated for all older clients or whenever there is any form of weakness, after operations, and in any form of lung disease. Care must be taken, in all the positions during and after exercises, that the client does not become dizzy. Stretching on the spine can cause a sensation of dizziness, particularly in hanging.

Derived positions

Basically derived positions are modifications of the fundamental positions by changing the positions of the arms, legs, head, and trunk. There are many derived positions in which exercises are performed. Here are some derived positions described in detail for use later in the chapter. The advantage of using the descriptive terminology is to cut out unnecessary repetitive and lengthy description. In a way it can be likened to shorthand. Exercises and movements today are generally based on the more natural positions of the body.

Standing

Stride standing: the feet are placed two foot lengths apart, the weight being evenly distributed between each foot. A steady firm position.

Walk standing: one foot is placed in front of the other, two foot lengths between the heels. Weight must be evenly distributed. Used very much together with stride standing in massage.

Curtsy standing: the hip and knee joints are flexed to right angles, with trunk kept upright; knees are apart.

Lying

Prone lying: client lies face down fully supported, or with head to one aide.

Crook lying: client lies with both knees bent, feet flat on the floor.

Sitting

Long sitting: client sits on floor with legs stretched out and knees together. Back must be erect.

Crook sitting: client sits on the floor with the knees bent according to comfort and requirements. Important to check upright position of head and back.

Kneeling

Prone kneeling: the body is parallel to the floor and is supported by the hands which are placed shoulder-width apart and vertical, hands pointing forwards, the knees are flexed at right angles, hip-width.

Progression of exercises

The means by which exercises are made more difficult is the progression of exercises. There are many ways in which to achieve this purpose.

1 **Starting** positions can be altered. The basic starting positions are lying, kneeling, sitting, standing, and hanging. There are many variations derived from these positions. By making the base of the starting position smaller the exercise becomes harder. By complicating the basic starting position, bringing into play a larger number of joints and muscles, the difficulty of the exercise is increased. For instance, lying is the easiest position as it has the largest base. Little effort, if any, is required from the muscles and joints to maintain it.

   Crook lying, or lying with the knees bent, is a progression, for the size of the base has diminished and also some effort is required to keep the knees bent. It is easier to do an exercise in stride standing (feet apart) than it is in close standing (feet together), or toe standing where the size of the base has now been considerably reduced and many more muscles are brought into action.
2 **Repetition** of movements should be increased.
3 **Altering** the centre of gravity by raising it makes the exercise harder. For example, trunk bending forwards is made more difficult with the arms stretched above the head.
4 **Lengthening** the lever increases the weight and resistance to the movement. For example, raising the arms sideways to shoulder level is easier with the fingertips on the shoulders and the elbows bent than with the arms fully stretched sideways.
5 **Increasing** speed.
6 **Decreasing** rest periods.

7 **Removing** the stability of the more fixed point (origin) of the working muscle is difficult. For example, side leg raises from stride standing rather than side lying.

8 **Increasing** the resistance to a muscle to its maximum is helpful. The resistance can be provided by apparatus, including springs, weights, pulleys, or by the therapist's manual resistance or by self resistance.

9 **Co-ordination** exercises can increase the difficulty and perfect the movements. These can be done by combining a series of actions of the trunk, head, arms, and legs into one exercise. The client has to concentrate throughout on performing the complicated exercise and maintaining a good starting position.

10 **Balance** exercises performed slowly are extremely difficult. They also improve co-ordination and posture at the same time, and are invaluable in any scheme of exercises designed to improve the general appearance.

Programme of exercises

There is little need to point out again the value of exercising. Most women welcome and grasp the chance to improve the contours of their body. Gone are the days when big bosoms, generous hips and spreading thighs represented man's pinnacle of beauty. Now it seems that it is desirable to have a firm bust line, trim waistline, flat tummy, slim arms and slender tapering legs.

By the means of exercise much can be done to achieve this ideal image. There need be no fear of turning into a muscular unfeminine figure; one has only to look at the female athletes of ice skating, tennis, or gymnastics to see that even after a lifetime devoted to sport the fair sex remains frankly feminine.

Like anything that is worth doing exercises require perseverance, practice, and patience. It is no good teaching clients some marvellous exercises if they are only going to do them once or twice a week with the beauty therapist. Clients must become sufficiently inspired and interested enough by the therapist to practise them at home.

Home exercises

Ideally they should be practised at least three times a day for a minimum of ten minutes at any one time. The client could be instructed to rise ten minutes earlier in the morning and retire ten minutes earlier at night, for the sole purpose of practising the exercises. Midday or when convenient would be a good time for the third ten minutes set aside to practise home exercises. Not more than four exercises should be given, otherwise there is a tendency to forget the detailed instruction of each exercise. Two or three minutes spent carefully and thoroughly on each exercise is not much to ask the client to do.

Simple home exercises that can be incorporated into a daily routine anywhere and at any time are another means of achieving clients' co-operation in helping themselves with their beauty project, if they are not too keen on the ten-minutes-a-time routine. For example, instead of climbing upstairs one at a time, increase this to two at a time, to improve all leg muscles.

For general posture suggest to the clients every time they pass through a doorway they pause, take a mental posture check, that is, abdominals in, back straight, chest up and out, etc. Whenever clients wash their hands or work at the sink, instruct them to push the palms of their hands hard together ten times to exercise the chest muscles, firming the bust line and upper arm. While sitting chatting on the telephone, lift the body just off the chair as though standing up, and then sit down again; no help with the hands. This last exercise is a bit disconcerting as concentration in listening to the person at the other end of the line tends to wane in the effort to perform the exercise, but what price is that to pay for a new hip- and thigh-line!

Most important of all is the posture, which clients should be made aware of whenever they see their reflection in a mirror or a shop window. An erect posture improves all contours automatically; clients must remember that all they have to do for a good posture regained quickly is merely to lift up their head with the chin in, pull back the shoulders, and pull in the tummy. Many chores require periods of standing, either at home, at work, or even waiting for a bus. Here is a good exercise for the clients to practise while standing, to exercise the internal muscles of the pelvis.

Cross one leg over the other and squeeze the seat muscles and tops of the legs tightly together as though trying not to spend a penny. Relax and change over legs. Very simply done without fuss, this exercise will help to prevent low backache and dragging pains in this area. The more it is performed the merrier, but up to about ten contractions each side at a time would be ideal.

Mobility exercises

Mobility exercises should be performed gently, loosely and freely without static holdings. The same movement should be repeated several times consecutively before the order to rest is given. A breathing exercise is more essential here before continuing with the same exercise several times again. Three or four repetitions of the same mobility exercise cycle is ample before moving on to another one, bearing in mind that the main function of mobility exercises is to warm up and loosen the body or parts through as full a range as possible prior to giving strengthening exercises.

Mobility exercises can be readily changed into strengthening exercises by reducing the speed of movement and adding a static holding of the contraction as explained previously. The variations possible on any one particular exercise, for any one muscle, are enormous by using different starting positions, ranges of movement, and muscle work. Exercise permutations are quite a fascinating study if not quite as numerous as football perms. Beauty therapists should be able to work out for themselves a balanced scheme of progressive and interesting exercises. The exercises have been described as though directed towards the beauty therapist and they should be tried out first, generally speaking, throughout the book.

Neck mobility

Starting position

Stride standing or sitting.

Exercise

Side turn: turn head to one side then back to the centre. Repeat turning the head to the other side.

   Tilting head forward: bring the head forward, chin to chest and then return to upright position. Do not take the head backwards.

   Half circles: tilt the head to the left shoulder, drop the chin to the chest and then tilt the head to the right shoulder. Repeat. Do not take the head back.

Shoulder mobility

Starting position

Stride standing or sitting.

Exercises

Shoulder rolls: relax arms and roll shoulders forwards together and then backwards together. Repeat.

   Shoulder shrugs: lift shoulders up towards the ears and gently lower. Repeat.

Trunk and lower back

Starting position

Stride standing.

Exercises

Curl and hollow the lower back: place the hands gently on the thighs and curl the back and then hollow. Repeat.

Side bends: slide the left hand down the left thigh while bending the trunk to the left. Return to an upright position and repeat. Repeat to right side.

Pelvic circles: bend the knees slightly and circle the pelvis one way and then the other.

Pelvic tilt: bend the knees slightly, contract the abdomen and tuck the buttocks under tilting the pelvis forwards and then back. Repeat.

Curl and hollow: prone kneeling, as above.

Pelvic tilt: crook lying, press the lower back into the floor and contract the abdominals. Relax and repeat.

Hip and knee mobility

Starting position

Stride standing.

Exercises

Knee lifts: lift one knee up towards the chest several times with each leg. Remember to concentrate on good posture.

Knee bends: standing with feet slightly more than hip distance apart, and feet slightly turned out, bend and straighten legs making sure the knees are angled over the toes.

Ankle mobility

Starting position

Stride standing

Exercises

Point and flex: flex the foot and then point. Repeat with each ankle.

Ankle rotations: lift the foot off the floor and circle to the right and left. Repeat with the other foot.

Strengthening exercise

When giving strengthening exercises, part of the cycle of the exercise is to order the holding of the contraction before giving the order to return the limb to the original position and to relax. At this point a reminder to breathe (not to hold the breath) is very often necessary. This is where the benefit of interspersing breathing exercises proves to be not only valuable in itself, but a useful resting point. The length of time that the contraction is held is entirely up to the judgement of the therapist and the condition of the client's muscles.

Generally speaking, a good guide would be to start off holding a contraction to the slow count of three (roughly three seconds). This can be increased by one second gradually, as the muscles strengthen. Different muscles will be able to sustain their contractions for longer periods of time than others, depending on their strength. To start with, the exercise itself should be repeated about six times.

Gradually the repetition is increased as the muscles gain in strength to a maximum of ten contractions. These guides apply to the normal average client. Obviously someone who is particularly weak, or excessively fit, would need special considerations. Relaxations of the muscles and the body after each contraction is an integral part of exercising, but it is important to understand that, until the limb or part of the body moved has been returned to the starting position, the command to relax is not given, otherwise it could be taken literally. For example, if a leg was still held up in the air and the command to relax given, the client might just let it flop down, causing bruising and strain. Apart from that fact, returning the limb to the original position belongs to the cycle of the exercise. Very often it involves using the muscles eccentrically on the return journey, and as such must not be overlooked. An experienced therapist should be able to balance and work out exactly how and in which range the muscles are required to be used, in order to achieve the maximum result.

Muscle building

Muscles can be built up considerably by exercise. If bulk is required for any one particular area, then usually weight lifting, or exercising the specific muscle against some form of resistance is necessary. The therapist must measure the girth of that particular muscle or area before treatment, and then regularly once a week.

A careful and accurate weight lifting chart must be made, recording details of weights lifted or resistances used. Concentric muscle work through full range is used. A general guide would be, for normally healthy muscles, to start off with a minimum weight, lifting it five times, contracting the required muscle. The static holdings in between each contraction must not be neglected.

The muscle is then rested before this procedure is repeated twice more making a total of fifteen contractions. If the muscle shows any sign of fatigue, such as trembling or an inability to contract fully or sustain the contraction statically, then the programme must be revised. Cut the basic number of contractions down to three and build up from there. The maximum number of contractions should reach ten, making a final total of thirty contractions at any one time. The weight depends on the strength of the muscle, but a one-pound or two-pound (half or one kilogram) weight to begin with should be easy to lift for the normal healthy muscle. If proper weight-lifting equipment is not available, improvisations can easily be made by self-resisting exercises, or with the therapist resisting, or with books, or tins of food, that could be brought and previously weighed by the therapist from home. These should be firmly attached to the right point on the lever of the body required to be lifted by the specific muscle or muscle group in question. Weight lifting for muscle building needs to be followed precisely. When the first weight is easily lifted ten times, then, and only then, can the weight be increased. The number of contractions is decreased to five again, and the procedure repeated and continued accordingly till the required effect has been produced. Self-resisting and therapist-resisting exercises are not an accurate means of weight lifting for muscle building. They are better than nothing, but are mainly used in free exercises when a little extra resistance other than gravity is required. The repetition of exercises will strengthen tone and will firm up the muscles to some extent, but, for a marked increase in bulk and girth, some form of regular progressive resistance must be added to the contracting muscle. These exercises should be practised daily at least once, and twice if possible, to see speedier results. At the end of six weeks there should be a marked improvement in the size of the muscle. Three months' diligent practising will produce excellent results for all schemes of exercising.

Explanation, command and cycle of exercise

Before the client is asked to perform the exercise, or exercises, the therapist must give a clear and precise explanation of what is required. The therapist should demonstrate the exercise and if necessary passively move the client throught the movement.

Clients are told what starting position to adopt, then the exercise explanation is given. This deals with correction of the starting position, which part of the body is to be moved, what movement is required, where to move it and, by a clear command, when to move it.

Muscular strength and endurance exercises

Abdominal strengthening exercises

It is extremely important before teaching abdominal exercises that the client can effectively execute a pelvic tilt. This involves the client in a crook lying position and while pulling in the abdominal muscles pressing the lower back into the floor therefore tilting the pelvis. It is also necessary for the client to contract the pelvic floor muscles. This position must be maintained whenever carrying out abdominal exercises.

Starting position

Crook lying.

Exercises

1 Curl up. In a smooth controlled movement, curl the trunk up to 45° from the floor. At the same time, slide the hands forward on the thighs.
2 As above with the hands on the chest therefore lengthening the lever.
3 As above with the hands supporting the head and the elbows back.
4 Bring both knees up and cross ankles. Keeping ankles close to buttocks, curl up from the hips. This will tone the lower abdominals.
5 As above but also lift the head and shoulders. This is obviously a more difficult exercise and would be prescribed when the client has mastered basic abdominal exercises.

Back strengthening exercises

Starting position

Prone lying, hands in lower back.

1 Keeping the chin tucked in and the neck long, lift the head and shoulders and lower. Repeat.
2 As above except on hand under forehead.
3 As above, both hands under forehead (lengthening lever).
4 Half stretch prone lying, lift torso and arms.
5 Stretch prone lying, lift torso and arms.

Quadriceps strengthening exercises

Starting position

Long sitting.

Exercise

1 Dorsi flex the floor and with the knee straight, lift the leg just off the mat. Repeat and change legs.
2 As above. Lift the leg and circle.
3 Reach stride standing, making sure the knees are turned out in line with the feet, bend the knees and 'sit back' using the arms to balance and keeping the chest up. Repeat.
4 As above, but bring the feet closer together and point the toes forward. Perform a squat, making sure the buttocks never drop lower than the knees. Repeat.

Hamstring strengthening and hip extension exercises

Starting position

Prone lying.

Exercise

1 With the left knee bent, raise the leg slightly off the floor and lower squeezing the gluteals.
2 Straighten the leg (lengthen the lever) lift and lower. Repeat with the other leg.
3 Prone kneeling, bend one knee and press the leg upwards (small movement).
4 Lift one leg backwards and upwards (again a very small movement).
5 Standing, bend the knee and press the leg backwards with short movements.
6 Swing alternate straight legs backwards keeping the abdominals in the hips and straight.

Abductor strengthening exercises

Side lying

Bend underneath leg for balance. Lift the upper leg keeping the knee facing forwards. The hip must stay forward throughout the exercise.

Standing

Lift the left leg to the side keeping the abdomen in and the hips square. The supporting knee can be slightly bent.

Adductor strengthening exercises

Lying

Push both legs inwards against the leg of a chair, hold, release and repeat.

Crook lying

Part the legs and close with the hands on the insides of the knees to provide resistance.

Support standing

Slowly swing the left leg across the midline of the body and return. Repeat and change legs.

Side lying with upper leg bent

Raise lower leg upwards and return. Repeat and change legs.

Gastrocnemius strengthening exercises

Starting position

Standing.

Exercise

Lift up on to toes and down.

Oblique strengthening exercises

Starting position

Crook lying.

Exercise

1 Lift head and shoulders off the floor and reach down to the right-hand side of the body. Repeat and change sides.
2 Left leg crossed over right, right hand on right thigh. Left hand behind head. Curl up and over towards right thigh. Repeat and change legs.

Triceps strengthening exercises

Starting position

Crook sitting.

Exercise

1 Hands facing forwards behind body, bend elbows and lower upper torso slightly towards the floor. Take the weight on the triceps. Repeat.
2 Lift gluteals off the floor and bending elbows lower body to floor and straighten arms.
3 For wall press-ups, stand with palms against the wall, bend the elbows and bring upper body towards wall. Straighten arms and repeat.
4 In prone kneeling position, keeping the back straight and abdomen in, bend and straighten elbows.
5 Extended prone kneeling, as above.
6 Fully extended prone kneeling, as above.

Controversial exercises

Any exercise is potentially dangerous if it is poorly executed or beyond the ability of the client. It is therefore essential that the therapist teaches the exercises accurately.

The following principles must be applied in order to ensure a safe programme.

Exercise

1 The exercise must be relevant. Choose the exercise that will have the most benefit but place the least strain on other parts of the body.
2 The movement must be controlled. Never use ballistic movements.
3 Posture must be correct and reinforced throughout the exercise.

4 Base must be stable to allow good body alignment.
5 Consider the length of the lever.

Joints

Joints must not be overworked or pushed beyond their normal range.

Muscles

Consider kinesiology, that is, prime movers antagonists, stabilizers, origins, insertions, direction of muscle fibre.

Stretching

1 Clients must be warm and muscles relaxed.
2 Use static stretching techniques.
3 Stretch should be taken to the point of mild discomfort only, never beyond.

The dangers of double leg raising

It is amazing that people persist with this exercise considering the extreme amount of damager that is caused by double leg raising.

The client lies on the floor and is told to lift both legs, keeping the knees straight. Unfortunately this exercise does not strengthen the abdominal but the hip flexers which tend to be strong already.

The work each group is doing is equal to the length of each leg multiplied by the weight of each leg. People think that they are lifting the weight of their legs but if you consider the laws of gravity, and in this case third class leverage, you will find that the flexor muscles are lifting not only the weight of the leg but is the weight multiplied by the length (Figure 10.14).

In any antagonistic muscle group reciprocal relaxation takes place, that is, if the agonists are working the antagonists will relax. In this case, the extensors will relax while the flexors work. The extensors of the hips (gluteals) tend to have a concentration of fat and it would be unusual for any women to want these muscles relaxed.

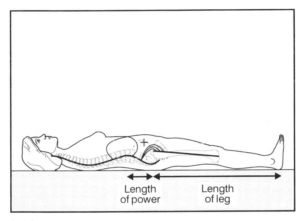

Figure 10.14 (a)

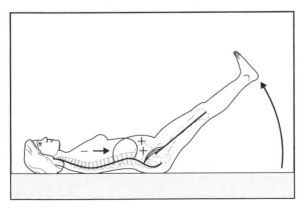

Figure 10.14 (b)

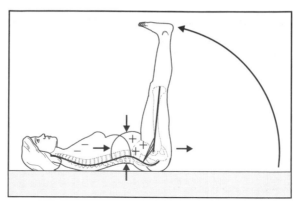

Figure 10.14 (c)

Now we have an enormous amount of work for the flexors to do. The flexors are attached above to the vertebrae of the lower back as well as inside the pelvis and below near the top end of the thigh bone. As the flexors are having so much difficulty raising the long and heavy legs, the upper end pulls the vertebrae forwards and the pelvis downwards and forwards. This stretches the lower attachments of rectus abdominus. At this point the lower back will come off the floor.

To try to stabilize the moving spinal joints the abdominal muscles try to work. They are now in a stretched outer range position and are trying to work statically. They are now very strained and may possibly quiver. Because the abdominals are attached to the ribcage above as well as the pelvis below they tend to pull at the ribcage. To prevent this movement and to stabilize the abdomen the clients hold their breath.

To summarize:

1 The flexors are being strengthened.
2 The extensors of the hip are being weakened and the lower back is being strained.
3 The abdominal muscles are being stretched.
4 The breath is being held which increases the pressure in the abdomen.

5 This area tends to be very weak in women and this pressure is very dangerous especially after the stretching imposed on the pelvic floor after childbirth.

At this point the sphincter around the urethra is unable to withstand the pressure and a slight gush of urine is experienced. This demonstrates the pressure downwards on the pelvic floor.

Sit ups with a straight back

This exercise lying flat and raising the trunk upwards is really the same exercise as double leg raising except the hip flexors are working in reverse in a way for which they were not designed. The trunk is even heavier than the legs to lift and so the strain is greater.

Cardiovascular endurance

If clients wish to improve the efficiency of the heart and lungs and lose weight then they must undertake some form of aerobic exercise, for example cycling, swimming, brisk walking, aerobics, step aerobics. That is, any type of exercise which will sustain the aerobic response of the body for at least 20 minutes in order to produce beneficial physiological adaptation. The exercise intensity must be maintained within the individual target training zone. This can be calculated from the chart in Figure 10.15 or a simple calculation:

220 – client's own age = maximum pulse rate.

Depending on the fitness level of clients, they should work at between 60–85 per cent of their maximum heart rate.

During exercise the pulse rate should be increased and decreased gradually to prevent blood pooling and fainting.

254 Body Massage for the Beauty Therapist

Flexibility

Flexibility exercises should be done as part of the warm up and cool down. Overworked muscles can shorten and thicken causing pressure on the muscle sheath. Stretching the muscle will help prevent post-exercise discomfort and also help to disperse lactic acid which accumulates in the muscle again causing post-exercise discomfort.

There are three types of flexibility:

1 Dynamic/active flexibility – the movement is repeatedly carried to the end range of movement in a slow controlled manner.
2 Static flexibility – slow sustained stretch held for between 8 and 30 seconds.
3 Passive flexibility – limb is moved to its end position and held by external resistance, for example therapist or physiotherapist.

There are two reflexes which are effective in stretching exercises:

1 Stretch reflex (in muscle spindle). This will be activated if a ballistic stretch is carried out. The muscle reacts by contracting to counteract the ballistic stretch therefore stretching must be carried out slowly and gently.
2 Golgi tendon organ (in tendon). This is a safety reflex designed to relax the muscle under extreme tension. It takes about 30 seconds to work so development stretches must be held for at least 30 seconds.

Values of flexibility

1 Increases flexibility.
2 Prevents injuries and soreness.
3 Relieves muscular tension.
4 Prepares muscle for activity.

5 Mental relaxation.
6 Maintains full range of movement.

Stretching exercises

Neck

Starting position

Standing or sitting.

Exercise

Pull the head down gently to one side. Remember to maintain the correct posture.

Side stretch

Starting position

Standing.

Exercise

Bend the knees slightly to take the strain off the lower back. Relax the shoulders and neck. Reach upwards with one arm at a time, swaying from side to side.

Triceps

Starting position

Sitting or standing.

Exercise

1 Drop one arm behind the head, with the opposite hand press the arm back. Keep the shoulders down and relaxed. Tilt the head slightly forward.
2 As above but with the other hand press down on the elbow.
3 As above but this time the hands are clasped behind the back.

Upper back stretch

Starting position

Inclined prone kneeling.

Exercise

1 Cat stretch. Drop the head and reach forward with the arms.
2 Crook sitting, lock the hands together and push forward allowing the shoulders to round.
3 Standing, as above, tighten the abdominals to provide lower back support.

Lower back/torso stretch/gluteal

Starting position

Crook lying.

Exercise

1 Drop the knees to one side and the arms to the other. Keep the knees parallel. Hold the stretch and repeat to the other side. Always drop the knees gently and ease into the stretch.
2 Crook sitting, sitting up out of the waist, reach round to the left and hold. Repeat to the other side.
3 Standing, as above. Remember to keep the lupus parallel and the abdomen in.

4 Crook lying, press the small of the back into the floor and bring both knees into the chest. Clasp the hands around the thighs and gently pull towards the chest. Hold.
5 Prone kneeling, contract the abdominals and round the back. Hold then lower.
6 Supine lying, bend the left knee to the chest then take the knee across to the right until a stretch is felt in the outer thigh. Hold then release.
7 Long sitting, bend the left knee and place the foot on the far side of the right leg until a stretch is felt in the outer thigh. Hold then release.
8 Place one foot over the opposite knee. Lift that knee and bring the legs towards the chest. Keep the lower back firmly into the floor and keep the neck and shoulders relaxed. Hold and change legs.

Hamstrings

Starting position

Crook lying.

Exercise

1 Hold one leg first below the knee and bring the bent knee towards the chest.
2 As above but straighten the bent leg slightly.
3 Stand with the weight on one leg which is bent, with the other outstretched to the front. Press the hips back. Rest the hands lightly on the thighs. Hold and change legs.

Calf stretching

Starting position

Walk standing.

Exercise

1 Using the wall as support press the hips forward until a stretch is felt in the back leg.
2 As above but free-standing.
3 Stand using a wall for support but stretch both calfs at the same time and take the legs further away from the wall.
4 Stand on the edge of a step, remembering to check posture drop one heel over the edge of the step until a stretch is felt in the calf. Hold and change legs.

Quadriceps stretch

Starting position

Prone lying.

Exercises

Bend the right knee towards the gluteals, grasp the ankle and keeping the knees together pull towards until a stretch is felt in the quadriceps. Hold and change legs.

Side lying, bend the top leg and grasping the ankle, pull towards the gluteals. Keep the knees together and press the hips forward. Hold and change legs.

Support standing, standing on one leg grasp the ankle of the other leg. Keep the knees together and press the hips forward. Hold and repeat with the other leg.

Abdominal stretch

Starting position

Prone lying.

Exercise

Put the hands under the chest and press up leaving the last rib on the floor until a stretch is felt in the abdominals. Hold.

Pectoral stretch

Starting position

Crook sitting.

Exercises

Clasp the arms behind the back and keeping the shoulders back hold until a stretch is felt in the pectorals.

Standing, as above.

Exercise, massage and obesity

Many hundreds and thousands of men and women all over the world are more weight- and figure-conscious than ever before. Why do they come to the beauty salons, health farms, and sauna baths to mention but a few of the places where advice and help in figure correction can be found? There are many reasons. Perhaps one may be some sudden spring sunshine and realization that summer holidays and revealing bikinis are not too far around the corner. Perhaps another is in preparation for winter sports, or to be able to wear a new dress with ease that now feels too tight, or to boost up the confidence of a teenager who feels that success in dating boy friends might be hers at last if her figure is righted.

Sometimes women who are experiencing the menopause feel that their youth and looks have ebbed away, and they need the reassurance that beauty therapy can give, by helping them to do something positive about it. For some men who seek physical fitness, their motives lie in the need to be successful with women, which they feel only comes with looks, health, and beauty.

Mental health and physical health go hand in hand, and everyone realizes that being overweight is hazardous and unhealthy for the heart and body. This is probably the main reason for doing something about it by asking the expert. Looking better makes one feel better, although the old saying that 'beauty is in the eye of the beholder' stands very true. Not everyone cares or is even interested in trying to alter their physical appearance, and sometimes this careless attitude is deliberately cultivated.

It really does not matter what the basic reason is for slimming or changing shape; the fact remains that most people, if given a chance to improve their figure and size by the wave of a magic wand would take it, and do so. The beauty therapist must respect whatever good reasons clients have, no matter how trivial they may seem, that bring them to seek professional advice and help which will build up the confidence and ego of the client.

Types of obesity

Before treating obesity it is as well to understand the different types that there are:

1 There is the type of obesity which could be called *hereditary*. This is the kind where no treatment seems to be of permanent benefit. When asked it will be discovered that the client's mother and grandmother were fat, and that indeed many members of the family tended towards obesity.
2 Another kind of obesity is attributed to the malfunctioning of the *glandular* system. For example, an under-secretion of the thyroid gland would result in the carbohydrates and fats being stored as body fat due to faulty metabolism. Fat, too, may be stored in the body during the menopause when the hormone balance is disturbed. This kind of fat, that is not oxidized properly nor broken down sufficiently in the process of digestion, seems to settle round the abdomen, hips, and thighs.

Middle-aged spread refers to these areas and the change of life between forty and fifty.

3 The most common reason for being overweight is that caused by *overeating*. This can take the form of generally eating too much, excess eating of the wrong kinds of foods, or an unbalanced diet coupled with insufficient exercise. These are the cases which can be treated most successfully. Very often it is the middle-aged person who has the means to indulge in richer foods, heavier drinking, and a more sedentary life, who finds weight is becoming a problem. However, these days it seems that carrying only one or two extra pounds of weight on the body constitutes a case for treatment. So the beauty therapist is faced with the task of prescribing and advising either general or localized treatments for all, no matter how slim or what age or sex.

Treatment

Treatment must only be undertaken after first having checked with the doctor to ascertain the cause, and to confirm that the general health of the client is good. The doctor will be able to prescribe a suitable diet which will probably cut down on starchy foods, sugars, and fats. There are many excellent diets some of which forbid certain foods entirely; others advocate the eating of more of one kind than another. The therapist should be able to supply the kind of diet to fit the case if required to do so. Crash diets are only advisable for a short period of time, and very often a drastic weight loss in a few days can result in making the client look haggard.

A slow steady loss over a period of weeks is healthier, better and more advisable.

It has been well established that the ideal form of treatment for obesity is by a combination of *diet*, *massage* and *exercise*, and even then there can be no guarantee. If the weight is to be reduced at all substantially then the full co-operation of the client is the most important factor of all. They must adhere strictly to the diet, not be allowed to expect too much from the massage, and be prepared to practise the exercises faithfully.

Consideration for clients is important, and if they are grossly overweight then exercises in the lying or sitting position could be more suitable until there has been a considerable weight loss, by which time the muscles would be improved in tone. Otherwise exercises in all positions would be given. Much encouragement must be given to clients to enable them to persevere, and they should be weighed and measured once a week. Even the smallest weight loss must be recorded and made known to the client, for encouragement to continue. Home exercises must be stressed, but they should be kept to a minimum and fairly simple.

Breathing and relaxation

The importance of correct breathing for health and beauty is underestimated. It is not quite as automatic as most people imagine. All the systems and tissues of the body require for their functioning and for body metabolism an ample supply of oxygen. This is ensured and promoted by the correct gaseous interchange which takes place in the lungs through respiration.

Resistance to infection is increased when the lungs are utilized thoroughly, maintaining and improving their elasticity and strength. If all the lung tissue is exercised frequently their secretions are less likely to stagnate and accumulate. Coughs and colds will be few and far between. Posture is improved with correct breathing; the mind becomes more active and alert, nerves are calmed by deep breathing, circulation is quickened, eyes are bright and clear, fat is oxidized and muscles are fed. The secret of correct breathing can control the speaking voice and the movements of the body, both of which are vital aides to being beautiful. Correct breathing assists relaxation, even in childbirth.

Mechanics of respiration

The air enters the body via the nose where it is filtered and warmed before it passes into the lungs. The lungs are two balloon-like structures each with an upper, middle and lower region or lobe, joined together at the top into one central passage known as the trachea. This links up to the back of the mouth and nose.

Respiration can be divided into two parts, namely inspiration, when the air is drawn into the body and expiration, when the air is expelled.

Inspiration involves the contraction of the diaphragm, intercostal and other respiratory muscles which enlarge the thorax in several directions. When the diaphragm contracts, it descends and expands, pushing out the abdomen. The rib cage is also pulled out vertically like a concertina. As the intercostal and other muscles contract they cause the ribs to be elevated laterally and anteroposteriorly like the lifting of a bucket handle, or the opening of venetian blinds. When the contractions take place the air rushes into all sections of the lungs.

If the diaphragm is not used properly then the lower regions of the lungs will not be ventilated or expanded and will become neglected. Breathing is shallower and is restricted to the upper part of the chest. A common fault on inspiration is to pull in the abdomen, which prevents the diaphragm from functioning correctly, limiting the breathing capacity.

Expiration normally involves a mere relaxation of all the respiratory muscles, returning the thorax to its original size. However, when the expiration is forced, the abdominal muscles contract and are retracted, flattening and even hollowing the abdomen; the diaphragm is pushed upwards and the chest hollows as the sternum and lower ribs are pulled down in an effort to expel the maximum amount of air from the lungs. Breathing becomes very deep.

Some important points

Breathing exercises can be practised in all positions so that whenever exercise is being carried out and in whichever position, a breathing exercise can and should always be incorporated. The breathing exercise can be purely for breathing, or for a combination of exercise and breathing. In this way clients are prevented from holding their breadth, a maximum oxygen supply to the working muscles is ensured, they can learn the difference between tension and relaxation in the muscles and when breathing is combined with arm and trunk exercises, the whole respiratory system is used to full advantage. However, the breathing should be in the client's own time but when combining the two it is generally carried out according to the therapist's instructions for guidance. Interspersing pure breathing in an exercise scheme has its advantages also. This method provides a useful resting point in which clients can relax and recoup their energy, regaining their normal rhythm of breathing after a particular strenuous bout of exercises. If they are placed in the lying position for the exercises, their knees should be bent as in crook lying to relax the abdominal muscles.

After the initial instruction and correction of the right way in which to breathe, clients should be allowed to breathe in and out in their own time. Too much deep breathing can cause light-headedness, dizziness and even fainting, especially if there is little muscle work taking place in the body. Restricting each exercise to three times, and to a maximum of three exercises at a time to be given consecutively, minimizes this temporary effect. In a general keep-fit scheme of exercises, both pure breathing and breathing combined with an exercise can be included. This helps to add interest and vary the exercises. Because even the fittest client may feel a little light-headed after too much deep breathing, it is as well to ask clients from time to time if they feel all right. Before the breathing exercises are begun, the client should empty the air out of their lungs by blowing out first.

Three kinds of breathing

Apical uses the upper lobe of the lungs and is shallow, high and rapid. High temperatures, illness, fear, excitement, anger, respiratory diseases, such as bronchitis or asthma, are some precursors to this kind of breathing. Sometimes athletes use it for a quick intake of oxygen and apical breathing takes place during childbirth while the diaphragm muscle helps to fix the thorax and push the baby out of the birth canal.

Lateral costal uses the upper and middle lobes of the lungs. It is deeper and slower than apical breathing and it is this kind of breathing that many people use unwittingly most of the time, together with apical.

Diaphragmatic uses the upper, middle and lower lobes of the lungs. It is deep and calm and should be used whenever possible at all times.

All three kinds of breathing exercises should be explained and taught to the client so that a complete overall picture of the breathing mechanism is obtained. However, in health and beauty, it is only the diaphragmatic breathing which is emphasized and practised. This guarantees full and correct use of the normal healthy respiratory system.

Technique

Apical breathing

Position: stride standing.

1 Place hands flat either side of chest just below clavicle; blow out.
2 Take a short breath in through the nose, pushing up the upper part of the chest under the hands, slightly lifting the shoulders.
3 To the short sharp sound of 'Sh', blow out the air through the mouth. The client will hear the air being expelled and feel the chest relaxing.
4 Repeat this breathing rapidly no more than three times as explained previously. The client will feel the chest lifting up and down.

Lateral costal breathing

Position: stride standing.

1 Place the hands flat on either side of the chest wall below the axillae and above the waist. Blow out.

2 Take a deeper breath in through the nose keeping the upper part of the chest and shoulders down and relaxed, pushing out the sides of the ribs. Clients will feel this expansion sideways with their hands.
3 To the sound of 'Ha' blow out the air through the mouth. Clients will feel their ribs concertina down and they can hear the air being blown out. It will be a longer respiration than apical breathing.
4 Repeat the breathing in the client's own time, emphasizing the expiration.

Diaphragmatic breathing

Position: stride standing.

1 Place the flat hand either side and across the front lower ribs. The fingertips should be touching each other just below the xiphoid process of the sternum. Blow out.
2 Take a long deep breath in through the nose, pushing up the hands in front and the ribs out at the sides. If the diaphragm muscle is being used properly, the fingers will be parted in front on expansion of the thorax. This can be felt with the hands guiding and encouraging the client to greater effort.
3 To the sound of 'S', blow out the air for as long as possible by pulling in the abdominal muscles as hard as possible at the same time. The client will hear the air being expired, feel the rib cage descending, fingers coming together again, and the abdomen pulling in.
4 The breathing is repeated in the client's own time.

Relaxed breathing

The *normal natural rhythm* of relaxed diaphragmatic breathing with a gentle rise and fall of the abdominal muscles on breathing in and out respectively is soon acquired. There should be no exaggerated heaving of the chest and shoulders. The air has to pass through the upper and middle regions when the lower lobes are being used as in the relaxed diaphragmatic breathing. With relaxed breathing the client should be instructed to breathe in and out of the nose.

Some general exercises combined with deep diaphragmatic breathing

Remember to breathe in through the nose and blow out through the mouth.

Position: stride standing.

1 Lift both arms sideways and up into elevation by the side of the head taking a deep breath in at the same time. When maximum inspiration is obtained, slowly blow the air out of the mouth, lowering the arms at a steady rate to the sides at the same time.
2 Place the fingertips on the shoulders, circle the elbows round beginning by lifting them forwards and upwards to point in the air, sideways and down. As they are lifted forwards and up, a deep long breath in should be taken; as they lower down sideways the air should be blown out of the mouth.
3 Bend the trunk sideways sliding the right arm down the right leg blowing out at the same time. Stretch the trunk upright to the middle again, breathing in. Bend over to the left side blowing out and up to the middle, breathing in.

Position: stride sitting.

1 Bend over to touch the floor between the feet, blowing out. Slowly sit up lifting arms above the head and breathing in deeply. Bend over to touch floor again breathing out.
2 Place fingertips on shoulders and twist over to touch right knee with left elbow, blowing out. Stretch upright to middle, breathing in. Twist over to touch left knee with right elbow, blowing out; sit up, breathe in.

Position: prone lying.

1 Place hands under forehead, lift head, shoulder, arms and hands backwards off the floor or bed, breathing in. Lower down, blowing out.
2 Lift both legs, head and shoulder backwards, breathing in; lower down, blowing out.

Position: crook lying.

1 Lift trunk and bottom upwards, tightening gluteal muscles, till body is in a straight line with the thighs; breathe in at the same time, lower hips, blowing out.
2 Bend both knees over to the right to touch the floor, blowing out. Bring them back to the middle, breathing in deeply. Bend them over to the left blowing out; to the middle, breathing in.

Relaxation

Relaxation can be defined as the release of tension in the mind and body and is a desirable state which is pursued by everyone in some form or other. It has long since been agreed by the medical profession that tension of the mind can cause muscle tension, disease, illness, pain and even proneness to accidents. These in turn can cause relaxation to be impossible, so creating a vicious circle. The beauty therapist knows and often sees the havoc that can be played in the face and in the general posture, from a mind racked by problems and tensions, or aches and pains, from which there seems to be no respite. Mental and physical tension cannot be easily separated, but one thing is for sure and this is, that a relaxed mind is housed in a relaxed and healthy body and a relaxed and healthy body relates closely to a relaxed and healthy mind.

Why relax?

Relaxation of the muscles of the body is used sometimes to enable them to be spurred on to greater physical efforts. Sometimes it is used to block out mental thoughts as a means to inducing sleep. Although it is said by certain authorities that sleep and total relaxation are not synonymous, for even during sleep dreams occur and some muscles maintain a strong degree of tone, yet usually most of the muscles are relaxed in sleep and dreaming is a normal phenomenon. However, to be able to drift into a deep relaxed sleep and wake up feeling vitally alive and refreshed, instead of tossing and turning half the night, sleeping lightly and waking up as though never having been to bed at all, is for many an enviable state.

Recreation, amusements, television, sports and hobbies, drugs, alcohol, sex and holidays are but a few of the means used as vital pathways to escape from the cares of life and work. They are mostly applied entirely to the mind and bring with them their own special brand of side effects which, if not harmful, can in turn be tension-provoking, so that even mental relaxation is only partially achieved. A change is not always as good as a rest.

Philosophy

Relaxation of the mind and body can become a philosophy and a way of life to be learned, being of great value to the individual. Ridding the body of unconscious mental and physical tension means that the mind can take it easy and refuse to become unnecessarily excited. Living slows down to a steady rate, instead of a constant rush with never enough days in the week. Holidays can be taken instead of being needed. Learning to relax for this aim in an art which needs to be practised in order to be mastered. Like an elusive pimpernel, relaxation may take weeks to accomplish. When once having acquired the ability to relax by whatever method, it can be utilized as a pacemaker for two or three minutes at a time whenever pressures begin to crowd in throughout the hustling rush and bustle of a busy day.

When to practise

The best time to learn how to relax is before going to sleep at night. For those who suffer from insomnia, relaxation can be a means of luring sleep. It has already been stressed that it must be practised regularly to be perfected and it would be best to advise the client to retire to bed half an hour earlier than usual to specifically practise the art of relaxation.

Aids to relaxation

A *brisk walk* before retiring is recommended as a preliminary to relaxation and sleep. It requires little effort depending entirely on available time and personal strength. Loose rhythmic movements of the arms and legs should be adopted which will produce a pleasant warm tired sensation and gentle muscular fatigue.

Active exercises are another preliminary which would prove to be helpful and conducive to relaxation. They need only take ten minutes. Each movement should be done five times or until slight fatigue is felt in the working muscles.

The sequence of exercises is as follows:

1 **Foot, ankle** and **toe** movements such as bouncing up and down on toes with heels raised.
2 **Knee** movements lifting first one knee up in the air and then the other.
3 **Hip** backward and forward swinging and then circling the whole leg round, holding on to a support.
4 **Wrist, hand** and **finger** movements such as quick fist and hand flapping.
5 **Trunk** forward bending and circling round in both directions to mobilize the spine.
6 **Elbow** movements involving bending and stretching elbows alternately by placing fingertips on shoulders from the sides of the body quickly.
7 **Shoulder** and whole arm swinging round in circles.

8 **Shoulder girdle** shrugging up and down and pulling back shoulder blades.
9 **Neck** and **cervical spine** movements consisting of head turning and circling.
10 **Scalp** movement consisting of linking fingers together across the top of the scalp and sliding them forwards and backwards at the same time as flexing and extending the neck.
11 **Brisk rub-down** all over the body with the palmar surface of the hands on the skin to stimulate the superficial circulation and leave a warm sense of glowing.

At *first* during the practising period avoid competitive games as they tend to leave the mind in a highly active state which will hinder relaxation.

Warmth by taking a hot bath or a warm drink is important for muscles cannot relax if they are cold.

Ventilation is essential, without producing a draught, to ensure an ample supply of fresh air. Stuffiness is unhealthy although the oxygen requirements are considerably less when the body is at rest.

Disturbance and noise should be avoided as much as possible; the client should ask for co-operation in this matter.

Darkness in the room will help to cut out visual impulses for, even though the eyes may be closed, a bright light can still penetrate through the eyelids.

Comfort by means of pillows and well-sprung mattress can make relaxation and sleep more of a certainty. The client should not be wearing tight restricting clothes. A comfortable sleeping position should be adopted and sufficient pillows for maximum comfort.

Ideal starting position

The ideal starting position is half prone lying. The client should lie on the right side, with head turned to the left, left leg and arm slightly bent in front of the body. The right arm is behind the body and the right leg slightly bent. A pillow can be placed underneath the left knee and leg.

Methods of relaxation: blocking out mental impulses

Contrast muscular relaxation and tension

In order to know whether muscles are relaxed or tensed they must first be deliberately tensed. Experiencing the sensation of strong muscular contractions is then contrasted with the sensation felt when it is released, which is known as relaxation of the muscle. There are no nerve impulses which produce relaxation, only those which produce a contraction and tension. One method is to contract and relax all the muscle groups consecutively in one session; and another method is to concentrate on one muscle group alone for the whole session before proceeding to another group at the next session.

Breathing

The use of deep diaphragmatic breathing, followed by shallower lateral costal and apical breathing is another method by which relaxation is taught.

Colour black or pleasing object

This method teaches the client to concentrate solely on emptying the mind and filling it with the colour of black allowing no other penetration of thoughts to enter. Concentration on a pleasant subject, one which fills the mind with warmth or a special person the client holds dear, the sun, sand drifting through the fingers, the sea, a star, are a few objects which could be suggested and which must be examined, dissected, analysed, criticized and thought about, blocking the way for anything else that might come creeping into the mind. This will lead eventually to the mind being completely blank, first perhaps for only a second or two and then gradually for longer periods of time. At first the client may drift into sleep but when the practice period is complete the client will be able to use this method, or the other, at any time to clear the mind and relax without sleeping.

Combination

All three methods of relaxing the mind and body can be combined to produce a greater effect, like a doctor's prescription which very often may contain several drugs for their cumulative effect. This is the method, the technique of which will be described in more detail in the following paragraphs. The beauty therapist should practise it first to be relaxed and to reap the rewards both health- and beauty-wise. The therapist will then be better qualified and able to teach the client how to relax. The same rules apply to the therapist as a client. If at first the therapist does not succeed in relaxing then the technique should be tried again. When teaching the client to relax, it is important to use a dull, monotonous tone of voice, the speed of which should be slow and consistent.

Technique

Feet first

Curl the toes and pull up the ankles as hard as possible. Go on tightening and pulling up. Now let go. Repeat this five times or until the tension can be felt flowing out of the muscles, the foot and ankle becoming heavy and relaxed. Concentrate on the lightening and relaxing, putting all other thoughts out of the mind.

Thigh and seat muscles

Brace the thigh muscles statically pressing the knees back but without movement. Squeeze the seat muscles as hard as possible together, then let go. Repeat even harder and stronger, then gradually let go, feeling the release of tension and muscle tone. Do not allow the mind to wander from tightening and then relaxing.

Hands, wrists and fingers

Clench the fists very tightly until the fingers dig into the palms of the hands and pull back the wrists as hard as possible. Hold these contractions until it aches, then let got and feel the relief as the aching dies away. Repeat this stronger and stronger about five times more. The rest period between each contraction will become longer as the tension takes longer to ease away after a hard contraction. All sounds around fade and drift away. Just tighten and relax.

Shoulders, upper arms and back

Press the upper arms into the sides of the body and pull back the shoulders tightly. Hold it and then let go. With each contraction squeeze and tighten a little harder, a little longer, before letting go. This should be done about five times in all. Keep on tightening and letting go, feeling heavier and heavier.

Facial muscles last

Press lips together, screw up the eyes tightly, depress the nose and clench the teeth, then let go. Again tighten and relax and yet again and again.

The difference between tension and relaxation of muscle groups should now have been learned. The body and mind should be prepared to float off into sleep.

The whole body

Tighten all the muscle groups of the body and while relaxing just concentrate on feeling heavy, limp and sleepy, shutting out the world completely. Become aware of the comfortable bed and sink into it deeper and deeper. Again, slowly tighten each muscle group and check how tight and tense it is before letting go. As the tension is relaxed, sigh out in relief with nothing at all in the mind but comfort, peace and physical heaviness. Over and over again. If the emptiness does not blur into a haze and then drift into sleep try the soothing, relaxing breathing. Remember there is no hurry; time; time should be taken the whole way through.

Deep breathing

Begin by taking a deep breath in through the nose allowing the air to fill and expand the chest and push out the abdomen. Slowly sigh out the air through the mouth. Breathe in again feeling heavy and relaxed. Repeat this deep breathing with emphasis on the sighing out. There is no hurry at all between each breath. Each sigh out should be accompanied by allowing the body to sink heavier and heavier like lead into the bed. No thought or sound should distract the mind from this rhythm of deep breathing. Breathe in through the nose even more deeply and sigh out again through the mouth. Gradually change deep breathing into a lighter shallower type by closing the mouth and breathing in and out naturally through the nose. Concentrate on breathing in, and out, in, and out. Push away any thought that creeps into the mind other than the movement of the chest which lifts up, and down, up and down. By now not even the breathing should be apparent and even the gentlest thoughts of regular rhythmic respirations will have become a hypnotic haze and deep sleep should have engulfed the body and the mind to become completely absorbed with the colour of black. When a tiny thought wanders into the corner of the mind, black it out, still breathing rhythmically and relax. Keep bringing the thoughts back to blackness and nothing, slip one second of nothing into the mind and then try another, and yet another . . . .

Having learnt to drift into sleep by one or another of the methods described above, the therapist should try to practise the relaxation without the sleep. The client should be advised to do the same. This can be done anywhere; there is no need to lie down. The client should be encouraged to take time off to relax and leave the rushing, running and racing for tomorrow.

About electrical treatments

To the professional beauty therapist a fundamental knowledge of electricity is essential. The range and variety of electrical equipment is so vast that it is impossible to keep track of the latest piece, but the basic principles of working retain the same for each type of current used. Galvanic, faradic, sinusoidal and high-frequency currents are those most commonly utilized for cosmetic purposes, although the direct current is little used today. Together with radiant heat, infra-red and ultra-violet radiation, they provide some of the many methods of treatment that therapists will be required to employ during their career. Both in electrotherapy and actinotherapy the highest level of skill, attention and care in use of machines is required to produce good results and legitimate effects safely. This basic knowledge of the currents being employed and the effects on the tissues of the body cannot be learned overnight, or with the manufacturer's instructions in one hand and the client in the other. There are several dangers resulting from poor technique, inexperience and inadequate knowledge which can be fatal and crippling for life. A doctor should always be consulted before electrical treatments are commenced, however well qualified the therapist is.

General dangers

Shocks

The greatest danger when using electrical machines is that of giving an electric shock by earthing as the client becomes part of the circuit. Metal pipes, radiators, wet or stone floors and metal beds are all conductors to earth if contact is made with a faulty piece of machinery or socket. The more current passing through the client the stronger the shock will be. If the machine is inadequately earthed very severe shocks could occur when treating the limbs in water. Strong currents through the head, neck or heart or if the client is totally immersed in water or steam, could be fatal.

To prevent earthing through the client, all apparatus should be properly insulated and each part earthed correctly so that there is no danger of touching a piece of an unearthed 'live' equipment. This is usually guaranteed by the good name of a reliable manufacturer who has to comply to a certain standard. The apparatus should be overhauled regularly by a professional electrical engineer and one who is preferably experienced in the maintenance of medical–electrical and cosmetic equipment. Keep the apparatus away from the client in case of leakage, faulty connections and wear and tear on insulations. As rubber is a good insulator therapists should wear rubber-soled shoes for safety so that they are protected in case of accidents and can safely touch the client in an emergency without themselves being earthed. A rubber sheet placed under the linen sheet on the couch, or a rubber mat under the client's feet on the ground is advisable when using electricity, especially with water.

Shocks may also be caused by pure carelessness, not being of the earthing kind at all, but merely an unpleasant and unexpected sensation from the electrical currents. The current sensations should always be explained carefully to the client first and tried out by therapists on themselves in front of clients. If the intensity control switch on the apparatus is not turned down to zero before switching off the equipment after each treatment, a large amount of current may be carelessly passed through the next client when the machine is used again. All apparatus control switches should be turned down to zero or off, before switching on. The selector switch must be carefully checked. Shock provoking tactics are caused through the current being suddenly increased or decreased due to faulty connections, broken leads, electric power failures and bad technique. Precautionary measures, in testing the current first to find out if there are any irregularities in the sensation which might give the client a shock, should be taken first before applying it.

Increase and decrease the current intensity slowly, especially in water. Contacts on the skin should be firm unless a special effect as in high frequency is required when the glass electrodes should be dry. Special lubricants and contact soaps should be used or talcum powder if a dry surface is required. Broken leads should not be used and the wall socket should always be switched off first before being unplugged.

Do not allow clients to regulate or supervise their own treatments under any circumstances, or come into contact with each other while undergoing electrical treatments.

Other untoward effects, such as burns and painful treatments, can be caused through bad technique of application. Faintness can occur due to too much heat or a current on the head or near the heart. The intensity of the treatment may be excessive and duration too long, causing a fall in blood pressure or other signs of stress in the client.

Further general precautions

1 Care must be taken not to use currents of electricity that would produce haemorrhage, especially after a recent injury to a part, though it is highly unlikely that the client would be at the beauty salon if they had badly injured themselves. This principle applies to varicosed and bruised areas.

2 A skin test must always be made before applying electrical currents to make sure that skin sensations are normal. The area

being treated is tested for hot and cold, and for sensitivity to a painful stimulus such as a pin prick. This latter can be done by applying the faradic current to the area.

3 Jewellery should be removed from the part to be treated, especially rings.

4 Skin rash due to sensitivity from currents should be noted and further treatment on this area avoided or delayed. Some skins are more sensitive to certain treatments than others. If there are any small skin lesions or spots in the area they should be insulated with Vaseline before treatment commences.

5 If there is a skin inflammation, treatment should never be given over the inflamed area.

6 Great care should be taken when applying any treatment near the heart.

7 The client must never be permitted to interfere with or touch the equipment.

8 The therapist should be within earshot of clients and be able to see them throughout the treatment, checking at regular intervals that they are all right.

Galvanic current

Precautions for the prevention of shocks, burns and injuries

1 The area must be properly washed, inspected and prepared before treatment to lower and equalize the resistance of the skin.

2 A skin test for hot and cold should be given prior to treatment and also to test whether the area is anaesthetized. This can be given by using a faradic current or a pin prick. Galvanism should never be given to an anaesthetized area.

3 Cuts or scratches should be insulated with Vaseline to prevent current concentration on them.

4 The client should be warm and comfortable.

5 The pads used to cover the electrodes should be made of lint towelling and should be neatly folded, allowing the edges to be even and at least half an inch thick or sixteen lint thicknesses. All the metal must be equally covered before the pads are placed in contact with the client. They should be preferably smaller than the size of the lint pad and made of malleable metal so that they will mould to the shape of the client. The corners should be rounded so that there is no current concentrations. The leads and metal clips must also be insulated from the client.

6 The lint should be soaked and wrung out evenly in a 1 per cent solution. The salt should be allowed to dissolve properly in hot water.

7 According to which effect of galvanism is required, other solutions containing drugs can be used and the pads placed accordingly on the part of the body.

8 The tingling sensation of galvanism should first be explained to the client before any current is experienced. Clients must be told most carefully to report if they feel an unevenness of current in the pads, or concentration of heat on one spot, or pain of any description. If this happens the area should be examined and if one small area is red then the treatment should be discontinued as continuation might lead to a serious glavanic burn, deep into the tissues. The amount of current passed through a client very often depends upon the information the client gives, but must not exceed 0.31 mA per square centimetre (2 mA per square inch) of pad under all circumstances. Usually it is much less.

9 Do not allow the client to be misguided into believing that the stronger the current the better the treatment, otherwise a serious burn may occur; therefore do not allow the density to be too high.

10 The current must be given time to adjust to the resistance of the tissues before increasing the intensity.

11 Pressure from bandaging to hold the pad and electrode in place must be even. Protect the bandage from the wet lint pads by rubberized jaconet or rubber, otherwise it may

conduct the current. Also protect the linen from becoming wet with a piece of rubber and a towel under the part being treated.

12 Rings and metal in the area must be removed.
13 The client must not touch any electrodes.
14 When in a sitting position, the client's feet must rest on a rubber mat.
15 A different area should be treated each day.
16 Depending upon which effect is required, so the length of duration of treatment will vary.
17 On completion of treatment the current must be turned off slowly.
18 The skin should be washed to remove acids and well dried.
19 The exact details and reaction of the treatments must be precisely recorded. This includes the size of pads, area of treatment, solution used, current intensity and duration of treatment.

Faradism and sinusoidal currents

Precautionary measures for the comfort of the client

1 Burns cannot occur with these currents but if technique is poor they can be painful and uncomfortable. If the client is totally immersed in a bath the current should be earth free. These currents must be surged to make the muscles contract and relax.
2 The beauty therapist should test the current first before applying it to the client.
3 The sensations of the current must be carefully explained before use on the client.
4 The client must be comfortable and warm, and all water used in treatments should be a hot 1 per cent solution.
5 Electrodes and pads can be conveniently fixed to the area with rubber straps. The pads must be thoroughly soaked in the water and the area moistened if necessary.

6 Smooth surging of these currents with a period of relaxation between the contractions is vital for comfort. A long sustained contraction is tiring and fatiguing.

7 For greater skin stimulation the sinusoidal current is preferable. Muscle contractions are obtained with the surged faradic current. Uninterrupted stimulation causes a temporary deadening effect.

8 When a group of muscles is stimulated the indifferent pad should be placed on either the nerve trunk or a convenient area of skin nearby or the origin of the muscles. The active electrode should be placed over the motor point of the muscles or over their insertion.

9 The duration of treatment should be rapidly progressed to a maximum of twenty minutes. Uninterrupted stimulation on a small area should last for only about 5 minutes. If the labile and bath methods are used, 10 to 20 minutes, depending on the current density, is sufficient.

10 The current density depends upon the client's tolerance of it, but for muscle toning with surged faradism a good strong contraction is required, to be of any value.

11 The current intensity should be turned on and off slowly at the commencement and end of treatment when all parts should be well dried and powdered.

12 The client should be allowed to rest if necessary but this is not essential.

13 The treatment should be recorded.

Infra-red and radiant heat radiation (IRR)

Dangers

1 Burns may occur if the client is too close to the lamp, if it gets touched or if the intensity is too high.

2 Some clients are misguided enough to think that the lamp has to burn and feel very hot for maximum benefit.

3 If the circulation is poor a burn may occur because the area heats up but the blood does not circulate and disperse the heat.

4 Skin should be washed clean and free from oils, unguents and linaments which could cause burning and painful blisters.

5 The muslin can catch fire if too near the lamp.

6 Earth shocks may occur if insulation is faulty and the client touches the lamp.

7 Dizziness and faintness can be caused, due to a fall in blood pressure produced by excess heat.

8 Headaches and nausea may occur with radiant heat bath treatments, especially if clients do not sweat. Cold compresses can be placed on the client's head.

9 Extra water should be drunk unless a weight loss is desired.

10 General irradiation in a heat bath is not given during very hot weather and the time for local irradiation is reduced to a minimum. This depends upon the size of the lamp but should be measured from its element. Usually 46–60 cm (18–24 in) is the correct distance away from the skin to produce a slightly erythema and gentle warmth of the tissues in 10 minutes.

   Many lamps carry the manufacturer's instructions which should be tested before use. Every client will have a different reaction so no rule is hard and fast. After the first 10 minutes the heat can be increased if required by turning up the intensity control or moving the lamp closer. Up to half an hour's exposure is sufficient.

11 The lamp must never be placed directly over the client as this can be dangerous and cause a burn in any part of it were to fall.

Radiant heat radiation (RH)

This form of heating feels milder than infra-red and radiant heat radiation, but it can still burn the skin and produce unpleasant scorch marks which could take several weeks to disappear.

Precautions

1 Test the skin sensation for hot and cold.
2 Cover sensitive areas with a muslin cloth to prevent scorching from the bulb.
3 Place a blanket over both ends of the bath type of radiant heat to allow a more even heating of the skin. If the ends of a bath are left open to allow air to flow through it, scorching is more likely.
4 The lamp should be placed at a distance of 46–60 cm (18–20 in) away.
5 Position the lamp parallel to the part.
6 Turn on the lamp before use to allow it to warm up, particularly with the bath cabinet.
7 Between 20 and 30 minutes is a sufficient length of time for exposure.
8 Check temperature of client before and during treatment in a bath. Do not allow a rise of more than half to one degree Centigrade (one or two degrees Fahrenheit).
9 Do not leave the client alone for too long; keep checking at regular intervals that the client is feeling all right.
10 Allow the client to rest and cool down after treatment.
11 A cool shower or bath to wash away sweat and reduce the body temperature to normal should be available before clients leave the salon.

Ultra-violet light (UVL)

There is no immediate effect of pinking to be seen on the skin on treatment with ultra-violet rays. This pinking is called an erythema and it appears four to six hours after irradiation. There are four degrees of erythema but only the first two are usually used in beauty therapy. A first degree erythema or E_1 fades after twenty-four hours and there is no skin peeling. A second degree erythema or E_2 is a stronger pinking or reddening of the skin and fades after two or three days followed by fine peeling. A suberythemal dose is one which does not produce any visible reaction in the skin at all.

Dangers

1 Severe burns can arise from careless use.
2 Blindness can occur if the eyes are not protected with special goggles.
3 UVL can be dangerous if given to people with heart disease, nephritis, arterio-sclerosis, Addison's disease, or exophthalmic goitre.
4 Irritation of the skin can occur.
5 Other eruptions of the skin can occur.
6 Headaches, vomiting, increased irritability, sleeplessness or other symptoms can develop through exposure to UVL.
7 If a client is taking certain drugs UVL could be dangerous.
8 Earthing could occur if the client touched the burner.
9 Chills can occur if the room is cold or draughty.

Precautions

1 Each time the lamp is used the number of minutes should be recorded in a special book, as the rays become weaker with use, and longer exposures are required with an old lamp than with a new.
2 The erythema reaction should be tested on the client first to ascertain the dosage. If the stated dosage produces an E_1 in 1 minute, the test doses would be given for 30 seconds, 1 minute and 1 minute and 30 seconds. The client would be asked to note very carefully how long afterwards the erythema showed up and for how long it lasted.
3 The distance from the lamp varies with each lamp and usually the manufacturer encloses a leaflet of instructions which should be followed precisely and tested. If these are not

available, the lamp should be tested at 33 cm, 67 cm and 1 m (1, 2 and 3 ft) away for the first degree erythema dose.

4 It is important to place the lamp parallel to the surface being treated so that the rays strike the skin at right angles and maximum absorption is obtained into the skin.

5 The temperature of the skin can alter the effect of the treatment for it is more sensitive to UVL when warm than when cold.

6 Infra-red and radiant heat rays can increase sensitivity if given before ultra-violet radiation but diminish the effect if given afterwards. In this way they can be used as an antidote to an overdose.

7 Skin colourings differ in reaction to UVL. Fair skins are usually more sensitive than dark skins. Certain areas of the body are more sensitive than others, therefore the erythema dose may vary from one part to another.

8 The dose is increased by lengthening the time of exposure to maintain a first degree erythema, up to 4 minutes can be added by increasing the time by 25 per cent each session. After that only 1 minute at a time should be added for a maximum of 20 minutes. Three times a week is desirable but daily doses can be given. If clients miss their treatment the dosage should not be increased up to 10 days, half the dosage up to 14 days and the original dose if longer.

9 If an overdose occurs, infra-red rays should be applied to the area immediately. This will have the effect of producing an IRR erythema which will reduce the intensity of the ultra-violet rays. Cold cream can be applied to the part and later, if necessary, calamine lotion is cooling and soothing.

10 Care must be taken to expose the same area of skin for each treatment.

11 If the lamp goes out the client must not touch the lamp.

12 The beauty therapist must wear special goggles all the time.

13 Good ventilation is necessary to keep the room free from fumes.

14 The room must be warm.

15 Keep the lamp low down and face down to the floor before use.
16 Strike the lamp 5 minutes before irradiation and leave on until all treatments are completed.
17 The parts around the area to be irradiated must be protected and until the lamp is correctly positioned the part to be treated must be covered.
18 The therapist must not touch the filament or burner of the lamp.
19 The lamp must never be positioned directly over the client.

High frequency

Precautions

1 Explanation of the sparking effect and a demonstration should be given first on the beauty therapist before use on the client.
2 The area to be treated must be thoroughly dry.
3 The electrode should be applied to the skin before turning on the current as this avoids frightening the client.
4 For a soothing treatment firm contact with the skin must be maintained to prevent sparking.
5 For stimulation the electrode should only be in light contact with the skin allowing the small sparks to produce a bright crythema effect. If strong stimulation is required the electrode should be lifted further away from the skin, but in these cases a rash may be produced.
6 The skin must be free of any lotions or preparations containing sulphur or alcohol.
7 Do not sit the client near metal pipes or allow jewellery near the area to be treated. A wooden chair should be used and the client should be comfortable and warm.
8 After use the glass electrodes should be cleaned and sterilized; care must be taken to dry the electrodes before use again.

Some conditions for treatment

It is not within the province of the beauty therapist to treat medical conditions. However, therapists will find that there are many clients who, while having massage, electrical or other cosmetic treatments, will be inclined to mention a pain in the back, a headache, or a gammy knee. These clients should be referred back to their doctor for such conditions, who may then give permission for the beauty therapist to apply heat or modify the massage to fit the case, and perhaps relieve discomfort in suitable cases. The following conditions are those most widely prevalent. They would only be treated if present to a lesser degree, and not in the acute stages, but the doctor would decide whether they were suitable cases for beauty therapy.

Arthritis, rheumatism and other conditions

These are terms used to denote a pain, ache or stiffness in joints, muscles and bones. In actual fact they can be likened to the surname of a large family of individual conditions which produce these symptoms.

Rheumatoid arthritis

Rheumatoid arthritis is a condition of the joints where the synovial membranes are affected, generally in the smaller joints of the body. It is apparently more common in females than in males and the onset is between twenty and forty years of age. The fingers and toes can take on a spindle shaped appearance because the joints swell and thicken, and the muscles above and below the joints dwindle and atrophy and they can become quite deformed in advanced cases. In the acute stages the joints are very hot and shiny and must be left alone.

Cause

The cause is thought to be a focal infection such as tonsillitis or excessive wear and tear if only one joint is affected. Generally the cause is unknown.

Treatment

Mild radiant heat, passive exercises, active exercises. Massage to the wasted muscles but avoided at all times on the affected joints. Wax baths can be given to the hands and feet and this is a most popular form of treatment.

Osteo-arthritis

Osteo-arthritis is less crippling than the bad cases of rheumatoid arthritis. It affects large weight-bearing joints mainly and is a disease of middle and later life. The cartilage of the joints wears away exposing the bone which hardens. The synovial membrane may calcify and chip off into the joint, limiting movement. Osteo-arthritis of the knees is most commonly seen in large obese women. The therapist may find the joints creak on movement and patella movements are restricted.

Cause

It is thought to be poor postural habits, metabolic changes, occupational stress and strain on joints.

Treatment

Heat treatment such as infra-red radiation. Vigorous joint massage, mobility and strengthening exercises.

Fibrositis

Fibrositis is a painful rheumatic condition affecting all ages, more common in men than women. It takes the form of deep-seated tender nodules which at times can be excessively painful and quite incapacitating. Sometimes during a massage the therapist may discover a tender spot particularly in the back muscles. The therapist should be able to feel these areas; the client certainly will.

Cause

The schools of though about fibrositis vary. Some say the nodules are fatty globules caught up in the muscle fibres; others say that they are areas of tension in the muscle fibres. Muscle strain, a focal infection such as a bad tooth or exposure to cold, wet and damp conditions are all contributory factors.

Treatment

Heat treatment such as IRR or RH or other available heat. Massage with deep frictions and effleurage. Exercises.

Tenosynovitis

Tenosynovitis is the inflammation of the synovial sheath and membrane of the tendon of a muscle. Most commonly found in the tendons of the wrist and ankle. In the acute stage there is much swelling, pain and even crepitus (creaking) on movement. The doctor will probably order rest and apply a strapping to the part. It should be left completely alone until it has subsided.

Cause

The cause is unknown – probably overuse or strain of the muscle.

Treatment

Gentle heat. Faradic hand bath may be given. Gentle finger kneadings.

Tennis elbow

Tennis elbow is a fibrositic condition round the elbow. Occurs not only in tennis players, but in many housewives who carry heavy shopping bags or who suddenly attempt to paint the house. The area is a tender spot found in the common extensor tendon of the forearm, around the head of the radius and around the back of the lateral condyle of the humerus. Sometimes it is the supinator muscle of the forearm.

Cause

Muscle strain is most commonly attributed to the cause.

Treatment

Heat treatment, infra-red, anodal galvanism. Massage with deep transverse frictions across the belly of the muscle into the affected area. Eccentric muscle work exercises for the extensors of the forearm.

Frozen shoulder

Frozen shoulder is a 'rheumaticky' condition around the shoulder area resulting in pain and stiffness on abduction of the arm. It can vary from complete loss of movement to a mild twinge in the shoulder region.

Cause

Fibrositis in the supra-spinatus tendon.

Treatment

Heat treatment. Massage and exercise for the shoulder girdle muscles.

Lumbago

Lumbago can describe the form of a dull heavy intense low back-ache in the lumbar vertebrae region. It may hinder movement.

Cause

Can be due to bad posture, extra physical exertion, lifting heavy weights, nursing mothers, bad stance in massage practice (occupational causes).

Treatment

Deep massage over origin of latissimus dorsi, the erector spinae muscles and the lumbar region. Ironing, finger kneadings and effleurage. Heat treatment. Back extension exercises.

Sciatica

Sciatica can denote pain in the lumbar region, sacral region down the back of the leg from the buttocks, sacro-iliac and hip joint.

Cause

Pressure on the sciatic nerve (which travels from the lower lumbar vertebrae down into the back of the thigh) due to wear and tear of lumbar joints and bones, bad posture, also tumours or tuberculosis both of which would not be treated.

Treatment

Heat treatment. Massage, ironing, finger kneadings and frictions around the lumbar, sacro-iliac joints and sacrum. Exercises correcting pelvic tilt and posture and back extension exercises.

Slipped disk

Slipped disk is the forward protrusion of the cartilage found between the bodies of the vertebrae. One or more lesions may occur and they are most commonly found in the cervical and lumbar regions of the spine. Great care is necessary at all times if a client is thought to be suffering from a slipped disk. Flexion of the spine should be avoided and the client taught how to bend from the knees and hips keeping the back rigid and straight. The client should have a doctor's note authorizing all cosmetic treatment to the body.

Cause

Lifting heavy weights, muscle weakness, strain on the joints, wear and tear of the joints.

Treatment

Heat treatment. Back extension exercises with particular emphasis on strengthening exercises.

Flat feet

This condition can be taken to mean one of several in the feet. It can mean an outward turning of the feet; it can mean a foot which is banged down heavily with each footstep like a piece of wood; or it can mean a complete or partial collapse of one or both arches of the feet. The most important aim when treating any variety of flat foot is to keep it mobile and functional.

Cause

Various causes are attributed to flat feet conditions. They can be due to hereditary factors, strain, overweight, injury, ill-fitting shoes or weak muscles, to mention but a few.

Treatment

Deep massage to the sole of the foot and to the tibialis anterior muscle which is one of the chief supports of the medial arch of the foot. Faradic foot baths to all the arches of the feet. Active exercises, both mobility and strengthening exercises should be given.

Skin conditions
Acne vulgaris

This is an unsightly condition occurring mainly in adolescence. It tends to clear up by itself after the age of twenty-one. The regions mainly affected are the face, between the scapulae, over the sternal region and possibly the neck. It is characterized by comedos (blackheads) and raised pustules on the skin which is usually greasy.

Cause

The cause is said to be a maladjustment of the sebaceous glands at this stage of life.

Treatment

Ultra-violet light (an E_2) is given to the areas, care being taken to clean and wipe off any grease first which would filter off some of the rays preventing them from penetrating. The face should be treated in sections so that the lamp can be accurately positioned parallel to its shape. All areas not being treated must be covered and an accurate skin test should be performed before treatment commences. The eyes should be protected with Vaseline and covered in cotton wool.

Blackheads

Blackheads can be expressed with a sterile blackhead expressor.

Boils and carbuncles

A boil is an inflamed and septic area of the subcutaneous tissues and skin containing pus and a hard core. A carbuncle can be several boils confined to one local area, or an exceptionally large local inflammation containing pus and a core.

Cause

Various causes such as lowered resistance to infection, or greasy, dirty clogged infected pores.

Treatment

After the inflammation has subsided and the infection cleared a general tonic course of sunlight treatment could be given. This would be a first degree erythema dose of three treatments weekly for six to eight weeks' duration.

Psoriasis

This condition is a non-infectious skin condition which can be confined to one small area or in sporadic patches all over the body. It is characterized by round red raised dry patches covered with silvery scales. It seems to appear on the extensor surfaces of the body, but can occur on either surface. For instance, it appears on the back of the arms, on the front of the legs and on the back of the trunk. The scalp can also be affected at the roots of the hair.

Cause

It seems to be constitutional and can appear in early childhood, then disappear and reappear again at any crisis in life.

Treatment

Oil massage has been found to be helpful. General sunlight treatment may help.

Pine baths may help, followed by a brisk towelling down and an oil massage to loosen the dry scales.

High frequency can be given to the scalp, the showers of sparks help to increase the circulation.

Note: By improving the condition of the skin, scaling may be prevented and also skin infections, common in this condition.

Alopecia

There are two types of alopecia:

1 **Alopecia areata** affects localized areas of the scalp and is characterized by small round areas of baldness mainly on the occipital region of the cranium, but it can spread to the parietal bones. The patches may be up to an inch across singly or in groups.
2 **Alopecia totalis** affects the whole scalp and eyebrows. 'Senile' alopecia affecting men, rarely women, begins in the thirties or perhaps earlier and is a condition in which the hair begins to recede from the temples, or on the crown of the head spreading outwards.

Course

When the hair begins to grow again it is at first white or blonde and very fair. After a length of time the downy hair is replaced by normal hair, but it is white and only after many months does the hair become pigmented again.

Cause

It is thought to be partly psychological, but unknown.

Treatment

This is usually given to relieve nervous tension and can take several forms, which will help to tone up the general health of the body. A course of massage and exercises could be given. The massage would be soothing and relaxing following the exercises, either a general course of sunlight treatment or a localized treatment of the area.

Localized treatment would try to improve the circulation of the scalp by using high frequency or a second degree dose of sunlight. It is passed over the area where the hair is expected to grow and is used every other day. Ultra-violet radiation, giving an E_2 in cases of alopecia totalis, would involve sectioning the scalp into four areas, that is the two sides, top and back. The face and ears should be covered and the client could hold a towel over them. The two sides would be treated first and then the top and back of the head would be treated four days after when the first E_2 had died down. The dosage may become longer as it is increased each time; however, if it becomes too long, then high frequency may be used instead every other day. A whole head should take about 20 minutes.

Impetigo

This is a highly infectious acute skin infection which should on no account be treated but referred immediately to the doctor. Small vesicles appear on the surface of the skin which are filled with a clear fluid thick with bacteria. It appears on the face and ears and is carried anywhere on the body by scratching. Wherever the fluid is spread impetigo will spring up. It is most commonly found on dirty people and spread around communities if it is not spotted and treated medically.

Naevus

This condition is a small area of dilated blood vessels to be found on the skin. Sometimes they form a purple area on the skin and are known as a port wine stain or birthmark. The port wine stain is very difficult to cure. With strong local doses of ultra-violet light they may fade but are rarely cured. The most superficial naevus may be treated by a galvanic current or high frequency in an attempt to try to disperse the fine vein-like threads of blood. It is doubtful that these conditions can be influenced at all by treatment and many beauty therapists leave them alone.

Superfluous hairs

This condition is thought to be due to the incorrect balance of hormones. Sometimes the cause is attributed to heredity but generally thought to be glandular. It can occur in young people who should be advised by their doctor, but more frequently, when the hormone balance is disturbed, it is during the menopause. It is a condition which requires a specially trained therapist with great tact and understanding.

Treatment

There are varying forms of treatment which range from waxing to using depilatories. Electrolysis is frequently and most satisfactorily used on the face but unless it is expertly administered the hair will grow again. The needle must be inserted down the hair follicle in order to destroy the root of the hair and care must be taken to use the right polarity to destroy the hair, otherwise a black charring scar will result.

Warts

Before attempting treatment of warts the doctor should be consulted. If treatment is recommended electrolysis, magnesium drugs or a third degree erythema dose of sunlight can be effective. High frequency is a popular method of treating warts.

Debility

A general tired run-down condition of the client which can be due to several factors. It would be anaemia, overwork, aftermath of illness, constant coughs and colds, poor appetite. The client would be advised to seek the advice of the doctor before commencing treatment to ascertain the cause.

Treatment

General light massage and exercises.

A course of sunlight treatment consisting of a sub-erythema dose, gradually increasing to a first degree dose of ultra-violet light, could prove to be most beneficial.

Care of equipment

A bad workman blames his tools and no matter how superb the technique of treatment may be, if the equipment is neglected, the final performance can only be at a substandard level. Great personal pride in handling and looking after equipment and materials lies in conjunction with good workmanship. To see a well-cared for department or salon is both encouraging and reassuring to the client. A neat shining orderly salon reflects the pride and interest taken by those who work in it. One which is higgledy-piggledy is not conducive to a peaceful and calm atmosphere, neither does it create a favourable impression.

Hints on orderliness

1 **Tidiness** of the couch and line is important. When folding sheets, blankets and towels, make a point of folding the edges neatly inside. Turn the pillow case opening away from the door. Tuck the corners of the sheets into the couch like an envelope corner. Place used towels neatly into a laundry bin. Place a bowl on the trolley for cotton wool or used tissues.

2 **Machinery** should be kept in one place, regularly dusted, the shining reflectors and chrome polished, enamel carefully washed. When not in use they should be covered with dust sheets which in turn must be regularly washed. The face of the heat and sunlight lamps should be turned to the floor and lowered down as far as possible, the wires wrapped carefully round the hooks provided on the machines. All switches and controls should be at zero and the plugs removed from the sockets which should be switched off. Any damaged or broken equipment should be repaired immediately and not left until required for treatment again. Leads should be neatly hung up or separated in a box; rubber straps and bandages likewise. Most manufacturers send cleaning instructions for their equipment.

3 The **store cupboards** must be thoroughly cleaned once a week and tidied every day.

4 The **floors** should be cleaned every day.

5 **Electrodes** must be stored dry and flat, especially if metal.

6 **Lint pads** washed out and renewed when necessary.

7 Sometimes **sterilization** of equipment is essential, especially needles which are used for electrolysis.

8 **Small jars** and **bottles** should be kept topped up from larger containers and drips wiped away.

9 A **waste bin** should be lined with paper, unless disposal bags are used.

10 All linen and gowns frequently changed and washed.

Help the client

1 The therapist can help the client to sit up by hooking the near arm through the client's, with the other arm firmly encircled round the client's back.

2 Stand near the client when the client stands up, from lying or sitting, or after having had a course of heat treatment, whether in a steam bath or dry heat, in case of dizziness.

3 Pick up clients' shoes for them and hand them a gown or their clothes.
4 Call clients by their name.
5 Show clients to the couch and show them right to the door when they leave.
6 Present the account simply after each treatment or at the end of the course of treatment.
7 Do not rush the client.
8 Be a good listener by being genuinely interested in the client's welfare.

New techniques

Cellulite

What is cellulite?

Cellulite is caused by the overloading of fat storage compartments beneath the skin. As the compartments become overfull
they bulge, compressing the blood and lymph vessels that run
between them. The blood vessels bring nutrition to the cells while
the lymph system removes waste products and maintains fluid
exchange. With both unable to function normally, stagnation is
set up in the cells and they become undernourished and steeped
in excess fluids and toxins. This is a vicious circle since the more
distended the cells become the more compressed and less able is
the circulation to relieve pressure by removing fluids.

Over a period of four to eight years, the fat cell membranes
harden giving established cellulite its gritty, lumpy feel. As time
goes by it becomes harder to break down and remove. The
resulting puckering of the skin gives the characteristic 'orange
peel' dimpling of cellulite. Pressure on nerves and blood vessels
can result in pain in those areas where cellulite exists.

Causes

There are many factors which contribute to the build-up of
cellulite particularly in women, for example the hormone

oestrogen triggers the laying down of fat. This is one of the reasons that men do not suffer from cellulite. Certain foods can also contribute to cellulite such as fatty foods which can cause toxicity, for example chocolate and dairy products, and foods which contain hidden fats, for example pastries, biscuits, meat, tea, coffee and alcohol.

Treatment

A *low fat diet*, for example eating plenty of fruit and vegetables which help with the removal of toxins, along with plenty of carbohydrates for energy and water.

Massage helps to increase the blood circulation which in turn helps with lymphatic drainage and removal of toxins.

Low intensity aerobic exercise again helps to maintain good circulation and aids the removal of cellulite.

All the treatments highlighted in this chapter help with the fight to combat cellulite.

Aromatherapy

The word 'aromatherapy' is derived from 'aroma' meaning odour of oil and 'therapy' meaning the art of applying.

Effects and uses

The more concentrated the oil the more effective it is, and therefore the more beneficial aromatherapy is to mind and body. It is claimed that aromatherapy improves health through the use of certain essential oils and gives the client a sense of well-being.

With the use of certain oils on some problem skins, aromatherapy can improve the texture and revitalize the skin giving it a feeling of beauty.

Certain aromatic colours can relax a nervous or tense client and this can be very beneficial. It is also claimed that some aromatic scents, if used on the correct problem and client, can stimulate the mind to make the client feel more alert and bright.

Procedure

The order and method of work and the preparation and procedure should be the same as described in Chapter 5 (the actual massage movements are explained below). A client record card should be filled in as normal with a note of which oil has been chosen and why. Therapists should use their skills in choosing a correct aromatic oil after talking to the client gently and assessing the problem for which the client most needs help. It may be that clients have certain skin problems on their body or face which they feel they would like to improve or perhaps they cannot sleep at night and have a need for relaxation. It is then up to the therapist to determine the real reason for the treatment so that the correct essential oil can be chosen.

The art of applying and techniques of aromatherapy

There are forty-three pressure points on the anterior part of the body which is where the therapist begins the massage. The client must be in a comfortable position and the room must be very warm so that the client will not feel cold when the towel is removed from the area on which the therapist is working.

The therapist sits at the end of the bed with the chosen essential oil in bowls at either side of the client's feet. Starting at the toes, the therapist works up the body applying the oil to each pressure point with a certain amount of pressure in the middle fingers. Once the oil has been applied to the pressure points on the client's body the therapist begins again using effleurage movements, working from the points at the feet to the arms from one pressure point to the next, massaging slowly and rhythmically until the client feels relaxed.

When the massage to the front of the body has been completed the client should turn over and the same procedure should be followed. There are ninety pressure points on the posterior side of the body, most of which are on the back. Care and time must be taken on the client's back for if the client isn't relaxed this is the last chance and the treatment will have been a success.

If the client is being given an aromatic facial, then again the same procedure must be followed. The pressure points of the face must be learnt thoroughly by the therapist before attempting this type of treatment.

Aromatic oils – their properties and uses

Rose

Anti-bacteriological, mature dry sensitive skins, soothing effect, headaches, anti-depressant.

Sage

Stimulant, astringent, fluid retention, stiff necks, rheumatism, fibrositis, all aches and pains.

Tangerine

Revitalizing, tonic for children and young people, pale complexions, improves circulation.

Thyme

Strong general stimulant, dermatitis, boils.

Eucalyptus

Chest rubs, nasal bronchitis, muscular pains, insect bite wounds.

Juniper

Antiseptic, astringent, acne, stimulates circulation and blood purifier, dermatitis, psoriasis, oily skins, cleansing, toning.

Lemon grass

Astringent, tired legs, venous conditions, strong anti-bacterial effects.

Marjoram

Nervous tension, good bath oil, warming, calming, relieving pain, rheumatics, sprains, stress, general body massage.

Neroli

Non-irritant, eau de cologne, sedative anti-depressant, calms and slows down the mind, all skin types, redness, dryness, broken capillaries, improves skin elasticity, insomnia.

Peppermint

Reduces inflammation, decongestion, cooling effects, burns, respiratory problems.

Sandalwood

Antiseptic, mild astringent, insomnia, nervous tension, dry skins, sedating purposes, high colour and broken capillaries.

Patchouli

Anxiety, depression, skin care, wounds, bactericidal action, aphrodisiac, stimulating in small doses, effect of sedation depending on individual, promotes formation of scar tissue.

Facial treatments

Geranium

For pale complexions.

Sandalwood

For broken capillaries, acneic skins, softening effect.

Basil

Antispasmodic, antiseptic, tonic effect, herpes.

Bergamots

Antiseptic, anxiety.

Benzoin

For redness, irritation, itching, cracked dry skin, relaxing effect, uplifting.

Camomile

Mother herb, burns, boils, dermatitis, acne, allergies, all skin types.

Rosemary

For migraine, rheumatism, muscular pain, dehydrating oil, fluid retention, facial, puffy eyes.

Lavender

For nervous tension, relaxing, uplifting, sensitive acneic skins, antiseptic diuretic properties, wounds, burns, bites, soothing

effect on eczema, psoriasis, boils, acne, dermatitis, invigorates
body and mind, skin rejuvenation.

Ylang-ylang

For depression, anxiety, nervous tension, oily skins, aphrodisiac,
pale complexions, effect of pushing out impurities.

Jasmine mix

For dry sensitive skins, dermatitis, skin elasticity, nervous
system, to relieve anxiety and depression.

Gyratory massage

A gyratory massage machine is used for general body work and
is normally floor-standing, with the weight of the motor
supported by the main shaft or pedestal of the apparatus.

Sometimes gyratory massage is used simply to complement
manual massage but mainly it is an adequate treatment for the
removal of cellulite while a client is trying to lose weight.

Gyratory vibrators operate in a vertical and horizontal plane
and the therapist can create a circular movement while the
massager vibrates up and down.

There are different types of heads and applicators which can be
attached to the massager and each one has different effects.

1 The **sponge head**. This must always be used first and has the
  same effect as effleurage.
2 The **hard rubber ball head**. The same effect as petrissage.
3 The **spiky three-pin head**. This has the same effect as
  tapotement.
4 The **pin cushion applicator**. This applicator gives stimulation
  but should not be used on fine skin

5 The **football applicator**. This improves the circulation and helps disperse deposits of fat.
6 The **eggbox applicator**. This gives a very deep massage and should be used on sense fleshy areas of the body.
7 The **heavy pronged applicator**. This gives a deep kneading massage (see Figure 13.1).
8 The **round sponge applicator**. A general purpose applicator often used as an effleurage movement. It should be used with continuous movements with light pressure. It is important to constantly keep in contact with client's skin. The movement should follow the direction of the venous blood flow. It can also be used as a kneading movement.

The feeling and effects of these applicators are totally different from those of manual massage. It is a far deeper massage and breaks down cellulite to the extent of grinding it to the bone on excessively large clients where manual massage would have no effect whatsoever.

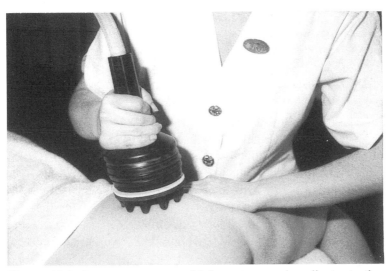

Figure 13.1 Gyratory massage with heavy pronged applicator to the back

Contraindications

1 Varicose veins.
2 Identified lumps, skin tags, hairy moles.
3 Thrombosis.
4 Pregnancy or during menstruation on abdomen.
5 Very thin or elderly clients.
6 Slipped discs on the back area.
7 Extremely sensitive skins.
8 Excessive hair (usually on men's legs as the pin heads could become caught on the hair and cause extreme discomfort).

Effects

1 Figure improvement, breakdown of cellulite.
2 Increases the blood circulation.
3 Improves the muscular system.
4 Relaxing, especially on large clients.
5 Muscular pain relieved due to the relaxation of tense muscle fibres.
6 Improves skin tone.

Method

The client must be prepared in the same way as for body massage and the contraindications must be carefully checked before commencing the treatment.

Once the therapist has decided which area of the client is to be treated, the gyratory massage talcum powder is spread on the area. This allows the applicator to be massaged over the skin without it dragging and causing discomfort.

The therapist must always begin with a soft foam head for effleurage which prepares the client's skin for a deeper massage. The treatment is applied with long sweeping strokes in an upward direction, always towards the heart. The movements will follow the natural contours of the body and enough pressure must be applied so that it does not cause unnecessary irritation.

The gyratory massage machine is a heavy piece of equipment but with practice and strength in the arms and wrists it becomes an enjoyable and skilful treatment for the therapist.

Depending on the intensity of the problem, the time taken with various applicators will vary. At the end of the treatment the sponge head must always be used as a calming and soothing end to the treatment.

Advantages of gyratory massage

1 Adds variety to body treatments.
2 Helps the breakdown of fatty deposits.
3 Less energy-consuming for the therapist.
4 Less personal, so that it can be used for treatment on men.

Looking after the gyratory massager

Gyratory massagers can be very expensive so adequate attention must be paid to this piece of equipment.

1 Regular servicing.
2 Correct use.
3 Correct cleaning and sterilizing of the heads when necessary. A number of each head should be purchased.
4 The heads should only be used with talc and on a clean skin.
5 Never use on oil and make sure that the skin is free from oil if the treatment follows a body massage.
6 Always wash the applicators after use with a mild detergent and allow to dry thoroughly.
7 Dust the dry sterilized sponge with a thin layer of talc before putting it away to keep it in good condition.

8 If the sponge begins to break away from the rubber an appropriate adhesive should be used to bond the two together again.

Physique Plus

Physique Plus is a slimming machine capable of giving lasting results and is a new improved type of faradic current. The treatment lasts for 30 minutes from start to finish leaving behind the faradic treatment which needs at least 45 minutes to build up the current. Inch loss is immediate and body toning and reshaping are results which can be achieved exactly in the areas required with the minimum effort required.

Using the modified faradic current the Physique Plus not only produces highly successful isometric exercise but also improves the lymphatic and blood flow helping to drain away waste toxins. The increase in frequency enables more energy to be emitted into the body which results in an increase in the localized metabolism. See Figure 13.2.

Contraindications

1 Pregnancy.
2 High or low blood pressure.
3 Diabetes.
4 Epilepsy.
5 Recent scar tissue.
6 Bruises or cuts and abrasions.
7 Varicose veins.
8 Metal pins or pacemakers.
9 Rheumatoid arthritis.
10 Heart disorder.
11 Skin disease.
12 Lack of skin sensitivity.

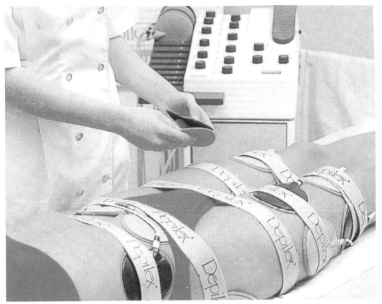

Figure 13.2 The Depilex Physique Plus unit

13 Pre-menstruation and during menstruation if the client suffers any discomfort.
14 Any severe medical condition.

Effects

1 Concentrated muscle toning.
2 Increase in blood supply bringing fresh oxygen and nutrients to the tissues.
3 Increase in lymphatic flow having a beneficial effect on cellulite which is present and helping prevent any that may occur.
4 Muscles are exercised (torsion effect on muscle).
5 Fat cells are mobilized thus helping with weight loss when combined with a calorie controlled diet.

Method

1 Carry out full consultation.
2 Choose padding layout. See Figures 13.3 to 13.6.
3 Wet discs thoroughly with warm water and place under pads.
4 Secure them firmly with straps.
5 Adjust the stimulation, interval and frequency dials.
6 Ensure all amplitude dials are at zero and switched off.
7 Switch the mains switch on.
8 Press the timer reset button. The clock should show 00m 00s.
9 Set treatment time to 15 minutes by means of the timer set button.
10 Press the start button.

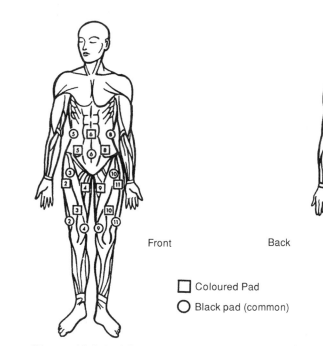

Front   Back

☐ Coloured Pad
◯ Black pad (common)

Figure 13.3 Padding up average client

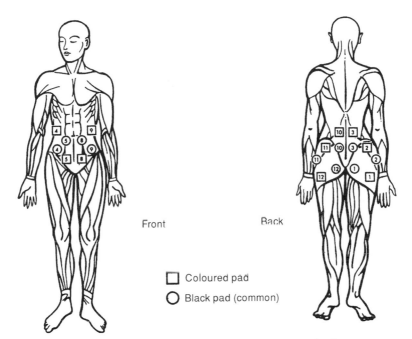

Front   Back

☐ Coloured pad
○ Black pad (common)

Figure 13.4 Padding up stomach, buttocks and lower back

11 Turn up each amplitude control unit until muscle contraction is achieved.
12 Cover the client with a towel.
13 Turn up the amplitude dials during the treatment if necessary.
14 The unit will sound a signal when the time is up. Switch off stop button.
15 Switch all dials back to zero.
16 Remove pads in reverse order.
17 Take measurements and write on client's record card.

Advantages

1 New improved current.
2 Less time-consuming.
3 Immediate inch loss is obtained.

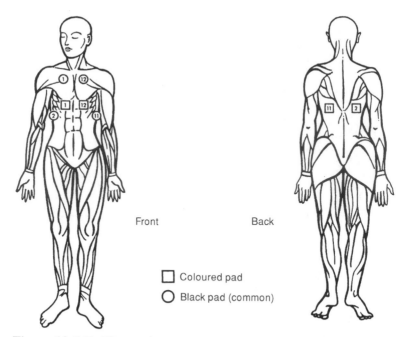

Front   Back

☐ Coloured pad
○ Black pad (common)

Figure 13.5 Padding up breast

Hydrotherapy

Water surrounds us both inside and out. Our bodies are made up of 70 per cent water and 70 per cent of the earth's surface is covered with it.

We can exercise, float, relax and beautify ourselves with water as the following examples show.

Hydrotherapy baths

With hydrotherapy hundreds of tiny jets in the bath, used in conjunction with essential oils, massage the body to relax and soothe.

The therapist can aim the jets at problem areas to improve circulation.

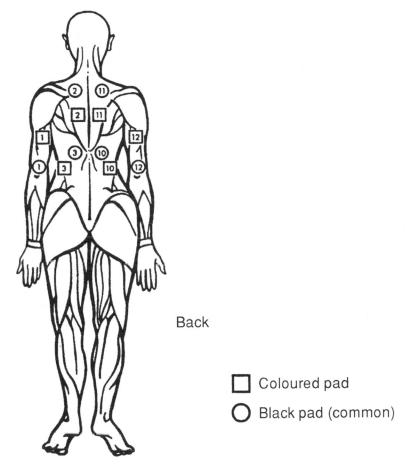

Back

☐ Coloured pad
○ Black pad (common)

Figure 13.6 Padding up back and arms

Flotation

The flotation tank is a small, insulated room with a floor of water at body temperature.

There is enough water in the tank to lie in but it contains so much Epsom salts (nearly 100 lb in 10 in of water) that it makes the body float like a cork.

Floating rejuvenates and relaxes the body but it stimulates the immune system and may help to overcome addictions such as smoking and alcoholism, lifting aching joints, stabilizing blood pressure and reducing stress.

Plunge baths

Plunge baths are very beneficial in raising and lowering the body temperature when used in conjunction with saunas and steam baths.

Clients will feel totally refreshed and invigorated after such a treatment.

Showers and jet showers

A shower cleanses the skin and can be used as a pre-treatment in the salon. It can also be used to lower the body temperature after various heat treatments. Showers also refresh and stimulate the skin.

A jet shower produces a higher pressure water spray which stimulates the body quicker and more effectively. It is very useful for poor circulation in areas such as buttocks and hips.

Turkish baths

Turkish baths were based on steam rooms of different temperatures, where people could progress according to their own individual tolerance. They would move through interlinking rooms where the level of heat started from moderate temperature progressing through extremely high levels of heat. The client could conclude their treatment by using the plunge pools. If this was too much they could simply reverse the procedure and move back through the rooms. This process is very useful as a form of relaxation and deep cleansing and was a very popular treatment in Roman times. Turkish baths can be found in some large health units.

Steam baths

These are cabinets constructed in metal or fibreglass and permit one person to sit comfortably inside. The head is placed through an opening at the top. The steam is produced by electrical elements heating water in a bath under the seat, controlled by a thermostat set to the desired temperature.

This is a relaxing heat treatment and can be used as a pre-treatment before massage or as a cleansing treatment. See Figure 13.7.

Foam and hydro-oxygen baths

The foam baths work on a principle of aerating the water of a bath to create stimulating and heating effects. Foam essence and water are combined and an air compressor forces air through tiny holes in duckboards placed on the floor of the bath. Heat is built up within the body and the client is virtually surrounded by the foam which acts as an insulator and holds the heat.

The same principle is a more elaborate form is used in the hydro-oxygen bath in which the client reclines to be stimulated with warm or hot jets while the cabinet is diffused with oxygen.

The client will feel refreshed and invigorated by the treatment.

The jets of air or water should always be directed along the limbs, muscles and tissues, towards the venous blood and lymphatic flow.

Vacuum suction

What does it do?

Vacuum suction creates reduced pressure within clear plastic cups applied to the body in patterns which relate directly to the lymphatic system of the body.

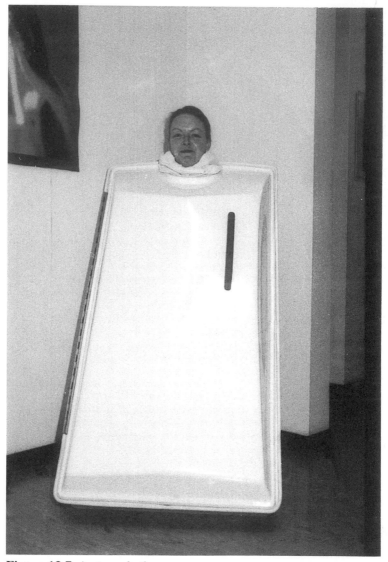

Figure 13.7 A steam bath

The cups are attached to the vacuum machine by plastic tubing and the suction effect produced by the combined pump and motor of the equipment.

The skin rises upwards into the cup by this suction effect. The cup should only be one third full with skin, otherwise bruising can occur. The therapist should follow the paths of the venous and lymphatic system of the body.

Uses

1 Heavy hips and thighs.
2 Abdomen and midriff weight accumulation.
3 Heavy lower legs.
4 Swelling of the ankles.
5 Heavy upper arms.
6 Subcutaneous fat on the back.
7 Large buttocks.

Physical effects

1 Increased vascular and lymphatic flow.
2 Aids tissue regeneration.
3 Produces erythema and aids desquamation.
4 Helps to remove fatty deposits from established weight accumulations.
5 Reduces swellings.
6 Helps to prevent chilblains.
7 Stimulates metabolism.

Contraindications

1 Varicose veins.
2 Recent scar tissue.
3 High or low blood pressure.

4 History of thrombosis.
5 History of phlebitis.
6 History of heart abnormalities.
7 Over the abdominal area during pregnancy.
8 Bony areas or areas with little flesh or fat.
9 Infectious skin conditions.
10 Extremely over-stretched skin.
11 Bruises, cuts, sunburn, etc.
12 Hypersensitive skin or skin prone to thread veins.
13 Hernia weaknesses.

Method

1 Prepare couch.
2 Prepare tables with oils, a bowl of water, tissues, cotton pads and a client record card.
3 Check that the machine is plugged in and that it is in good working order.
4 Check client for contraindications.
5 Small areas use a cup of one inch.
6 Fairly thick areas use a cup of two inches.
7 Very thick areas use a cup of three inches.
8 Buttocks use a cup of four inches.
9 Check that the skin rises into the cup first.
10 At the end of each stroke slide the tip of index finger under the cup to release suction.

See Figure 13.8.

Galvanism iontophoresis

Galvanic current

A galvanic current is a constant direct current which flows in an uninterrupted path with no change of intensity. Thus iontophoresis is the effect produced in beauty therapy. The current helps to

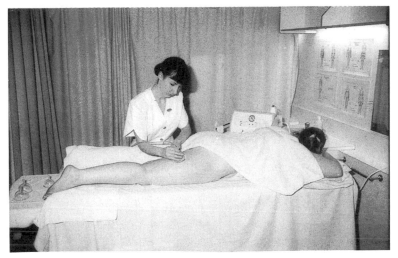

Figure 13.8 Vacuum suction to the thigh

introduce active substances into the skin which in time will penetrate and help to improve the function of the tissue in the area and assist in the elimination of excess fluid and toxins.

When the positive and negative pads are applied to the body on a specific problem area the active substances are applied to the same area and will pass through the skin on a galvanic charge.

The main emphasis of treatment being given is on the negative polarity which is particularly effective for treating cellulite.

The electrodes are given their polarity from the machine, initially determined on the positive setting. The active electrode is the negative, the indifferent electrode is the positive.

Effects

Negative pole cathode

1 Irritation due to the production of alkali.
2 Softens skin tissue and relaxes pores which increases skin's receptivity.

3 Production of erythema and heat by vasodilation.
4 Stimulates nerves.

Positive pole anode

1 Mild irritation due to the production of weak acid.
2 Hardens tissues, tightens and firms, refines pores.
3 Production of erythema and heat by vasodilation.
4 Soothes nerves.

Index

330   *Index*